HIGH-TECH
Teaching Success!

A Step-by-Step Guide to Using Innovative Technology in Your Classroom

HIGH-TECH
Teaching Success!

Edited by
Kevin D. Besnoy, Ph.D.
and **Lane W. Clarke,** Ed.D.

PRUFROCK PRESS INC.
WACO, TEXAS

Library of Congress Cataloging-in-Publication Data

Besnoy, Kevin D.
  High-tech teaching success! : a step-by-step guide to using innovative technology in your classroom / Kevin D. Besnoy and Lane W. Clarke.
    p. cm.
  Includes bibliographical references.
  ISBN-13: 978-1-59363-384-4 (pbk.)
  ISBN-10: 1-59363-384-X
  1. Educational technology--United States. 2. Computer-assisted instruction--United States. I. Clarke, Lane W.
  II. Title.
  LB1028.5.B4395 2010
  371.33'4--dc22
                          2009030473

Copyright © 2010, Prufrock Press Inc.
Edited by Lacy Compton
Cover and Layout Design by Marjorie Parker

ISBN-13: 978-1-59363-384-4
ISBN-10: 1-59363-384-X

Printed in the United States of America.

At the time of this book's publication, all facts and figures cited are the most current available. All telephone numbers, addresses, and Web site URLs are accurate and active. All publications, organizations, Web sites, and other resources exist as described in the book, and all have been verified. The authors and Prufrock Press Inc. make no warranty or guarantee concerning the information and materials given out by organizations or content found at Web sites, and we are not responsible for any changes that occur after this book's publication. If you find an error, please contact Prufrock Press Inc.

Prufrock Press Inc.
P.O. Box 8813
Waco, TX 76714-8813
Phone: (800) 998-2208
Fax: (800) 240-0333
http://www.prufrock.com

Contents

HIGH-TECH
Teaching Success!

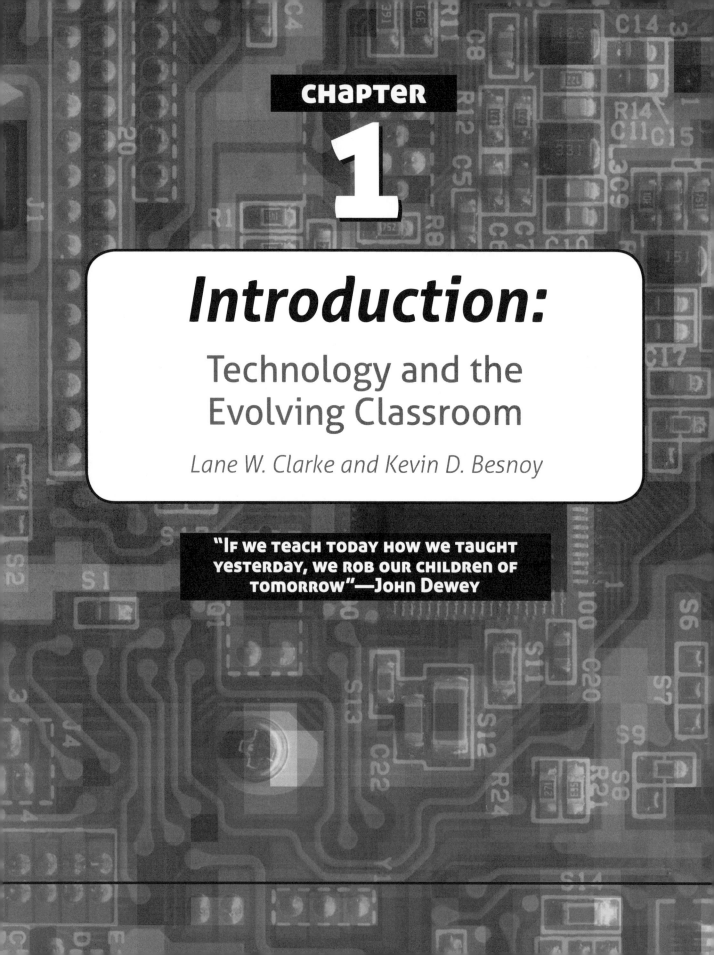

CHAPTER

1

Introduction:

Technology and the Evolving Classroom

Lane W. Clarke and Kevin D. Besnoy

"IF WE TEACH TODAY HOW WE TAUGHT YESTERDAY, WE ROB OUR CHILDREN OF TOMORROW"—JOHN DEWEY

The four of us sat in a stuffy room, lined with packed-up boxes of teaching materials, sanitized desks, and the background hum of the school corridor floors being polished. It was July at P. County Middle School and most teachers were enjoying their summer by the pool or at the lake, but the four of us were huddled together navigating the stylus and screen of the new class set of Palm handhelds that we had just received. We eagerly envisioned the wealth of classroom applications that this new device offered for the upcoming school year. The two eighth-grade social studies teachers and we, two university professors and researchers, were eagerly brainstorming endless possibilities for enhanced instruction.

"Could the students access digital images of Native American habitats, make notes, and beam the answers to their partners?"

"Could the students read original documents from Columbus' journey and then hyperlink to corresponding images?"

"Could the students beam me the main idea of this passage after reading it off the handheld?"

The possibilities seemed endless and as we worked through that day and many subsequent days we began to get excited at the possibility of transforming another year in eighth-grade social studies with an exciting way to integrate technology into powerful and engaging learning for the students and ourselves.

Like the excitement and eagerness that the four of us had as we came together on that hot July afternoon, this book came out of a vision that technology and content-area curriculum could be partnered in such a way to enhance not just learning for the students, but also increase enthusiasm for the teachers. As two university professors, we spend a lot of time in teachers' classrooms and see technology changing rapidly. We see a changing student body that looks nothing like the students that we grew up with or even the students that we both taught only 10 years ago. We see the classroom changing as technology is incorporated in new and innovative ways. Computers, SMART Boards, and multimedia production are now the norm, and teachers are inundated with technology ties from every textbook that they use. Not only is the classroom changing to meet the new technologies, but technology continues to evolve to meet the demands of newer students. One example of this phenomena can be viewed though the evolution of the Internet.

In recent years, the Internet has morphed into an application-based tool that allows users to create content, post ideas, and share experiences.

Initially, the Internet was highlighted by the act of browsing for information that fed an individual's interest. Few individuals were interested in developing the ability to create and post their own knowledge. The days of surfing the net, where the Internet was constructed of static content and resembled a digital warehouse of random information, have passed. Today, the Internet is a dynamic digital forum where people of any interest can have shared experiences.

This new form of the Internet is commonly referred to as Web 2.0 and is fundamentally different than the original version. Although initial Web sites were simple dispensers of information to the generic public, today's Web sites serve as social gathering places where people are free to express themselves. Web 2.0 is a collection of Internet-based applications that allow users to easily create and post content (O'Reilly, 2005). Popular examples of Web 2.0 technology include but are not limited to: blogs, wikis, and podcasts. As a result of these developments, the Internet has undergone a shift from being something that one passively browses to something to which users are actively contributing. In essence, Web 2.0 technology has transformed students from simple readers of content to conscientious participants of written discourse.

In the past couple of years, the development of Web 2.0 has drastically changed an individual's experience. Programmers have created computer code, manipulated computer language, and socialized with computer peers to enable average computer users to personalize their experiences. An individual can open up the Internet and immediately receive content catered to his or her specific interests. It is no longer necessary to surf the Internet for information, rather, content is delivered automatically to an individual's personalized homepage. By utilizing the tools of Web 2.0, rather than searching the Internet for content themselves, individuals are training the Internet to do the surfing for them (O'Brien, Friedman-Nimz, Lacey, & Denson, 2005).

At the same time, computer interfacers use Web 2.0 to establish and maintain robust Internet sites that enable average computer users to plug themselves into the global society. The interfacers have provided platforms for people with similar interests to locate one another and to establish a purely digital relationship. Of course there are the common social networking sites like Facebook (http://www.facebook.com), MySpace (http://www.myspace.com), and LinkedIn (http://www.linkedin.com), but there also are sites that specifically cater to educators like ePals (http://www.epals.

com) and Classroom 2.0 (http://www.classroom20.com). These networks provide an opportunity for people with similar interests to congregate, communicate, and collaborate (O'Brien et al., 2005).

More exciting is the promise that technology integration will continue to expand and enrich our lives. This book is a response to these trends: changing students, changing classrooms, and changing technology. Our goal is to share some instructional ideas and technology tools that can help teachers to dynamically integrate technology across the curriculum. It is our hope that this information will allow teachers to adapt and shift with changing times.

Changing Nature of Students

Sophie gets off the bus barely missing the last step, as she is too busy texting her best friend whom she just saw 20 minutes ago. She saunters into the house and slings her backpack on the table and with a quick "hey" to her mom, goes upstairs to log on to her computer. She immediately updates her blog on the newest gossip from the day, downloads the latest episode of *Gossip Girl* onto her iPhone, listens to her favorite song on her iPod, and checks all of her friends' MySpace accounts. Hours later, her mom comes up to ask about her homework, to which Sophie replies, "Mom, I'm too busy for homework."

Sophie, like many students, is immersed in a world of technology. Students today have at their fingertips access to a variety of Information and Communications Technologies (ICT) that simply did not exist when their teachers were school-aged children. Teachers who still remember taking typing class, going to the library to do research and dusting off voluminous encyclopedias, or trying to fold a map after locating a destination are amazed at the technological landscape in which today's students are acculturated. According to Besnoy, Housand, and Clarke (2009) many of today's students seamlessly integrate new technologies into their lives in ways that mystify many adults.

Recognizing the need for seamlessness is key when discussing how technology should be integrated into the classroom. Kids' use of technology is so commonplace that many of their technologies are considered invisible, meaning that the user does not even realize that they are using a technological advancement. This line of thinking is analogous to the development and popularizing of the wooden pencil.

There was a time when the wooden pencil, first mass-produced in 1662, was seen as a technological leap forward. It is still more efficient to use than many other popular writing instruments that have been developed over the past 400 years. The use of this tool has allowed countless people to more easily write down their thoughts and share them with others. However, there are very few people today who consider the wooden pencil a modern technological advancement. Basically, its use is so commonplace that its novelty has long been extinguished. This is happening to the computer as we speak as it too is becoming an accepted means of communication.

Now, while the novelty of new technologies still exists, their use is becoming so commonplace and seamless that many young people could not imagine living without them. Take a look at any gathering of kids today and pay attention to how they communicate with each other. How much time is spent texting one friend while talking face-to-face with another? Try taking away a kid's phone and you will quickly see how seamless its use has become. For example, when we interviewed a group of eighth graders we were a bit surprised at their hesitancy to actually call a friend on the phone. Rather, it is more socially acceptable to simply text questions and responses back and forth. One girl commented, "If I want to see if a friend wants to go to the mall, I'm not going to call her because then we will end up talking about other stuff. I am just going to text her and she'll answer yes or no." Texting to her was more immediate and to the point, and texting was something they could do all day long versus constantly calling up a friend. Having grown up in the 1980s, we found this an odd statement because our generation relied on the phone for such communication and still cannot imagine not having this personal contact. As educators, we are so frightened and out of touch that we ban the use and possession of this technology from most educational settings without realizing how woven it is into students' perception of human interaction.

New technologies are powerful. They allow young people to maintain social connections through digital social networks; students navigate the Internet better than they can find the drawer for their clean socks; and they compose complex text messages with amazing accuracy. Young people are becoming accustomed to having access to the depth of human knowledge at their fingertips; playing virtual games on handheld devices; engaging in computer-based, life-like simulations; and participating in synchronous communication with peers from all over the globe. Their proclivity to fluently socialize with the latest technology is mystifying.

It is as if today's students speak in a tongue all their own; thus, if older generations want to communicate with their younger peers, they need to learn a second language.

According to Prensky (2001, 2006), today's students have morphed into technology natives that are profoundly different from their predecessors. Labeled "Generation M" (M for media), the Kaiser Foundation (2006) surveyed 2,000 third through twelfth graders and found that current students spend an increasing amount of time using "new media" such as computers, the Internet, and video games. In an effort to explain the generation gap that exists, Prensky (2001) labeled these students "digital natives" and asserted that they are qualitatively different from the types of students to which educators are accustomed. As a result of growing up in a media-saturated environment, "Today's students think and process information fundamentally differently from their predecessors" (Prensky, 2001, p. 1). That is not surprising given the results of the recent Pew Internet and American Life Project survey. This study found 93% of all U.S. students between the ages of 12–17 reported using the Internet, 87% use e-mail, 75% have cell phones, and 97% play computer/video games (Rainie, 2009). Yet, many of our pedagogical approaches are based on meeting the needs of digital immigrants, which do not allow digital natives opportunities to utilize their evolved literacy skills.

The digital native (i.e., today's student) expects teachers to allow him or her to complete assignments with the aid of instructional technology (IT) tools. Many of these natives want to demonstrate the depth of their knowledge in a digital medium (Kirschner & Erkens, 2006). It is with this in mind that we must confront the reality that the characteristics of students who are currently populating our classrooms are appreciably different than their predecessors. This irrevocable shift is so pronounced that, according to Dr. Bruce D. Berry, it is likely that our students' brains have physically changed—or at least their thinking patterns have changed (as cited by Prensky, 2001).

This profound difference in student interests, characteristics, proclivities, and brain patterns has created a disjunction between the students' world and that of the traditional pedagogical world. Prensky (2001) stated, "Today's students are no longer the people our educational system was designed to teach" (p. 3). Rather, their seemingly innate ability to simultaneously process content from multiple sources renders many 20th-century teaching practices obsolete. The concern that today's schools are not changing fast enough to keep up with these changing students is one that is echoed in many different educational spheres. Students have evolved, the educational tools have evolved, and now it is time for the curriculum to evolve.

Changing Classrooms

It is the mid-1980s and there are 20 of us huddled around 10 computers in the computer lab during our half hour of computer time that we get every other week. The computer teacher epitomizes all stereotypes about computer geeks prevalent at the time—tall, thin, greasy hair, thick glasses, pocket protector—making the PC guy from today's popular commercials look like a star. We are learning basic programming that day—a skill that I never once relied upon in all of my subsequent interactions with computers. After creating flow charts with arrows and if-then boxes, we filed out of computer class for the week and went back to handwriting our term papers or, if we were lucky, typing them on a typewriter.

Many of us can remember typewriters and the biweekly computer class. However, today's landscape is dramatically altered and as a result our classrooms look nothing like the one described above. As Nagel (2007) stated, "For more than a generation, the nation has engaged in a monumental effort to improve student achievement. We've made progress, but we're not even close to where we need to be" (p. 1). Although schools have been changing, Nagel believed that it is imperative that the classroom landscape keeps up with technological advances in order to keep pace with other sectors (like business and industry) and that our country's competitive advantage lies within our ability to shift our classrooms to incorporate technological advances.

Just as technology has become a more integral part of our students' lives outside of the classroom, the same thing must happen inside the classroom. Now wireless Internet access is the norm vs. the exception and the increase of accessible computers and handheld devices such as PDAs, cell phones, and portable gaming systems have bonded with the everyday world of our students. At the 2008 meeting of the National Educational Computing Conference (NECC), the International Society for Technology in Education (ISTE) issued new technology standards for students (see "ISTE Unveils," 2008). One of the most profound shifts in these revised standards (from the initial ones introduced in 2000) was that they no longer are trying to get teachers "on board" with technology, but rather now they see a need to push teachers and students even further with technology integration. As Lajaene Thomas, Chair of ISTE Standards, pointed out, "We began with the assumption this time that every teacher recognizes the importance of technology and how it can transform teaching and learning" ("ISTE Unveils," 2008, p. 1). Unlike the standards of 8 years ago, we are no longer convincing teachers to use technology, but instead helping them use it better.

Unlike years prior where just having a computer was seen as integrating technology, today's schools are experimenting with innovation in order to harness these new technologies and to capitalize on their learning potential. Some schools have readily embraced this shift. For example, the Maine Department of Education has undertaken a groundbreaking initiative by signing a contract with Apple to equip all of the state's seventh- and eighth-grade students and teachers with one-to-one access to wireless notebook computers and the Internet. A school district in Arizona has abandoned textbooks in favor of digital resources in their one-to-one program where students have laptops and teachers use online resources (McHale, 2008). Teachers also are embracing new technologies that let students experience content. One example is the popular computer program Second Life. This program enables students to experience virtual worlds that are a bit out of their reach—such as the NOAA Earth System Research Laboratory, where students can soar through a hurricane, float through the atmosphere on a weather balloon, or navigate an underwater cave from the perspective of a submarine.

Today, many classrooms are now equipped with SMART Boards, multimedia production capabilities, and computers that can do a lot more than simple word processing or presentations. Teachers are expected to integrate technology as part of their normal course of instruction. For example, all states are requiring their teachers to integrate technology appropriately into their daily instruction (e.g., it is one of the 10 new teacher standards in the state of Kentucky and new teachers there must demonstrate the ability to integrate technology in order to receive certification). Other states have technology standards by grade level and even specific technology competencies that students need to meet by each grade. For example, Michigan breaks down its technology standards by categories such as basic operations and concepts; social, ethical, and human issues; technology productivity; technology communication tools; technology research tools; and technology problem-solving and decision-making tools. Under each of these headings the state identifies proficiencies that the students will be able to complete by each grade level. Not only are classrooms now more technologically advanced, but teachers are expected to be as well.

Promise of Technology

Although teaching in various schools and districts, Mrs. Slovinsky, Mr. Rosenfeld, Mr. Wang, and Mrs. Gomez all teach students with a variety of instructional needs. Some are behind their age peers, some are on par with their age peers, and others are ahead of their age peers. At some point during the school day, each teacher will instruct the students to pull out their handheld computers (which are about the size of a stenograph notepad), enter the global virtual community, and continue collaborating with group members who are solving the virtual simulation that they have been working on the past couple of weeks. Even though great distances physically separate each classroom, all of the students can collaborate to solve simulated problems thanks to a robust network, dynamic software, and cost effective resources. Whether collaborating synchronously or asynchronously, collaborative projects that allow diverse students from physically distant places to engage with one another will be the norm. In these settings, students will learn how to create answers to questions of which we have not yet thought.

Although this story may seem far-fetched to us now, no one is disputing the fact that technology is here to stay. It has changed our world, our students, and our educational environment. However, how technology impacts the future of schooling is terrain that is still being mapped. Certainly, technology has proliferated the classroom and changed the landscape of educational contexts forever, but many of us still struggle with how to effectively and efficiently incorporate this new medium in ways that enhance student learning and promote critical thinking skills. Norris and Soloway (2003) highlighted the range of positive impact that computers in the classroom has had on teaching and learning. For example they found that computers have shown an increased time on task, higher test scores, and increased motivation by the students. Although they credited many reasons why using computers benefit students, they maintained that given the time and money spent in this area we as a nation need to improve how we use technology in the classroom. Norris and Soloway asserted that "K–12 schools have not enjoyed the expected positive impact of technology—we have more technology in schools than any other country but student achievement has not really increased" (p. 26).

What could be the reason for this? One theory is that we have not used technology in ways that truly change the landscape, but rather that we try to fit technology into old models of educating. In his book *Silicon Snake Oil: Second Thoughts on the Information Highway*, Stoll (1996) worried that technology can be used as an inadequate substitution for education and that we need to be careful how we incorporate the new into the accepted ways of doing things. Roblyer (2006) asserted that we need to use technology as a channel for helping teachers communicate better with students and enhance instructional delivery: "It can make good teaching even better, but cannot make bad teaching good" (p. v). It is not uncommon anymore to go into a classroom and see a teacher use Microsoft PowerPoint, but is this really enough of a difference in instruction or is this more of the same just masked in the veil of incorporating technology?

A report by the State Education Technology Directors Association (SETDA), the International Society for Technology in Education (ISTE), and the Partnership for 21st Century Skills called *Maximizing the Impact: The Pivotal Role of Technology in a 21st Century Education System* set out some recommendations for the promise of technology use in schools. The report stated that "Technology can be an extraordinary support for teachers who can use it to become more effective in their classrooms" (p. 9), and that it is imperative that schools embrace technology in order to stay competitive in the global environment. They believe that educators need to broaden the narrow approach of the use of technology in the classroom and to offer more rigorous, relevant, and engaging opportunities for students to learn and apply their knowledge and skills in meaningful ways. In their most recent reissue of these standards in the summer of 2008, this organization has delineated five categories of technology integration in the classroom. The five goals for the next generation of teachers include:

- Facilitate and inspire student learning and creativity.
- Design and develop digital-age learning experiences and assessment.
- Model digital-age work and learning.

- ☼ Promote and model digital citizenship and responsibility.
- ☼ Engage in professional growth and leadership.

There is an old saying in business that with the advent of technological advances we need to not pave over the old dirt roads but rather create new superhighways. Technology has the promise to create new superhighways to advance learning in new and exciting directions. Technology needs to be seen not as an improvement on old tools but rather as a vehicle to chart new avenues—this is where the promise of technology lies in education.

21st-Century Curriculum and Digital Literacy

What does it mean for a person to be literate? The criteria for being considered literate in any given society generally boils down to a few basic criteria. Throughout the course of human history, the notion of what it means for a person to be literate constantly has evolved (Besnoy et al., 2009). However, the basic criteria of literacy have not changed. According to Morgan (2001), basic literacy is made up of three broad categories. Literacy is *functional* (accomplishing tasks with the use of words), *social* (communicating for some social purpose), and *shaped by contextual variables* (utilizing technology advancements to facilitate communication). Given Morgan's ubiquitous criteria, it could be argued that literacy rates during the Neanderthal period were quite high.

Certainly, based on today's standards, humanity at that time was able to survive on what we today would consider an illiterate skill set. Yet, that is judging Neanderthal society through the lens of today's advancements. However, if we attempt to measure the literacy rates of that time by looking at the three elements of literacy (Morgan, 2001), perhaps literacy rates were quite high. For example, given the depth of human knowledge 130,000 years ago, Neanderthals were able to functionally communicate (even though their lexicon was probably quite small), they were social (certainly they were able to use their limited lexicon for a social purpose), and they were able to utilize technological advancements to facilitate communication (as is seen on the cave walls of Altamira). Certainly a typical Neanderthal man would not be considered literate by today's standards, but by the standards of the time, an average person was as literate then as the average person is today.

Given this point of view, the definition of literacy can be interpreted as a dynamic construct that evolves depending on the technological tools and societal demands of a particular time period. As such, there has emerged in literature a notion of new literacies, or digital literacies. According to researchers, these digital literacies have evolved as a result of the most recent advancements of the digital age and demands to implement them. In the past 3 to 5 years, the Internet has evolved from a place where people were consumers of information to a place where they have begun to socially construct knowledge. According to Eshet-Alkalai and Amichai-Hamburger (2004), current contextual variables mandate that in order for people to functionally operate in the world to use their words to facilitate communication, they must possess the following basic literacy skills:

- *Photo-visual literacy:* Our students must evolve from a text- to graphic-based environment. Photo-visual literacy refers to a person's ability to read and interpret messages in a visual-graphic form. For example, conducting research, collecting data, and creating landmarks with Google Earth fosters students' proficiency with photo-visual literacy.

- *Reproduction literacy:* One of society's requirements for success is the ability to use digital production technologies (e.g., digital cameras, scanners, camcorders, or graphic editing tools) to create messages in a multimedia format. For example, students should be able use a digital camera to capture images of any experience, edit the pictures with graphic editing tools, use a movie editing tool to create moving illustration with narrations, and present their final product through a video server such as YouTube.

- *Branching literacy:* Now, and for the foreseeable future, information is presented in a medium that requires us to be able to retrieve, interpret, and create information in a hypermedia, nonlinear-based environment. The Web environment is a typical media that requires students to have proficient branching literacy. Through carefully constructed lessons, students can learn to choose the right branch of information and how to navigate in an environment in which information is presented in a multidimensional format. For example, students must be able to manage and navigate information in an article about microbiology that contains hyperlinks, which branch the reader from one subcategory to another.

- ☼ *Information literacy:* Given the ease by which bogus information can be published, presented, and disseminated as authentic, we much teach students the ability to validate the credibility and the value of the information. Living in an era where people are bombarded with vast amounts of information, educators must nurture students' abilities to critically seek, analyze, and use information in ways that generate research questions, investigations, and solutions. For example, teachers should require that their students triangulate resources by finding a minimum of three sources that support their conclusions.

- ☼ *Social-emotional digital literacy:* Students will be required to communicate with others synchronously and asynchronously through the use of video conferencing tools, social networks, wikis, and Weblogs (or blogs). This literacy skill enables students to know how to use the communicational tools in a responsible and respectful way to work with other people. For example, teachers in various locations can facilitate group work to solve complicated mathematical problems. Classrooms from all across the globe can collaborate through instant messengers, video conferencing, discussion boards, Weblogs, or social networks to find a solution to the problem.

Given this latest evolutionary step in how literacy is defined, it is necessary for educators to reevaluate both pedagogical practices and IT tools to determine how to best pair them in ways that promote 21st-century literacy skills. Through each of these chapters we will return to these categories of digital literacy and highlight how the technology tools capture the multidimensionality of literacy in today's digital environment.

WHY THIS BOOK: TECHNOLOGY AS AN INSTRUCTIONAL TOOL

It is with the knowledge that students are changing, that classrooms need to change, and that technology holds a wonderful promise for the future of education that inspired this book. We believe that technology can be used as a powerful instructional tool to enhance classroom instruction and push the boundaries that challenge all students to think and learn in meaningful ways. We believe that technology has the potential to push content-area thinking and conceptual understanding in new directions. We believe that through thoughtful integration, teachers and students can engage in meaningful inquiries and investigations where they apply new skills and knowledge to their work in the content areas with meaning and purpose.

By gathering those in the field who are working to use technology as a tool to enhance learning in the content areas, we hope to demonstrate how technology can help educators pave new roads and chart new directions. This book is the culmination of thinking about how to best incorporate technology into content-area classrooms in a practical, user-friendly, and transformative manner.

Each chapter in this book tackles a different content area that is found in most K–12 classrooms: literacy (i.e., reading, writing, and language arts), mathematics, science, and social studies. The authors present a picture of the current state of technology in their discipline, a justification for why technology integration will enhance content instruction, a tie to current standards in each field, and three technology tools that can be integrated into instruction to move the students' thinking and learning forward in new and innovative ways. Each chapter is written for teachers as they imagine how technology can be used to push their boundaries and each gives practical and step-by-step guidance as to how these tools might be used. The goal of this book is to help you, as a classroom teacher, explore new ways to integrate technology into your content area. To facilitate this, each chapter opens with guiding questions and teacher exercises and closes with some guidance for goal setting. Furthermore, the concluding chapter explores how you can use this information to create a Personal Technology Integration Plan (PTIP). This is explained in depth in the last chapter and is to be used in conjunction with the content chapters relevant to you.

The mission of this book is not to present all possible technology integration ideas—rather to be used as a starting point for imagining the possibilities. There are many technology tools that are addressed in this book as a whole (see Table 1.1).

It is important, however, that we are specific in how we use the term *technology*. It is crucial to understand that we see technology not as an add-on or a substitution of the old with the new. We use the term technology as a tool—not purely a productivity output device. The authors in this book have articulated how technology can be used as a tool to push

TABLE 1.1
Technology Tools in This Book

- Blogs
- Digital Media
- Digital Diaries/Storytelling
- Podcasting
- Probeware
- Really Simple Syndication (RSS) Feeds
- Screencasting
- Second Life/Virtual Worlds
- Student Response Systems
- Web 2.0 Technologies

the boundaries of instruction and learning in the content areas. Through them you will see what our vision of technology is but below is a list of what we think technology is *not*.

Technology is *not*:

- reiteration of the information from a textbook through a software presentation program,
- using a word processing program to write a paper,
- projecting a document using a document projector,
- using the Internet as a reward for completing class work early,
- plugging students into a software program during free time,
- substituting a CD-ROM for teacher instruction, or
- watching a video through a computer's streaming application.

We hope that this book will explore how students can be more than consumers of technology and demonstrate how these tools can impact learning for all students.

You could hear a pin drop in Mr. Smith's third-period social studies class as his students concentrated on their work. The eighth graders had previewed a digital photo of Greek democracy, manipulated the size and color of the font of the text, bolded key facts, and beamed questions about the text to a partner using their Palm Pilots. The engagement of the students was everything we had hoped for as one student proclaimed, "The more control you have over it, the more you want to read." The teacher joked that he had never seen a class so excited to read from their history books. The Palm Pilots had not only energized the students, but we too were excited to continue to explore the many instructional possibilities that we had envisioned when conceptualizing this project way back in the summer. By enhancing the curriculum with this technology tool, we were reaching students through motivating and engaging lessons and using this technology in a way to facilitate engagement with the content.

References

Besnoy, K. D., Housand, B., & Clarke, L. W. (2009). Changing nature of technology and the promise of educational technology for gifted education. In F. A. Karnes & S. M. Bean (Eds.), *Methods and materials for teaching the gifted* (3rd ed., pp. 783–802). Waco, TX: Prufrock Press.

Eshet-Alkalai, Y., & Amichai-Hamburger, Y. (2004). Experiments in digital literacy. *CyberPsychology & Behavior, 7*, 421–429.

ISTE unveils new standards for teachers: Group outlines what teachers should know to help digital-age students learn. (2008). *eSchool News, 11*(8), 1.

Kaiser Foundation. (2006). *The teen media juggling act: The implications of media multitasking among American youth* (Publication Number 7592). Retrieved from http://www.kff.org/entmedia/upload/7592.pdf

Kirschner, P. A., & Erkens, G. (2006). Cognitive tools and mindtools for collaborative learning. *Journal of Educational Computing Research, 35*, 199–209.

McHale, T. (2008). *Tossing out textbooks.* Retrieved from http://www.technlearning.com/showArticle.php?articleID=196604929

Morgan, M. (2001). Computers for literacy: Making the difference? *Asia-Pacific Journal of Teacher Education, 29*, 31–47.

Nagel, D. (2007). 21st century learning: "We're not even close." *The Journal.* Retrieved from http://thejournal.com/articles/2007/11/14/are-schools-failing-kids-in-21st-century-skills.aspx

Norris, C. A., & Soloway, E. M. (2003). The viable alternative: Handhelds. *School Administrator, 60*(4), 26–28.

O'Brien, B., Friedman-Nimz, R., Lacey, J., & Denson, D. (2005). From bits and bytes to C++ and Web sites: What is computer talent made of? *Gifted Child Today, 28*(3), 56–64.

O'Reilly, T. (2005). *What is Web 2.0?: Design patterns and business models for the next generation of software.* Retrieved August 28, 2007, from http://www.oreillynet.com/lpt/a/6228

Prensky, M. (2001). Digital native's digital immigrants. *On the Horizon, 9*(5), 1–7.

Prensky, M. (2006). Listen to the natives. *Educational Leadership, 63*(4), 8–13.

Rainie, L. (2009). *Teens and the Internet.* Retrieved from http://www.pewinternet. org/.../2009/2009%20-%201.9.09%20 %20Teens%20and%20the%20internet-%20 CES.ppt.ppt

Roblyer, M. D. (2006). *Integrating educational technology into teaching.* Upper Saddle River, NJ: Prentice Hall.

State Educational Technology Directors Association (SETDA), the International Society for Technology in Education (ISTE), and the Partnership for 21st Century Skills. (2007). *Maximizing the impact: The pivotal role of technology in a 21st century education system.* Retrieved from http://www.setda.org/c/document_library/ get_file?folderId=191&name=P21Book_complete.pdf

Stoll, C. (1996). *Silicon snake oil: Second thoughts on the information highway.* Burnsville, MN: Tandem Library Books.

2

It All Adds Up!

Using Technology in the Math Classroom

Jesse Lubinsky

GUIDING QUESTIONS

1. (a) How can teachers employ traditional and innovative technology applications to enhance student learning? (b) What instructional activities will help me achieve this?

2. What technologies are available to enhance mathematics teaching and learning?

Needs Assessment

1. *Keywords*

   Look over the keywords found in this chapter listed below. Rate yourself from one to three on your familiarity with each word. Then use this rating to help you set some goals for reading this chapter.

Word	1 Don't know at all	2 Some familiarity with this word	3 Very familiar with this word
Web 2.0			
Screencasting			
Mathcasting			
RSS (Really Simple Syndication)			

2. *Tools*

   Look over the four key technology tools listed below. Rate yourself from one to three on your familiarity with integrating these tools into your math classroom. Then use this rating to help you set some goals for reading this chapter.

Tool	1 Don't know at all	2 Some familiarity with this tool	3 Very familiar with this tool
Wiki			
Blog			
Podcasting			
Student Response System			

3. *Goal(s) for the Chapter*

   Fill in your goals below:

   a. By reading this chapter I hope to _____

   _____ .

   b. By reading this chapter I hope to _____

   _____ .

In a middle school mathematics classroom in Irvington, NY, a hush comes over the class as the teacher approaches the front of the room with a pensive look on his face. After taking a moment to think, he finally speaks up. "Alright guys, I need Steve Smith to score 23 points tonight in order to win the teachers' fantasy football league. If a reception is worth one point, every 10 yards is equal to another point, and a touchdown is worth six points, which of the following games can Steve Smith have and still win me the league?" An explanation of the league scoring system was probably unnecessary because the class has been following their teacher's fantasy league exploits all season long. In the teacher's own words: "When you roll with Evans, you roll with a winner!"

On the board, a PowerPoint slide lists four possible options, each labeled A through D. The students pick up their Texas Instruments graphing calculators and enter in their choices. After a couple of minutes, Mr. Evans stops the class and says, "Let's go over the results." At the click of a button, we see how the class did, with the results displayed instantly on the screen. Out of the 22 students in the class, 19 chose the correct response, which was Choice C (eight catches for 95 yards and one touchdown). The other three students chose Choice D (six catches for 110 yards and one touchdown). In examining the results, Mr. Evans asks the class what could have caused the three students to choose the incorrect response. Several students point out that Choice D gives exactly 23 points while Choice C gives 23.8 points. "Maybe," suggests one girl, "they thought the number had to be exactly 23 to win and not more." Mr. Evans smiles while other students nod in agreement.

Don Evans has been teaching middle school mathematics in the Irvington Union-Free School District for the past 6 years. His classroom has gained a reputation for being both a great place for students to learn as well as being fun. Despite this, Mr. Evans felt like there was something lacking. According to him, "I never felt like there was anything wrong in my classroom. I just wanted to mix things up." As with many other districts, Irvington began rolling out large numbers of electronic whiteboards to classrooms in all of its buildings. After seeing other teachers doing some impressive work with the new technology in their classrooms, he became curious: "I wanted to see if I could find new ways of doing some of the work I was already doing in my classes. We brought in graphing calculators and began working with those and from there, things kind of took off." Working with electronic whiteboards and graphing calculators were just the start. Over the past year, Mr. Evans has been working with other math teachers at the school to incorporate innovative new technologies into the math classroom. In the process, he has changed his classroom from a traditional "chalk and talk" model into an exciting and cutting-edge learning space for all of his mathematics students.

Introduction: Technology Integration in Mathematics Education

Technology has always been an integral part of the classroom but, perhaps, in no subject more so than mathematics (Owens, Song, & Kidd, 2006). Even before computer technology arrived on the scene, there were always innovations that allowed technology to become part of mathematics education. Prior to written numbers, the abacus made it possible for people to count large numbers (Fernandes, 2007). The use of this device also allowed for a greater analysis of complex problems. Much like the use of the abacus, today's technologies are impacting the way that mathematics is presented.

From a technological standpoint, the mathematics classroom of today differs greatly from that of even a decade ago (Dyck, 2003). Many classrooms now contain electronic whiteboards, Internet-connected pods of computers, laptop carts, projectors, scanners, manipulatives, and sets of graphing calculators. Most textbook vendors provide robust software programs that contain presentations, activities, and exercises mapped out by the standards. Furthermore, in recent decades, math students have had more access to manipulatives and advanced computers.

The most glaring example of technology is the role that the calculator has in the modern mathematics classroom. Its initial introduction to classrooms in the mid-1970s allowed students to perform simple four-function calculations in a quick and effective way (Chase, 1980). Today, graphing calculators permeate the classroom. Almost every student owns a calculator, with some students, depending on the grade level, carrying calculators that wield more processing power than the computers of only a few years ago. Rather than tediously solving equations on scratch paper, the graphing calculator's computational power allows students the mental freedom to analyze and synthesize the solutions to complex mathematical equations.

In many cutting-edge classrooms, teachers are using innovative technologies to push the limits of what is currently possible. Students are working collaboratively on developing solutions, demonstrating their answers to their peers, and taking ownership of their own learning. By using technology tools to complete computational tasks, it is now easier for the math teacher to assume the role of facilitator.

These changes work nicely within an established framework for 21st-century learning skills published by the Partnership for 21st Century Skills (2007). Specifically, the framework calls for students to develop learning and innovation skills combined with information, media, and technology skills. The framework goes on to state that a 21st-century skill set requires that students have the ability to be creative and innovative, think critically, problem solve, and communicate and collaborate. Furthermore, they must be able to carry out these processes in a digital environment. As such, students must be literate in what is referred to as ICT, or Information and Communications Technology. Students who are not fluent in these skill sets will be ill-equipped to successfully navigate 21st-century life and work environments.

Obstacles to Technology Integration

Although there has been access to technology for mathematics educators, using it has brought its own share of controversy and criticism (Pomerantz, 1997). For instance, even in recent years, the use of calculators by students has been looked upon as a potential pitfall in the area of mathematics education. Critics have argued that students use calculators as a crutch, replacing the basic skills necessary for students to compute solutions to fundamental math problems (Pomerantz, 1997). Meanwhile, proponents counter that neglecting to demonstrate the use of calculating tools will adversely affect students' mathematical thinking (Bing & Redish, 2007). In order to develop the skill set proposed by the Partnership for 21st Century Skills (2007), these proponents contend that teachers and students must be given appropriate training on how to use calculators and other ICTs (Kastberg & Leatham, 2005).

Critics of integrating technology into the classroom have centered on three arguments (Wenglinsky, 1998). First, critics argue that many teachers resist changes because they lack basic computer competency and comfort level. Not only are they intimidated by new technology, but they also resent those teachers who can easily integrate technology into the mathematics classroom. Next, the critics have argued that the cost of integrating new technologies does not equal the results that could be demonstrated as a result of their inclusion. Finally, they point to educational theories that suggest that there may be a social, noncognitive element of learning that technology limits. They point to the antisocial behavior that students may exhibit while working with technology.

Much of the criticism leveled toward classroom technology integration directly addresses some of the problems still facing mathematics classrooms today. First, there will always be some teachers who are ahead of the curve in trying to bring the latest and greatest technologies into their classroom to improve instruction. These teachers often spend countless hours developing new learning activities and new ways of introducing mathematical concepts. Rather than ostracizing their efforts, these individuals' instructional approaches should be held up as models of best practice and their ideas shared among the educational community.

Next, while there are still a large number of teachers who are not incorporating technology into mathematics classrooms, it is not due to a lack of monetary investment. Billions of dollars are spent annually in the K–12 system on technology expenditures to improve education (Sivin-Kachala & Bialo, 2000). In fact, many classrooms have added electronic whiteboards, computer labs, graphing calculators, and data analysis programs. Unfortunately, a scant amount of that money has been spent on professional development and training on how to appropriately integrate these tools with the mathematics curriculum.

Finally, the level that technology permeates the lives of digital natives is amazing and is a trend that will not change for the foreseeable future. Rather than condemning technology as a contributor to adolescent delinquency, students must be taught how to use mathematical ICT tools for productive purposes. One of the biggest challenges that proponents of incorporating technology into mathematics classrooms face is that of convincing math teachers that it is worth the investment in time and energy to bring these technologies into their classroom.

Successes of Technology Integration

A new set of technologies has begun to take the changes that have occurred in mathematics classrooms and drive them even further as well as address the concerns of critics. Many of the newer technologies are cost effective, easy to use, and require social collaboration in order to be used successfully. In recent years, the Internet has transformed from a place where information was simply posted for people to obtain to a model where the creation of information has become the key facet of many Web sites.

This trend has led to the establishment of the term *Web 2.0*. This updated Internet has been designed to reflect the next generation of Web sites and the movement toward more social interaction on the Web. Driven by user contribution to human collective, this social Internet has spawned new technologies and software that has allowed for users to socially construct knowledge through digital interaction. Such software includes, but is not limited to, blogs (virtual public journals), wikis (virtual collaborative spaces), podcasts (syndicated online media), and Really Simple Syndication (RSS; a way of subscribing to online content). When combined with innovative uses of electronic whiteboards, the proliferation of both subscription-based online services and software packages, and education's movement toward the use of student response systems, one can see the variety of innovative technologies that are available to mathematics classroom teachers.

Importance of Math Technology Integration and Technology Standards

There has been significant research and evidence produced by reliable sources that have indicated the positive impact that technology can have in the mathematics classroom. A report by the Educational Testing Service investigated technology's effectiveness and arrived at the conclusion that using technology to teach higher order thinking skills such as problem solving, reasoning, and puzzling were positively related to academic achievement in mathematics and the social environment of the school while also stating that using technology to drill lower order skills had a negative correlation to academic achievement (Wenglinsky, 1998). Also, in 2008, the National Mathematics Advisory Panel of the U.S. Department of Education produced a report entitled "Foundations for Success," which stated that technology could be used to improve curriculum. It noted that "technology-based drill and practice and tutorials can improve student performance in specific areas of mathematics" (U.S. Department of Education, 2008, p. 50). The report also stated that the use of instructional software in mathematics classrooms produces higher student achievement than in classes that do not have the software.

The National Council of Teachers of Mathematics (NCTM, 2008) has identified six principles for school mathematics that are designed to provide guidance to educational decision makers. The six principles are equity, curriculum, teaching, learning, assessment, and technology. NCTM noted that the mathematical landscape is being reshaped through the use of calculators and computers and that students can achieve a deeper understanding of mathematics through the use of technology. In an ideal classroom setting, all students would have access to technology that would enhance and deepen their understanding of mathematics. NCTM also made note of the benefits that technology can provide mathematics learners with special needs and added that some students can only achieve a deeper understanding of mathematics through technology use.

In March 2008, NCTM released an official position on the role of technology in the teaching of mathematics:

> Technology is an essential tool for learning mathematics in the 21st century, and all schools must ensure that all their students have access to technology. Effective teachers maximize the potential of technology to develop students' understanding, stimulate their interest, and increase their proficiency in mathematics. When technology is used strategically, it can provide access to mathematics for all students. (para. 1)

Furthermore, they observed that the use of technology can help students make progress in an assortment of areas related to mathematical learning such as the ability to "extend mathematical reasoning and sense making, gain access to mathematical content and problem-solving contexts, and enhance computational fluency" (NCTM, 2008, para. 2). It also is noted that the use of technology can "contribute to mathematical reflection, problem identification, and decision making" (NCTM, 2008, para. 2). Further, the organization put the responsibility of determining how to incorporate technology into mathematics classrooms onto teachers. Among the specific technologies it referenced for inclusion into the math classrooms were "appropriate calculators, computers with mathematical software, Internet connectivity, handheld data-collection devices, and sensing probes" (NCTM, 2008, para. 3).

NCTM's position meshes nicely with the standards released by the International Society for Technology in Education (ISTE; 2007). In ISTE's NETS for Students (NETS·S), the organization referenced similar themes as the NCTM position. It called for students to use technology to help promote critical thinking skills and solve problems. It also looked for students to be able to utilize technology to gather, evaluate, and use data. ISTE took things a step further by stating that students should be able to creatively think, construct knowledge, and apply existing knowledge using technology. What the standards put forth by NCTM and ISTE make clear is that in order for a child to be successful, in mathematics or in any other subject, technology must play a critical role.

Although there are many new technologies that are available to math teachers for implementation in their classrooms, the rest of this chapter will discuss three of them: wikis, podcasts, and student response systems.

Wikis

Before discussing all of the uses of a wiki, it is important to make one important distinction about wikis. Wikis often are compared to another technology driven by Web sites—blogs. In a nutshell, a blog (also known as a Weblog) is a Web site that functions as a personal writing space with dated entries that are posted in reverse chronological order. Comments can be provided to the posts, which the author publishes on his or her blog. Teachers sometimes ask whether a wiki or a blog is more appropriate for their classes. It is a common dilemma for teachers to have, due to the fact that blogs and wikis share a lot of common characteristics. Understanding the difference between them is the key to answering that question. Both make it extremely easy for users to post data. Both feature search capabilities as well as the ability to tag data. However, there are critical differences that make it essential for teachers to understand the nature of both technologies. Table 2.1 describes these differences.

What Is a Wiki?

A wiki, in its most basic form, is a Web site that allows visitors to make changes, corrections, or contributions. The meaning of the word *wiki* itself, the Hawaiian word for "fast" or "quick," says a lot about the technology it stands for. All that is usually required in order to use a wiki is access to a computer with Internet connectivity. Students and teachers are able to modify the page without needing prior knowledge of Web page authoring tools or any degree of technical expertise. A wiki provides users with a document that is open to revision by any number of authors. Wikis are searchable, easy to navigate, and allow for categorization of information and file management.

Wikis have multiple uses in the classroom. Table 2.2 provides a few suggestions for educational uses of this technology tool.

TABLE 2.1
Wiki vs. Blogs

Wiki	Blog
With a wiki, the organization of the page is flat. If another page is needed, you can simply create another page and link to it.	In a blog, the basic organizing principle is the reverse chronological order in which the posts appear (Doyle, 2006). The date and time of each post determine where data will be classified in the structure of the blog, meaning that newer data will always appear at the top.
Wikis act as a knowledge repository, storing data in whatever format and context that the users working on the page choose to render it.	Blogs post data in terms of the date and time the data is posted.
Wikis are designed to be edited and read by many users.	Blogs are meant to be written by one and read by many.
If the goal of your site is to provide structured information (using a table of contents) or a space for students to collaborate, then a wiki would be an ideal choice.	If the only goal of your Web site is to distribute information (e.g., you need a way to post homework assignments or information for your class), then a blog might be a useful choice because the latest assignment or announcement would appear on top for students to see.

TABLE 2.2
Educational Suggestions for a Wiki

- ☀ Students can use wikis to collaboratively develop research projects.
- ☀ Students can use a wiki page as a place to gather and organize research notes.
- ☀ Students can create detailed resource pages on topics by linking research found on the Web to their wiki pages.
- ☀ Teachers can allow students to use a wiki to summarize their readings and create a virtual, collective annotated bibliography.
- ☀ Teachers can use wikis to post course resources such as links to Web sites, handouts, or assignments.
- ☀ Teachers can use wikis as a knowledge base where they can share ideas, reflections, and thoughts about teaching practices. This idea is designed to allow teachers to collaborate with each other about best practices.
- ☀ Groups of students can use wikis as a substitute for more traditional presentation software such as PowerPoint. By doing a presentation using a wiki, students can edit and comment directly on the presentation while it actually is occurring. This can wind up being an enormous time saver because it eliminates the need to collate and organize feedback after a presentation.
- ☀ The entire class can use wikis for concept mapping and brainstorming.

Note. From Duffy and Burns (2006).

Uses of a Wiki

The structure of a wiki page is fairly simple. The layout of the basic wiki page contains several buttons and tabs that make it easy to create a navigational structure comprised of additional pages you wish to create. Figure 2.1 shows a basic wiki page from the site Wikipedia.

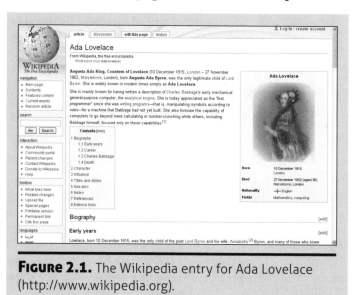

FIGURE 2.1. The Wikipedia entry for Ada Lovelace (http://www.wikipedia.org).

The beauty of such simplicity is that you and your students do not have to concern yourselves about the aesthetics of the site but, rather, can focus solely on the content they wish to produce. Additionally, the lack of complication in implementing changes to the wiki page also limits the technological hurdles involved for your students to work on the site. Despite the fact that there are not a significant number of customizable options on the page, most wikis will provide your students with the ability to post various types of media such as videos, pictures, or audio to the page. In addition, your students can easily insert text and add as many hyperlinked pages they wish.

In addition to the wiki page itself, there are two tabs present on each page that provide additional functionality for you and your students: the history and discussion tabs. The history tab links to a page where anyone with access to the page can see the history of the page, including any edits that were made to the page as well as who made those changes (see Figure 2.2). This can be especially valuable because it lends some insight into which students are contributing more than others and to what degree. Additionally, you have the ability to look at the nature of each of the edits. By looking at each of the entries on the history page, you can see whether the edit was collaborative in nature (meaning an edit of already existing work) or new content as well as whether or not the new content provided value to the page.

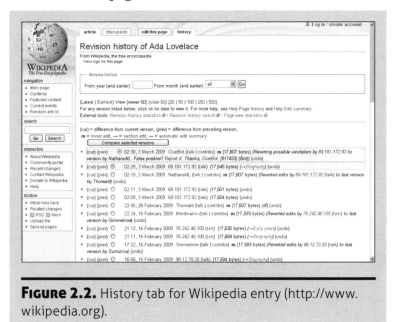

FIGURE 2.2. History tab for Wikipedia entry (http://www. wikipedia.org).

The discussion tab is where you can provide an area to respond to student questions as well as facilitate discussions about the work (see Figure 2.3). You can ask questions, make suggestions, and stimulate the learning potential of each activity by making recommendations about the wiki page without directly making edits to the page itself (Lund & Smørdal, 2006).

When students collaborate on a project, the traditional model has been for students to work on a document and send it to one another, allowing others to work on it. This presents some obvious problems, because it can be difficult for groups of students to keep track of the latest edits and revisions. If students work on one document, it creates a situation where some students are waiting for another student to finish working. If several students work on a document at the same time, all of their revisions may not be included in the edited document. If students all work on separate documents, then an effort must be coordinated to merge all of the changes into one cohesive document.

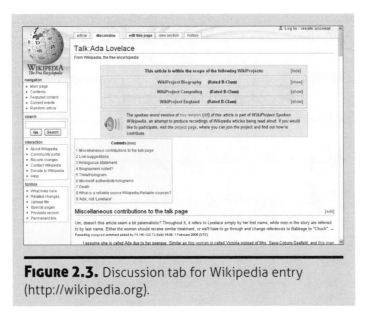

Figure 2.3. Discussion tab for Wikipedia entry (http://wikipedia.org).

One of the most important functions of a wiki is the fact that a wiki forces users to work on one document only. It resides on the wiki's host site so it is not necessary for students to send a document back and forth. In addition to allowing multiple students to work on a document at once, it also keeps track of the changes that each student makes so that it is easy to find out how much each student contributed to a project.

Benefits: Why Should I Use a Wiki in My Classroom?

Wikis provide several educational benefits, primarily due to the fact that they address a number of learning paradigms. The first learning paradigm addressed is that of collaborative learning. In collaborative learning, students work in groups where each individual member of the group depends on and is accountable to the other members. This often occurs when groups of students work together to search for solutions to a problem or to create some type of end product of their learning. The collaborative nature of wiki technology makes it an ideal solution for activities that promote collaborative learning and, particularly, computer-supported collaborative learning, which is collaboration through the use of technology to promote and increase learning. One thing that can enhance collaborative learning is when it occurs within a community of practice (Parker & Chao, 2007). This is a process that occurs when people are collaborating and working toward a common goal within the same context.

Wikis are an ideal tool toward this end because they serve as a knowledge platform where the users can contribute various types of information to help meet the goals of the group (Schaffert et al., 2006).

Wikis also address constructivist learning. Because constructivism focuses more on knowledge that is constructed rather than given, a wiki would seem to fit that model quite well. According to Seitzinger (2006), "Wikis seem to be the ultimate tool for constructive learning, providing a problem manipulation space, cognitive tools, learner-centeredness, and social presence through communities of learners, interactivity, and support, all in one place" (p. 11). An illustration of how the community of learners comes into play can be found by examining the fact that any student who is a member of the wiki can change anything within the wiki. However, students generally will not make changes that do not fit into the context that they have created on the page. Students have to add their work but only in a way that will gain acceptance by the rest of the group to ensure that the newly added data will remain. Additionally, the ability for wikis to show all of the previous versions in the history tab allows the teacher to see the evolution of the students' thought processes as well as to see how they are interacting with each other. Because wikis are very easy for students to use but also very flexible in terms of the functionality that they provide, they create opportunities to offer collaborative, constructive learning throughout educational environments (McMullin, 2005).

Another benefit of using a wiki for educational purposes has to do with how group work is conducted. In the past, in order for students and teachers to work on a group project, it involved coordinating many people to be present at the same time in the same place. The nature of a wiki allows anyone to access it from any location provided that he or she has a Web-enabled computer. This means that physical location is no longer as large of a consideration when assigning group work. Also, because many students have crowded daily schedules, wikis allow them to meet the rigors of their daily schedule while still collaborating on group projects.

How to Create Your Own Wiki

Once you have decided whether or not to host your own wiki or to use an online provider, you can get started with working on your own. The process is extremely simple. For the purposes of this example, we will create a wiki using the online wiki hosting service, PBWiki (also known as PBworks). The steps are as follows:

Step 1: Locating and Initiating the Process
1. Go to http://pbwiki.com
2. Click on the "Academic Solutions" link. This will bring you to PBWiki's information on classroom integration.
3. After reading about classroom integration, click "Try It Now!"
4. On this page, you will be given several pricing options for obtaining your own wiki. If you are not sure what your needs are, you can choose to create a free wiki now and upgrade to a higher priced model at a later time. Click on "Select" under the Basic category to get a free wiki.

Step 2: Creating Your Wiki Account
1. First, you must choose a domain for your wiki. If I choose, for instance, a domain name of mrlubinsky, then I will be able to access my wiki by going to mrlubinsky.pbwiki.com.
2. Second, enter in what the wiki is for, the company type, and wiki (work-space) purpose.
3. Third, enter your name, e-mail address, and password in order to create your account.
4. Finally, click "Next."

Step 3: Confirming Your Account
1. A confirmation e-mail will be sent to your inbox to verify your identity (see Figure 2.4).

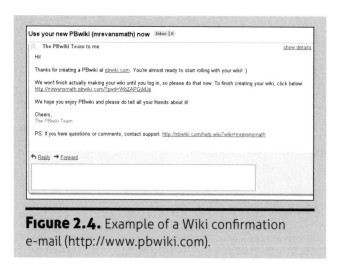

FIGURE 2.4. Example of a Wiki confirmation e-mail (http://www.pbwiki.com).

2. You will have to go to your e-mail inbox, read the confirmation message from PBWiki, and then click the confirmation link that is embedded in the message.
3. When you click on the link contained in the message, you will be brought to a page that asks you to select some security settings for your wiki.

Step 4: Creating Security Settings for Your Wiki
1. First, you will have to choose who can see your wiki. You can leave it viewable to anyone or only to those people who you invite or approve. The default option is to allow anyone to view your wiki.
2. Second, you must choose who is permitted to edit your wiki. The options are anyone can edit the page or only those who you invite or approve. The default option is only those users who you've invited or approved.
3. Once you have made your choices, you must read and accept PBWiki's Terms of Service.
4. Click "Take me to my wiki."
5. At this point, you will be on your wiki page (see Figure 2.5). There are a series of manuals and quick 30-second videos designed to help you navigate, edit, and allow users to access your page.

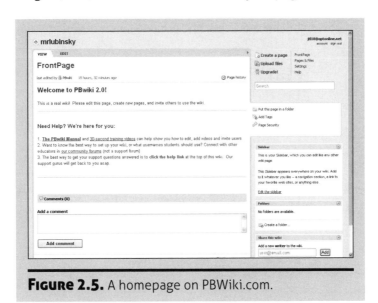

FIGURE 2.5. A homepage on PBWiki.com.

Step 5: Creating Student Accounts
1. You can click on the "Settings" button on the right hand side on the wiki page.
2. Click "Users" under "Access Control."

3. Click on the link that says "create accounts for your students" (see Figure 2.6). This will bring you to an easy-to-use wizard that will allow you to create accounts for all of your students.

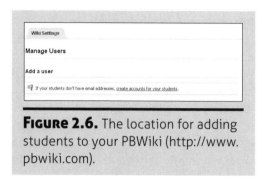

FIGURE 2.6. The location for adding students to your PBWiki (http://www.pbwiki.com).

4. The first step will be to create classroom accounts (see Figure 2.7). You are prompted to enter in the number of students who need accounts. Additionally, you are asked to assign a role (or level of access) to cover all of the users. The levels available are Writer, Editor, and Reader. The value you enter here will be the default value entered for each student. If you would like to customize particular students to have different values, you will have the opportunity to do so on the next page.

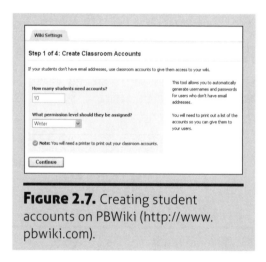

FIGURE 2.7. Creating student accounts on PBWiki (http://www.pbwiki.com).

5. Once you select the number of accounts needed and their level of access, you will have the opportunity the enter in the names of each of your students, each student's role (if it is different than the default), and his or her username and default password. PBWiki will suggest usernames and passwords that you can use but you may choose to use your own standard usernames.

6. You will be asked to confirm all of the details that you just entered. Be sure to check the spelling as you will not be able to change the account names once they are created. If you need to change any information, click "Edit Accounts." Once you are sure all of the information is correct, you can click "Create Accounts."
7. After creating the accounts, you will be able to print out the list of accounts in order to distribute them to your students. A copy of the accounts created also will be sent to your e-mail address.

Considerations

Although wikis are an excellent technological tool to introduce into the classroom, there are still some issues that merit consideration. The first has to do with preparation. It is important for you to spend time with your classes introducing them to the details and features of the wiki as well as appropriate use (Notari, 2006). Also, the writing style that is used within wikis often is different than that of traditional essay writing. Many of the recommended wiki activities for educational use require different structures and procedures so outlining the differences are an important task for you to spend time on prior to engaging in wiki activities.

From a technological standpoint, not all wikis allow pages to be locked; meaning that if two students are working on a page at the same time, the possibility exists that one student will overwrite the second student's work without notifying the student losing the work. Wikis that do not allow you to see and restore to earlier edits of a wiki page should not be used. Versioning is a critical feature of educational wiki use and must be present in order to maximize the ease of use for both teacher and student. If someone deletes critical information or adds inappropriate content, the wiki page can simply be reverted back to an earlier version.

As a teacher, there also can be some issues with implementing a wiki into your classroom. Among the challenges that can present themselves are that tracking changes, while managed through the history tab, can be a time-consuming process. Also, because many wiki pages start off as being accessible to anyone, you should consider ways to restrict access so that only students of you class can edit pages on the wiki. Without assigning appropriate access rights to students, you will not be able to track who is making which changes.

Determining a way to grade students for work done on a wiki also can be a challenge because the end product is a collaborative effort. Teachers can go through the history of the revisions in order to see how often changes were made by individual students as well as what the changes were comprised of. However, it is wise if the teacher has given consideration to these issues in advance and perhaps created a rubric to assist with assessment.

Selecting the Right Wiki

Choosing where to host your wiki is another decision you must consider before beginning wiki work with your students. There are routes to take for both beginners as well as advanced users. An excellent site called WikiMatrix (http://www.wikimatrix.org) can walk you through a wizard to help you choose which options might be right for you. There are two ways of running your own wiki. You can choose to either set up wiki software on your school's hardware and host the wiki yourself or you can simply subscribe to a hosted service on the Internet that will run the wiki for you (Alexander, 2006). Running your own software installation gives you more control over the Wiki, but also involves more overhead and requires a greater level of technology expertise. For those looking to host your own site, there are several good wiki software packages to use. Two good options are MediaWiki (http://www.mediawiki.org/wiki/MediaWiki), the same software used to drive Wikipedia, and TikiWiki (http://www.tikiwiki.org).

Most hosted services are free and provide premium add-on services for educators. For instance, PBWiki (http://www.pbwiki.org), which already has been discussed, offers all of the key wiki functionalities needed such as the ability to embed audio and video as well as see past revisions and reverse any changes. Although all of this is free, in order to provide access control an add-on must be purchased. Another site, WikiSpaces (http://www.wikispaces.com) has been providing ad-free, private K–12 classroom wikis for several years containing functionality that allows for customized security.

Integrating Wikis Into Math Instruction

Wikis can be an excellent tool in mathematics for both teachers to use to provide students with information as well as to create pages for students to create collaborative work (Lightle, 2008). One good example of a fifth-grade wiki used for math is Mr. Ferrell's Class Wiki (http://mrferrell.pbworks.com/Math; see Figure 2.8) from Pioneer Ridge Middle School in Gardner, KS. On this page, the teacher not only uses the wiki to provide pages for students to post their projects and response to math questions but also to post resources to math resources online. In this example, student group pages are created underneath each project's page. Students have a safe environment where they can personalize and take ownership of the content on the page and post questions as well as information related to the project.

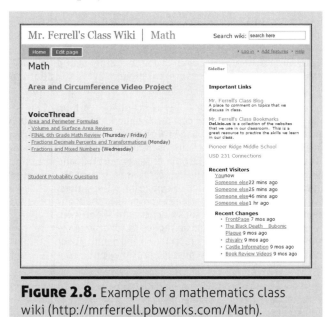

FIGURE 2.8. Example of a mathematics class wiki (http://mrferrell.pbworks.com/Math).

In elementary and middle school mathematics courses, there are a number of useful applications that wikis can provide from a collaborative perspective. Table 2.3 provides only a few suggestions.

Before you create a wiki in your classroom, you should consider the following questions to help you plan for creation and implementation of the wiki:

☀ What features would you like the wiki to have? For example, do you need versioning capabilities or the ability to make wiki pages private?

☀ Will you need to host the wiki at your school or use a wiki hosting service? Does the service have all of the features you need?

TABLE 2.3
Useful Wiki Applications and Benefits

Activity	Example	Benefit
Real-World Math	This idea helps teachers introduce the concept of the wiki to their classes. Students can use this wiki to finally answer the age-old question of "When will I ever need to know this?" Teachers would create a wiki page for the entire class to work on and students can collaboratively work to fill in the page throughout the year with real-world examples and applications of the mathematical concepts they are learning in class.	This project can be worked on by whole classes at any level. The upside to this type of assignment is that it will keep students thinking and watching the world around them for evidence of math for the duration of the school year.
A "Numbers" Wiki	Students can use a wiki to post examples of various numbers in as many ways as possible. For instance, students can show the number 20 as a product of 5 and 4 or 10 and 2. This can be done graphically so that students get a solid grasp of the idea of multiple representations.	This is great for new users of wikis because it is relatively basic conceptually but provides students with an opportunity to work with wikis.
Unit Summaries	As classes start to introduce new concepts or work on units with a large number of new terminologies, teachers can either create an empty page for the unit or have the students populate it with definitions of terms, or teachers can start the page off with just the terms themselves and have students fill in the definitions for those terms. At Ms. Barnes-Cardinale's Pre-Algebra wiki page (http://bc-gators.wikispaces.com), she uses this idea to post pages about different prealgebra concepts for students to post notes on. One area where this idea could be applied to, for example, is geometry. Students can post information and details about each of the shapes as well as post pictures they find of the various shapes.	This is a particularly nice strategy for younger students as this helps them to hone their word processing skills as well as work on definitions of math terminology.
Math Writing	Teachers also can have students work in groups and assign mathematical writing assignments to each group such as having them write out procedures to math concepts that require multiple steps. Examples could range from simple concepts, such as converting numbers from one form (such as fractions or decimals) to another; to more advanced concepts such as, for algebra students, factoring polynomials. One way to organize this type of assignment would be to create a wiki page for the assignment and then create additional pages for each of the groups. The teacher would then have to assign access rights to each group page so that only members of that group can edit the page. Finally, the teacher would create links to each of the group pages on the main assignment page. In general, this is a good procedure to follow when trying to create individual wiki pages for groups for any assignment.	This type of activity provides several benefits. First, students engage in writing about the mathematics they are learning in class. Second, they work collaboratively within the framework of the wiki. Finally, the end-product is a resource that can be used as a reference for the students in the class.
Problems of the Week	For longer, more difficult problems, such as Problems of the Week, teachers can post them on a wiki page where students can post their thoughts and work together on devising a strategy to solve the problem. Teachers would create the wiki page where the problem would be posted and students act as contributors to the page.	Using a wiki for this type of activity allows students to collaboratively engage in solving problems. The solutions can then be used as a source for studying for tests.

- ☀ Have you prepared your students to use the wiki before assigning them projects? Have you modeled correct usage for them?
- ☀ Have you given thought to how students will be assessed for their work on the wiki? Have you created a rubric?
- ☀ Are the activities you are assigning appropriate for a collaborative technology such as a wiki or would they be more appropriate for other technologies like a blog?

"Mathcasting" (Podcasting)

Mathcasting is a form of podcasting, which is a way of distributing types of media called podcasts (made up of audio or visual content) over the Internet. The term podcasting originally came from the words "iPod" and "broadcasting," as the first podcasts were essentially audio content distributed over the Internet onto iPods. Despite the fact that iPod is a part of the actual name, having an iPod is not a requirement to accessing a podcast. Although a portable media device would be useful for accessing podcasts, only access to a computer is necessary.

Over time, as more devices were able to access podcasts, the term *podcasting* came to stand for Portable On Demand Broadcasting. Listening to a podcast is similar to listening to a radio broadcast or watching a television show, except that the user does not have to tune in at a set time in order to watch or listen. A user can watch or listen at whatever time or day he or she prefers. The difference between a podcast and a simple audio or video file saved on the Internet is that, through the use of another technology called Really Simple Syndication (RSS), you can subscribe to a particular podcast and receive any newly posted content without having to go out and get it.

The way that podcasting normally works is that the person creating the podcast (known as the podcaster) first creates the podcast. Once the podcaster has completed the creation and editing of his podcast, he must publish the podcast to the Internet. This is done by uploading the file to a Web site that allows for RSS technology to create a feed. This feed, in turn, allows users to subscribe to the podcast. Once users subscribe to the podcast, new content is pushed out to them and they are able to listen to or watch the podcast.

Uses

As with many technologies, podcasts first made their appearance in the classroom as a way of making teachers' lives easier. Initially, podcasting was used in education at the university level, where professors found that they could save their lectures and have students download them for later use. However, educators quickly discovered that podcasting could be much more than simply converting classroom lectures into downloadable audio content. Educators began building onto their original use by overlaying audio to their PowerPoint presentations and streaming them out as video podcasts that were viewable on students' computers. From there, the number of uses began to grow. Table 2.4 provides some suggestions for using podcasting in the classroom.

Benefits

Podcasts can provide a great deal of value whether they are generated by teachers for the benefit of their classes or by students as part of a class activity or assignment. There are many benefits to podcasting but among the most prominent is the fact that teachers are able to reach large numbers of students by utilizing a technology that is both engaging and meaningful. If you walk through almost any school, you will see students with any number of devices such as iPods, cell phones, or digital audio players that all have the capability of listening to (or some cases, watching) content that they download. Even many students who do not have access to mobile devices can still leverage the power of the content by using their home computers. Using podcasting for educational purposes allows teachers to capitalize on the fact that students will be able to access content at any time. Table 2.5 provides additional benefits of teacher-created podcasts.

When the discussion changes to podcasts that are student-created, there are additional benefits that can be found. When students work in groups to create podcasts, they are engaging in activities that are essential to 21st-century skills such as collaboration. Also, when students create and edit their own podcasts, they are meeting ISTE technology standards that require students to be able to use existing knowledge to create digital content. Students then are provided with a "richer learning environment" (Seitzinger, 2006, p. 8).

TABLE 2.4
Educational Suggestions for Podcasting

Here are just some of the uses of podcasting in the K–12 classroom:

- ☀ Audio or visual recordings of classroom lessons can be accessible for students outside of the classroom.
- ☀ Mathcasting is a form of podcasting that involves creating podcasts where the content is mathematical in nature (Fahlberg-Stojanovska, Fahlberg, & King, 2008). Creating a mathcast usually involves digitally recording on-screen writing and overlaying it with voice narration.
- ☀ Recorded interviews with classroom guest speakers can be accessible for students online.
- ☀ Screencasts where information from the screen can be captured and overlaid with audio. One example where this might be useful is if a teacher is showing some useful Web resources for students to use for a project. The teacher actually can give a tour of the site and capture the audio while browsing the sites. This captured visual content then becomes a podcast.
- ☀ Video podcasts (also known as VODCasts) can capture video such as student performances or presentations.
- ☀ Student work such as presentations or group projects can utilize podcasts.
- ☀ Younger students can use podcasting to assist in a variety of learning activities such as learning vocabulary.

TABLE 2.5
Educational Benefits of Podcasting

Here are just some of the benefits of using teacher-created podcasts in the K–12 classroom:

- ☀ In a traditional classroom setting, if a student misses something the teacher said, he or she is limited to options like asking a neighbor (potentially disruptive to the class) or relying on another student's notes (not necessarily an accurate interpretation of the teacher's statements). With podcasting, students receive unlimited access to a lesson and can replay it an unlimited number of times.
- ☀ Not only can podcasts be replayed an unlimited number of times, but they can be replayed at any time or place depending on a student's access to a portable media device. Students also can multitask and listen to podcasts while conducting other work as well.
- ☀ Students with disabilities find significant value in having access to both audio and visual podcasts. These help students to better retain and gain a greater understanding of the material presented during lessons.
- ☀ The presence of podcasting can reduce the amount of time that students spend during class taking notes. This is particularly true if the teacher creates visual podcasts containing the teacher's presentation as well as the audio to go with it. The reduction in time needed to take notes will allow students to focus more on trying to comprehend and absorb the material contained in the teacher's lesson. This also can lead to greater interaction between student and teacher.
- ☀ The podcasts themselves not only reduce the amount of time needed to take notes in class but become an excellent supplement to traditional class notes.
- ☀ Students who benefit from auditory learning may get more value from podcasts than from traditional class notes or handouts.

Considerations

Despite all of the benefits and educational opportunities that podcasting brings to the table, there are still some issues that need consideration when implementing podcasts. One of the major benefits of this technology is the portability aspect of the podcast, but there is no guarantee that all students will have access to technology that will allow them to take advantage of that benefit. And although students can still access the content using a computer, losing the ability to take the podcast on the go is a big detriment.

Depending on the podcasting setup, there can be a steep learning curve for both teachers and students. Unlike may other technologies used in the classroom, the technical requirements for podcasting can be cumbersome. The more complicated the setup, the more difficult it will be for teachers and students to not only learn how to create podcasts, but to train others as well. The catch is that easier-to-use setups can tend to produce lower quality podcasts. The problem can be compounded by the fact that many podcasters are not trained to create high-quality audio recordings.

Selection

Selecting a setup for podcasting differs from many other technologies because rather than subscribing to one service or purchasing one piece of software, there are several considerations that need to take place when purchasing equipment for podcasting. This includes solutions that range from the inexpensive to the very expensive. Understanding what you need will help determine what type of podcasting setup is best for your needs.

At a bare minimum, in order to create a podcast you must have access to a computer, high-speed Internet access, and a microphone. However, there are some things that need to be taken into consideration when selecting the various resources needed. Here is a short guide to help you wade through all of the considerations involved in getting started with podcasting:

Step 1: Choosing Your Computer
1. *Operating System:* The computer is used to record, edit, and upload the podcast and can be either a PC or a Mac. The choice you make for your operating system can determine which software packages are available to you (e.g., many Macs come preloaded with GarageBand, a tool for

creating audio output). Be sure to consider the software you plan on using when selecting your operating system or vice versa.

2. *Memory/Processor:* Working with audio and video can be a very resource-intensive process and using a computer with insufficient memory and processing power can create a frustrating situation for the podcaster as performing even simple tasks can be very time-consuming.

3. *Hard Disk Space:* Hard drive space also is important as working with large media files can take up huge portions of the local hard disk. Podcasters who are planning on creating large amounts of content should consider purchasing an external hard drive, which is a cost-effective way of obtaining additional storage space.

Step 2: Selecting Your Microphone

1. Microphones come in many shapes and sizes but are critical to the creation of a podcast because they capture all of the audio that will be contained in the podcast. For basic podcasting purposes, podcasters can pick any unidirectional microphone that connects to their computer. Unidirectional microphones are ideal because they only capture audio input from one direction and ignore background noise and sound from other directions. There are some options to consider when choosing the type of microphone to get:

   a. *Headset microphone:* This is essentially a set of headphones with a microphone attached to it.

   b. *Freestanding microphone:* A freestanding microphone is a more traditionally known form of microphone but when used for podcasting purposes should be acquired in combination with a shock mount, a stand that minimizes bumping, as well as a pop filter, which is a filter that protects the microphone and prevents certain popping noises that occur when people speak from making it onto the recording.

   c. *Wireless lavalier microphone:* Also known as a lapel microphone, podcasters can attach this type of microphone to their shirt as well as hook an attached transmitter to their pants. All of the audio information is transmitted to a receiver that is connected to the computer. This is a good solution for users who plan on making live recordings of classes because the podcaster will not be physically limited to the computer and can walk around the room (provided that the distance is still within range of the receiver).

   d. *Alternative solutions:* There also are some excellent alternative solutions to consider for microphones.

      i. *Microphone attachments:* One way that teachers have students participate in group podcasting activities is to utilize sets of iPods (or other portable media devices) by using attachments that convert the iPod into a digital recorder.

Students can use the iPod to work in class and create recordings that then can be connected to the computer and downloaded for editing. Teachers who are considering group work or are looking to have students do audio recording outside of the classroom may want to consider this into their initial costs as this provides an excellent means of getting technology into the hands of students who may not otherwise be able to access technology to record their own audio.

    ii. *Audio capture sites:* There also are Web sites out there that will capture audio from a cell phone and convert it into usable content. This can include interviews as well as simple, one-person recordings. One example of a service like this is http://www.voice2page.com.

Step 3: Selecting Other Components

1. *Audio Mixers:* Although not required to create a podcast, audio mixers allow podcasters to mix multiple audio sources into one recording as well as adjust all of the audio levels. Many audio mixers are relatively inexpensive and can be purchased for less than $100. Rather than use an attachment for their personal media device, some podcasters prefer to simply purchase digital recorders and, although these are pricier than the attachments for the personal media devices, they often provide better quality

2. *Software:* Software is another consideration when working with podcasting. There are several types of software that play a part in podcasting. For audio files, editing software will be needed to convert your audio into a podcasting format (such as an MP3 file). For both PC and Mac users, one popular option for free software is Audacity (http://audacity.sourceforge.net). Although many people love the software, the one downside to consider is that an additional component, called a LAME MP3 encoder, also must be downloaded in order to give it the functionality to create MP3 files. However, this is a small downside as the Audacity site contains detailed information on how to download and install the additional component. (You can find that information here: http://audacity.sourceforge.net/help/faq?s=install&item=lame-mp3.) One software package that is only available to Mac users is GarageBand. This is part of Apple's iLife package and is a very comprehensive audio editing solution.

3. For podcasting solutions that involve either screencasting or mathcasting, there are some additional software and hardware components that need to be obtained:

    a. *Screen recording software:* The first is screen recording software. One popular option is Camtasia Studio (http://www.techsmith.com/camtasia.asp; see Figure 2.9), which is an easy-to-use software package that contains many excellent features for podcasting. Podcasters can record content on the screen synched with audio as well as with video content if desired. It contains editing software and also optimizes the final edited content to be exported for various formats such as iPod, Web, blog, and the like. Another option that many podcasters have used is Jing (http://www.jingproject.com) which is free. This is not as robust as Camtasia but it allows to you capture short screencasts (of up to 5 minutes in duration) and upload them directly to http://screencast.com where it provides you with a URL to the video. For a fee, Jing can be upgraded so that the videos created can be exported to a variety of file formats.

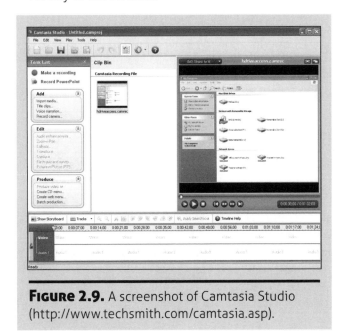

Figure 2.9. A screenshot of Camtasia Studio (http://www.techsmith.com/camtasia.asp).

b. *Input capture device:* Mathcasting requires some additional components as well. Because the goal of mathcasting is to capture math work, there needs to be some type of input device to capture the writing necessary to perform math problems. One option is for a full electronic whiteboard to be used (such as a SMART Board). Another option is for a wireless tablet to be used that performs the same functionality as the electronic whiteboard. With either solution, you will need software that can capture the writing and allow for annotation. Many solutions come with their own software to capture the writing done on the board or tablet. Once set up, users simply start recording using the screen recording software (such as Camtasia) and begin working on the input device (the whiteboard or tablet) while speaking into the microphone. Once he or she stops recording, the podcaster will have the raw mathcast and simply has to edit it in order to make it ready for distribution.

Another factor that needs to be considered when working with podcasts is distribution. As with almost all of the other aspects of podcasting, there are both free and cost models of distributing your podcast. In this case, using a free model involves several more steps than paying. If you are working with using a free-distribution model, you must follow the following steps:

Step 1: Uploading Your Podcast
1. You can upload your podcast to a site that offers free media hosting (such as Ourmedia at http://www.ourmedia.org).

Step 2: Creating a Blog
1. Once your media is uploaded, you must create a blog at any blogging site such as WordPress (http://www.wordpress.com).

Step 3: Obtaining an RSS Feed
1. The key to distributing your podcast is to create an RSS feed, which the blog should provide for you. If the blog service you choose does not have an RSS feed that supports audio you can use a free service called Google FeedBurner (http://www.feedburner.com), which converts non-audio RSS feeds into audio-supported RSS feeds. Once your blog and RSS feed are set up you are ready to go.

Step 4: Adding New Podcasts
1. Whenever you have an episode of your podcast to upload, you can add it as a post on your blog with information such as the title and number of the episode, a description of the show, and a link to the actual media file online. Listeners then only need subscribe to the RSS feed of the blog in order to subscribe to the podcast.

GETTING THE WORD OUT: DISTRIBUTING YOUR PODCAST

If you want your podcast to gain viewers outside of your immediate classroom, you also will need to publish your podcast feed to a podcasting directory. podCast 411 (http://www.podcast411.com/page2.html) features a list of podcast directories to choose from. The list is updated to keep track of any directories that may no longer be active. Each site contains instructions on how to list your podcast in its directory so that it can be searched by Internet users. You also can have your podcast linked to iTunes for free after it's published. This linking allows people browsing and searching for material on iTunes to find your podcast when they otherwise may not have discovered it.

Paying an online service is much easier. Podcasting hosts (such as Liberated Syndication at http://www.libsyn.com) manage all of those steps for you. They host your media files, create a blog, and set up the RSS feeds as well. Although this is a much easier approach, there is a cost associated with it and cost models change from host to host depending on the storage space you need.

Math Integration

One way that podcasting has impacted the mathematics classroom is through mathcasting. Mathcasts can be created by either teachers or students. Table 2.6 lists some of the useful applications and benefits of mathcasts.

One of the inherent advantages of mathcasting is that once a mathcast is created and published, it becomes a permanent part of the class' knowledge base. At the end of the school year, it is still there and as each year passes, teachers can work with classes to create additional mathcasts that address the same topics but with different questions or levels of difficulty. As this knowledge repository grows, teachers will have material that is differentiated for students of all ability levels. Having this available to students as a resource would be invaluable to helping improve the math performance of students. After several years, the teacher will have accumulated various examples from all topics in the curriculum. Students will be able to access these at any given point to assist in their learning. The potential power that mathcasting holds for education is enormous.

Many teachers who mathcast choose to upload their mathcast to an online video site such as YouTube. By doing this, the teacher then can import the video into a class wiki and have it directly accessible from the rest of the class information (Polizzi, 2008). However, several additional steps must be taken if you wish to add an RSS feed to the video in order to turn it into a podcast that users can subscribe to. If you have not already converted your file into an MP4 video file, you must do so at this point. There are several free online converters available for you to work with (any of which can be found by doing a search for "free online MP4 converter"; one good site is Movavi: http://online.movavi.com). Simply go to the site, browse your computer for your file (there is a limit of 10 minutes or 100 MB), add your file, select MP4 as your output type, and convert. Once you have the file, you can upload it to a video site such as Blip TV (http://www.

TABLE 2.6
Useful Mathcast Applications and Benefits

Activity	Example	Benefit
Capturing Specific Math Examples	With teacher-created mathcasts, the content usually is tied directly to class lessons. For example, a teacher may have taught a lesson on adding fractions and had concerns that students might run into difficulty finding the common denominator so he recorded himself solving three problems and posted it for students to view outside of the classroom.	This is particularly useful because students may not realize that they need assistance on a topic until they actually sit down to work on the problems themselves. Having access to video where the teacher is explaining the problems step-by-step can make a significant difference in a student's ability to understand the material.
Capturing Entire Lessons	Teachers can capture entire lessons to be viewed by students at a later time. They can be captured live or the teacher can select a time after doing the lesson with students to sit down and produce the mathcast by going through the slides on his or her computer. After class would be an ideal time because the teacher would have had an opportunity to see the types of questions that students had during the lesson. The teacher would then be able to answer those questions during the recording of the mathcast. Recording live can pose potential issues due to the unpredictable nature of the classroom as well as outside sources (such as PA announcements, fire drills, or monitors from the main office).	Students can access any aspect of the lesson they wish on-demand. This could mean accessing an explanation of a topic or focusing on examples. Additionally, by producing the lesson in a quiet, calm environment, the audio quality of the mathcast would more likely be much greater than that of the production quality generated by the live, in-class environment.
Student-Centered Mathcasts	Student-centered mathcasts are created by students such as the example illustrated before where the students solved math problems on the whiteboard while explaining them. One creative way that students can use podcasting for math is to come up with songs or mnemonic devices for math words or procedures.	Students have a lot of fun creating podcasts that allow them to explore their creativity and as an added bonus, they often increase their math knowledge as well.
Mathcast Assessments	Teachers also can use mathcasting as an assessment tool (Fahlberg-Stojanovska et al., 2008). Students can produce podcasts and give teachers insight into the thought processes that students undergo while solving problems.	An advantage of this is that it could help teachers pinpoint what difficulties students are having in solving a problem and allow them to address those weaknesses.

blip.tv), which provides you with an RSS feed. You can use this RSS feed in iTunes, or any other podcast directory, to create a podcast.

Before you choose to create a mathcast, you should consider the following questions:

- ☼ What type of podcasts do you want to create? Are you creating audio podcasts or do you want to screencast as well?
- ☼ What hardware and software will you need to create the podcasts?
- ☼ How will you make the podcast available to listeners? Where will you host the podcast?
- ☼ Do the podcasting activities you have planned address educational goals for your class?

Student Response Systems

Student response systems (also known as SRS, audience, classroom, or personal response systems or even more simply, clickers or remotes) have actually been around for a long time and have been used in education at the university level for years. Simply put, a student response system is comprised of a set of wireless devices (that often look like a pared-down television remote) that are distributed during class to students. Each student would receive one of the devices at the beginning of a classroom activity or lesson and, depending on the teacher's preference, each device can be registered to a particular student by having the student log in to the device. These devices communicate student input via infrared or radio frequencies to a receiving station often connected to the teacher's computer. Using software installed on the teacher's computer, teachers can use the information that is collected from the receiving station and use it in a variety of ways to further instruction in their classrooms and give teachers a sense of a class' understanding in real time (Tuttle, 2007).

Uses

There are three categories of activities that teachers can leverage using a student response system (SRS) in their classrooms (Deal, 2007). Table 2.7 describes each type in detail.

Note. Suggestions from Deal (2007).

An example of how a teacher can affect instruction through questioning in his or her classroom using a SRS is that a teacher could introduce a new mathematical concept and show an example, and a slide can be presented with a multiple-choice question related to the newly introduced concept. Now this may appear to be analogous to simply writing the problem on the board, but there is a critical difference. Students respond to the question by entering in their answer on the remote, giving you an instant assessment of the class' understanding while maintaining each student's anonymity. This creates a safe environment for your students to answer questions without fear of embarrassment for getting an incorrect answer.

In addition to creating a safe learning environment, you can immediately display the results in graphical form for the class, store the results for later use, and analyze whether particular students achieved mastery of the presented material. You are not limited to multiple-choice questions either. Depending on the make and model of the SRS, questions can range from multiple choice or true/false types of questions to text-based answers such as short answer or long-response questions (if the SRS selected supports alphanumeric responses).

Using an SRS to display student responses is beneficial for several reasons. First, students can instantly assess where they stand in relation to the rest of the class. Even though the names of the students who submitted the various answers are hidden (although teachers can display this information if desired), students can access information that normally would only be accessible to them after a final assessment on the concept was already conducted (assuming that teachers share that information with the class). Once students see where their understanding is, the teacher can take an alternative approach to teaching the concept. Teachers can have the class discuss the displayed results in small groups, allowing students to determine the best response and teach each other.

The data management and analysis tools of a SRS also are very powerful. Because the technology lends itself to assessment, teachers can use the SRS to give assessments and store the information compiled. Teachers then can use the data to pinpoint need areas for both individual students as well as the whole group. Many SRS models allow data to be exported into formats that most teachers can use such as Microsoft Excel, XML, or, in some cases, a teacher's grade book system.

Benefits

Using an SRS provides teachers with several benefits. One obvious benefit of using an SRS is that student learning is improved. Teachers are able to remove the stigma from students of incorrectly answering a question in front of their peers and allow them to become more involved in their own learning (Miller, 2007). A challenge that teachers have always faced is that usually the same group of students raise their hands to participate during a lesson while others choose to never become involved. Teachers can create a situation where they are calling on all students to respond to a question rather than calling on one raised hand. Because the technology is interactive, students are less-inclined to sit back in their chairs and allow the lesson to happen in front of them. Students today are looking to interact in the classroom in a way they are familiar with (Guthrie & Carlin, 2004).

By creating a classroom environment where students cannot be passive and must respond to a prompted question, teachers are able to manage the class and ensure that students are remaining on task. The anonymity created by an SRS helps produce near or full participation of the class when they are presented with questions (Ward, Reeves, & Heath, 2003). During the course of a question, the SRS software can display how many users have responded to the question and which students still need to respond. Because the actual results are not displayed until the teacher chooses to display them, teachers can follow up with the students who have not responded to ensure that they are participating.

From the student's perspective, even if he or she does not respond immediately, there is no fear of having other students in the class identify his or her answer choice, because the teacher is responsible for posting that information. Additionally, because the SRS requires students to pay more attention during lessons, they demonstrate better retention of the material learned (Lowery, 2006). Students also can be provided with increased opportunities to learn collaboratively from peers using peer instruction (Cline, Zullo, & Parker, 2007). Using a peer instruction approach to SRS implementation has been shown to have a significant effect on student learning in mathematics (Miller, Santana-Vega, & Terrell, 2006). Another benefit is that students are more satisfied during lessons involving an SRS than those in which they are learning passively.

From the teacher's standpoint, he or she now has access to invaluable information that previously was extremely difficult to obtain: He or she can instantly assess the class' understanding of a presented concept. By giving a quick assessment to a class using an SRS instead of a traditional paper quiz, teachers are able to save time (the time required to grade the assessment) as well as the paper costs associated with it. Additionally, because an assessment can be given at any point during the lesson, teachers can adapt or modify their lesson based on the results of the SRS assessment. For example, if a teacher is doing a lesson on adding monomials together, after presenting the topic and doing some examples for the class, a couple of questions could be presented to the class to gauge its level of understanding. If a teacher sees that, based on the results, a good portion of the class does not understand the concept or is making common mistakes such as adding the exponents together instead of the coefficients, he or she can revise the lesson plan and spend more time teaching the fundamentals of the concept. In the past, this type of information could not be obtained midstream and much time would be lost or wasted on the part of the teacher. An additional benefit is that many vendors now provide databases of questions to accompany their textbooks, making creation of an assessment a breeze.

Considerations

Although using an SRS can produce great results for a teacher, there are several drawbacks. One of the issues involved with an SRS is cost. Although many new technological tools for teachers, such as Web 2.0

applications, are free or of minimal cost for a teacher to use, SRSs do involve a little more of a financial investment. Prices on SRS classroom sets continue to drop but still run hundreds of dollars (or more depending on the brand and model chosen) per set. Many college courses often require students to purchase their own clicker ahead of time as a class supply; it may be unreasonable to expect students at the elementary or secondary level to do the same, making cost a definite consideration for teachers planning on using an SRS in a K–12 setting. In addition to the costs involved with the purchase of a unit, there are maintenance costs to consider as well. Each remote runs on its own set of batteries and as they run out, costs must be set aside to replace them. Additionally, while the remotes themselves are fairly durable, their use in a K–12 classroom, where it is possible for them to experience a good deal of wear and tear, may make it necessary to purchase replacement remotes or, at the very least, factor in the cost of some spare remotes initially so that there is no interruption in use of the SRS due to broken remotes.

From an instructional standpoint, another potential pitfall is that additional planning time must be put aside in order to figure out how to appropriately incorporate an SRS into a teacher's instruction. This means finding time to create learning activities and questions that leverage the educational benefits of the SRS. Teachers also should spend time initially going over policies, procedures, and rules for using the remotes during class. Initially, teachers may not have a complete grasp on which rules to put in place but, with more experience, they will be able to better define the way their classes should look with an SRS in place. Although using an SRS is an excellent way to increase participation of all students, it is possible that some students with disabilities may have some difficulty pressing the small buttons on the remotes or with seeing the lights on the remote.

Selection

When it comes to choosing an SRS for your classroom, there is no lack of choices in the marketplace. The challenge becomes finding the system that best suits your specific needs. Most systems come with three components: student input devices (the remotes), the receiver that attaches to the teacher's computer, and the software that must be installed on the teacher's computer. It is assumed that with any system, you have a projection system installed in your classroom to display the teacher's computer to the class. If you do not have one in place, the cost of obtaining one should be factored into the total cost of selecting an SRS. Set up of an SRS generally is a fairly painless process. Installation is relatively simple and the only area where teachers need to put some thought is the creation of login IDs for the students so that there is a way of clearly differentiating which responses belong to which students.

The input devices generally fall into two categories: inexpensive devices that utilize infrared or radio frequency keypads or expensive devices that are more sophisticated. The choice between infrared or radio frequency keypads basically boils down to whether or not you require one-way or two-way communication. Infrared keypads generally are one-way devices, meaning that when a student submits a response to the teacher, he or she can only confirm that the response has been received by checking the screen to see which users have not submitted responses. With a radio frequency device, students can receive a signal from the system letting them know that their response was received. This is a feature that is more useful in situations where the SRS is being used to maintain attendance records or is being used for graded assessments. Infrared devices also tend to more simplistic in their design, featuring response buttons, while radio-frequency devices often feature alpha-numeric keypads as well as screens that allow students to see questions and answers on them. At the elementary level, choosing a device that has fewer features and might not be as overwhelming to the students would be a preferable option.

The more expensive class of input devices is comprised of devices that have additional functionality outside of the SRS such as cell phones, laptop computers, calculators, or personal digital assistants such as Palm Pilots. Each of these devices has various features that make them extremely attractive outside of the classroom and that can tie in directly with particular SRSs. However, in elementary or middle school classrooms there are some downsides to working with some of these devices. Many schools have cell phone policies that prevent students from using cellular phone technologies in the school building. Additionally, although there is a definite benefit to leveraging a technology that many students may already have access to, it could prove difficult to work against established district policies when there are similar technologies that will provide the same functionality. Another impediment to using some of these devices is that laptops and Palm Pilot-type devices are quite expensive and not the most durable options for a middle or elementary classroom setting.

The one type of device that does have potential in the math classroom is the calculator, specifically the graphing calculators compatible with the Texas Instruments SRS, the TI-Navigator™ Classroom Learning System.

Math Integration

A study of K–12 teachers who were each given an SRS for use in their classroom showed that while a large number of elementary teachers were most likely to use their SRS across various subjects (probably due to the fact that elementary teachers are responsible for teaching a wide array of subjects), a large number of middle school teachers used their system for mathematics (Penuel et al., 2005).

The TI-Navigator is a good solution for mathematics classrooms beginning with the middle school grades. The student's input device is a graphing calculator, which in many schools is a required school supply. For the high school level, Navigator systems can currently handle TI-83 Plus and TI-84 Plus calculator families (with support soon coming for the TI-Nspire models), while at the middle school level, the TI-73 Explorer graphing calculators are supported. Because the calculators have the ability for users to enter alphanumeric data, when connected to the Navigator, they become a more advanced SRS device for students to use (see Figure 2.10).

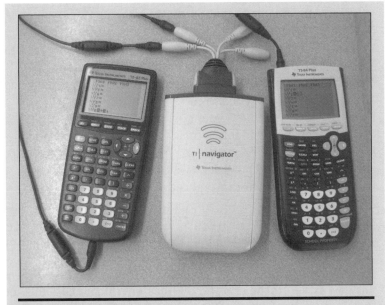

Figure 2.10. The TI-Navigator system.

The Navigator setup is comprised of the Navigator software, a Wireless Access Point that connects to the teacher's computer, a series of hubs that are placed around the room, and a set of charging bays where the hubs can be stored when they are not in use. Each hub can connect to four graphing calculators, giving them the wireless capabilities that they do not possess by default. Once students are connected to the hubs, they can login to the system directly from their calculators. Although the Navigator package contains comprehensive documentation on how to set up your system, it is worthwhile to understand what is involved in terms of classroom setup as well as getting all of your students' calculators ready to work. Here are the steps involved:

Step 1: Setting Up the Computer
1. It is necessary to install the TI-Navigator software before beginning the set up or installing any hardware. This is due to the fact that your students' calculators will need to be updated in order to work.

Step 2: Setting Up the Navigator Hardware
1. Documentation is provided in order to assist with the installation of the hardware. It is important to note that you must charge the hubs in the docking bays for several hours prior to first using them.

Step 3: Setting Up Your Calculators
1. Two things must happen to each of the student calculators. They must have the most current operating system and they must have the Navigator applications installed on the calculators.
2. Determine the operating system version. Currently, using the Navigator 3.0 software, the version of the operating system must be 1.90. You can check this by pressing 2nd and MEM. On the Memory screen, choose 1: About. This will show you the current version.
3. If the version is not 1.90, you must use the TI-Navigator software to update it. You will need this software to install the applications as well. In order to perform this update, you must make sure that the calculators are connected to the hubs and that the network is available.
4. In order to install all of the applications, select the Tools Tab and click on the App and OS Transfer Tool. The five applications that you need to send to the calculators (LearnCheck, NavNet, θAlgACT, θnavstk, and θMSact) are already loaded and ready to transfer. You also must make sure that TI-73 Explorer™ Family is the selected Class Type.
5. If any of the calculators need the latest operating system, you can install this now as well. In the App and OS Transfer Window, click the Add File... button. Using the Navigator CD, browse to the Calculator Software\TI-73 folder and select Base190.73u. Once this is selected, do not worry about

where it is in the order. By default, the new OS will be installed prior to any applications.

6. Click Start Transfer. If this is done while all of your students' calculators are connected, you will ensure that all of them receive the latest OS as well as the needed applications.

Step 4: Setting Up Classes

1. Using the documentation provided, you must set up a class on the Navigator software as well as login names for your students. Once this task is done, you should be ready to take full advantage of the Navigator.

Math teachers can find numerous ways to create age-appropriate activities that utilize the Navigator. Some of the features can be found in Table 2.8.

Using the Navigator, students can do a variety of activities that address math standards such as investigating number patterns, performing operations on stacked fractions, and plotting data in histograms. Software also is provided that allows students to explore operations on real numbers using a graphical expression as well as the tools to estimate a given area. The Fraction software that is provided allows students to visualize fractions pictorially in a variety of ways such as fractions, decimals, and percents. In addition to all of the math-specific content that is provided by the Navigator, the system also provides all of the functionality that other SRS models contain. For instance, the ability to poll students as well as assess them is present. However, the additional functionality that the Navigator provides (such as the ability to take snapshots of the student's calculator and save them) makes it a valuable addition to a mathematics classroom.

Students enjoy using the Navigator because it makes them feel as though they are partners with teachers in the learning process. They also enjoy the instantaneous nature of the feedback that they receive from the system. Teachers are able to use it in a variety of ways such as assessing their prior knowledge through a several-question warm-up at the beginning of class to Activity Center exercises, which challenge students to identify different types of graphs and predict what points will belong to each graph. Although there is a great deal of value in having the Navigator in the math classroom, there also are some challenges that can be encountered. Each calculator must be updated to have the latest operating system on it and because each student owns his or her own calculator, it can be a somewhat time-consuming process to have each student connect to the Navigator and download the latest version. Also, because the Navigator

Table 2.8
Useful TI Navigator Applications and Benefits

Activity	Example	Benefit
Activity Center	The Activity Center provided with the Navigator allows for a wide variety of lessons and activities that are interactive and meaningful for the students. An example of an activity that would be appropriate for younger grades includes data collection activities where students enter in data that the teacher can save as a list and send out to all of the students to perform operations on such as finding measures of central tendency. The data can be data that students might find interesting such as favorite numbers, birthdays, number of states visited, and so on.	Making this data meaningful to the student will increase student interest throughout the class.
Poll Center	The Poll Center allows teachers to poll students and receive, display, and review the students' responses to questions. The questions can range from multiple choice to short answer questions.	Students receive instant feedback on how they are progressing in their understanding of the course material.
Learning Check	This tool allows teachers to distribute assessments that are done on the calculator and then collected automatically. The data from these assessments can be stored and used later.	Teachers can more easily assess their classes to gauge understanding of concepts.
Screen Capture	This Navigator tool allows you to see what is on each of your student's calculator screen at any given time and capture an image. Teachers can take screenshots of student solutions and incorporate them into lessons or documents.	This tool is useful as both a classroom management tool to ensure students are remaining on task as well as to capture screen shots of student work. Students who demonstrate solutions to complex problems can show their peers how to solve them on the calculator.

hubs must be set up at the beginning of each class it may be necessary to train monitors to set up the hubs around the room at the beginning of the class period as well as put them back in the charging bays at the end of the class. Additionally, the time to set up each class in the Navigator software can be a nuisance but once it is set up, it does not need to be redone until the next year.

There has been evidence that the TI-Navigator enhances learning in the middle grades. A recent study showed that a group of mathematics students in an introductory algebra class using the TI-Navigator in conjunction with their graphing calculators outperformed students who solely used their graphing calculators (Owens et al., 2008). Another study conducted by the University of Hawaii did a similar comparison between those groupings and found that students who used the TI-Navigator in their classes demonstrated greater conceptual understanding and improvement in areas such as the quantity and quality of student responses as well as time spent on task (Dougherty, 2005). It also has been shown that the TI-Navigator is useful in helping improve outcomes related to state examinations (Stroup, Carmona, & Davis, 2005).

Before implementing an SRS in your classroom, consider the following questions:

- ☼ What types of activities do you want your students to participate in? Does the student response system you have selected allow you to work on those activities?
- ☼ Have you discussed your selection with people who work in your district to ensure that your classroom can support the selected student response system?
- ☼ Has time been spent rethinking your lessons and how you can integrate appropriate student response system activities?
- ☼ Will you be collecting and analyzing the data that can be captured by the student response system?

Conclusion

> Mr. Evans is catching up on some e-mails during his prep period when there is a knock on the door. It's two of his students from the earlier class. "Great!" Mr. Evans says, "let's get started." Over the next 20 minutes, Mr. Evans works with each of the students at his whiteboard, having them alternate turns solving problems at the board. At first glance, it might appear as though the students are coming to see him for extra help, not an uncommon situation in the school. As we are about to find out, they are there for a more exciting reason.
>
> The teacher explains the purpose of the work session. "Today we were learning how to multiply binomials, and these students both had really nice solutions to two of the problems so I asked them to come during their lunch period to record their solutions." One girl stands at the board wearing a wireless microphone and looking to Mr. Evans for her cue. "Now," he says. With that, she begins writing on the board and going step by step through the problem. Mr. Evans explains that software is installed on his computer to record all of her audio and sync it with what she is writing on the whiteboard. "Once we have it captured, I can export it and save it online for students to view or download. The cool part is that instead of just a bunch of videos with me talking, the students are the ones explaining the solutions in their own words."
>
> His goal is to create an online repository of videos for the students, by the students. They can watch them online or download them into their iPod to watch on the go. Because many of the students are very active in the community and participate in numerous extracurricular activities, the ability to have access to solutions and explanations on the go is something that many students in the class find appealing. Eventually, he plans to try to record some of his lessons to add as well. As he puts it, "I like the idea of one-stop shopping."

Only a few short years ago, these type of activities would never have been possible. In a brief period of time, the number of opportunities for mathematics teachers to expand the classroom experiences of their students has exponentially grown. A large reason for this is the number of new technologies available for teachers to incorporate into their instruction. These technologies help to break down the walls of the classroom and provide students with the ability to learn in ways that best suit their learning styles. Without the wiki, students would have to be in class or meeting in person in order to collaborate on a problem. Without the podcast, students would not be able to hear a teacher's explanation of a concept when they get stuck while studying or doing homework. Without a student response system, students would have to wait until a formal assessment to get a sense of what level of understanding on a concept they possess. Fortunately, for math teachers and students, the traditional mathematics classroom model of "chalk and talk" is quickly becoming a thing of the past and, with the help of technology, the new collaborative classroom is becoming both our present and our future.

REFLECTION

Now that you have read this chapter, reflect on your opening exercise and the information presented to do the following:

1. Write a technology goal:
   a. What skills would you like to acquire?
   b. What hardware/software would you like to acquire?
   c. Identify the resources that you need to make this happen.
2. Set a timeline for achieving your goal.

REFERENCES

Alexander B. (2006). *Web 2.0: A new wave of innovation for teaching and learning?* Retrieved from http://net.educause.edu/ir/library/pdf/ERM0621.pdf

Bing, T. J., & Redish, E. F. (2007). *Symbolic manipulators affect mathematical mindsets.* Retrieved from http://arxiv.org/ftp/arxiv/papers/0712/0712.1187.pdf

Chase, G. C. (1980). History of mechanical computing machinery. *Annals of the History of Computing, 2,* 198–226.

Cline, K., Zullo, H., & Parker, M. (2007). *Using classroom voting in mathematics courses.* Retrieved from http://archives.math.utk.edu/ICTCM/VOL19/C035/paper.pdf

Deal, A. (2007). *A teaching with technology white paper: Classroom response systems.* Retrieved from https://www.cmu.edu/teaching/resources/PublicationsArchives/StudiesWhitepapers/ClassroomResponse_Nov07.pdf

Dougherty, D. J. (2005). *TI-Navigator technology and algebra 1.* Retrieved July 8, 2009, from http://education.ti.com/sites/US/downloads/pdf/research_dougherty.pdf

Doyle, B. (2006). *EcontentMag.com: When to wiki, When to blog.* Retrieved from http://www.econtentmag.com/Articles/Column/I-Column-Like-I-CM/When-to-Wiki,-When-to-Blog-16900.htm

Duffy, P., & Burns, A. (2006). *The use of blogs, wikis, and RSS in education: A conversation of possibilities.* Retrieved January 1, 2009, from https://olt.qut.edu.au/udf/OLT2006/gen/static/papers/Duffy_OLT2006_paper.pdf

Dyck, B. (2003, Summer). When technology goes to math class. *Meridian: A Middle School Computer Technologies Journal.* Retrieved from http://www.ncsu.edu/meridian/sum2003/math/index.html

Fahlberg-Stojanovska, L., Fahlberg, T., & King, C. (2008). Mathcasts: Show-and-tell math concepts. *Learning & Leading With Technology, 36*, 30–31.

Fernandes, L. (2007). *The abacus: A brief history.* Retrieved from http://www.ee.ryerson.ca:8080/~elf/abacus/history.html

Guthrie, R. W., & Carlin, A. (2004). *Waking the dead: Using interactive technology to engage passive listeners in the classroom.* Retrieved from http://www.audienceresponseinfo.com/interactive-technology-classroom

International Society for Technology in Education. (2007). *The ISTE national educational technology standards (NETS•S) and performance indicators for students.* Retrieved from http://www.iste.org/Content/NavigationMenu/NETS/ForStudents/2007Standards/NETS_for_Students_2007_Standards.pdf

Kastberg, S., & Leatham, K. (2005). Research on graphing calculators at the secondary level: Implications for mathematics teacher education. *Contemporary Issues in Technology and Teacher Education* [Online serial], *5*(1), 25–37.

Lightle, K. (2008, August 28). *Teacher tools that integrate technology: Wikis.* Retrieved from http://expertvoices.nsdl.org/middle-school-math-science/2008/08/26/teacher-tools-that-integrate-technology-wikis

Lowery, R. (2006, April). *Clickers in the classroom: A comparison of interactive student-response keypad systems.* Paper presented at the National Technology and Social Science Conference, Las Vegas, NV.

Lund, A., & Smørdal, O. (2006). *Is there a space for the teacher in a wiki?* Retrieved from http://www.wikisym.org/ws2006/proceedings/p37.pdf

McMullin, B. (2005). Putting the learning back into learning technology. In G. O'Neill, S. Moore, & B. McMullin (Eds.), *Emerging issues in the practice of university learning and teaching.* Dublin: AISHE. Retrieved from http://www.aishe.org/readings/2005-1/mcmullin-D01-M10-2004.pdf

Miller, J. (2007). Pick and click: Interactive assessment goes to school. *Edutopia.* Retrieved from http://www.edutopia.org/assessment-classroom-response-systems

Miller, R., Santana-Vega, E., & Terrell, M. (2006). Can good questions and peer discussion improve calculus instruction? *PRIMUS, 16,* 193–203.

National Council of Teachers of Mathematics. (2008). *The role of technology in the teaching and learning of mathematics: A position of the National Council of Teachers of Mathematics.* Retrieved from http://www.nctm.org/uploadedFiles/About_NCTM/Position_Statements/Technology%20final.pdf

Notari, M. (2006). *How to use a wiki in education: Wiki based effective constructive learning.* Retrieved from http://www.wikisym.org/ws2006/proceedings/p131.pdf

Owens, D. T., Pape, S. J., Irving, K. E., Sanalan, V. A., Kim Boscardin, C., & Abrahamson, L. (2008). *The connected algebra classroom: A randomized control trial.* Retrieved from http://www.ccms.osu.edu/pub/Publications/ICME11_TSG22CCMSpaperFinal1.pdf

Owens, E., Song, H., & Kidd, T. T. (2006). *Socio-economic disparity and technology use in the urban classrooms.* Retrieved from http://www.texasacet.org/journal/ACETJournal_Vol4/Socio-EconomicDisparityAndTechnologyUse.pdf

Parker, K. R., & Chao, J. T. (2007). Wiki as a teaching tool. *Interdisciplinary Journal of Knowledge and Learning Objects, 3,* 57–72.

Partnership for 21st Century Skills. (2007). *Framework for 21st century learning.* Retrieved January 1, 2009, from http://www.21stcenturyskills.org/documents/frameworkflyer_072307.pdf

Penuel, W. R., Crawford, V., Haydel DeBarger, A., Kim Boscardin, C., Masyn, K., & Urdan, T. (2005). *Teaching with student response system technology: A survey of K–12 teachers.* Retrieved from http://www.audienceresponseinfo.com/teaching-with-student-response-system-technology

Polizzi, C. (2008). *Mr. Polizzi sixth grade math wiki* [Wiki]. Retrieved January 1, 2009, from http://mrpolizzi.wikispaces.com

Pomerantz, H. (1997). *The role of calculators in mathematics education.* Retrieved from http://education.ti.com/sites/US/downloads/pdf/therole.pdf

Schaffert, S., Bischof, D., Burger, T., Gruber, A., Hilzensauer, W., & Schaffert, S. (2006). *Learning with semantic wikis.* Retrieved from http://ftp.informatik.rwth-aachen.de/Publications/CEUR-WS/Vol-206/paper9.pdf

Seitzinger, J. (2006). *Be constructive: Blogs, podcasts, and wikis as constructivist learning tools.* Retrieved from http://www.elearningguild.com/pdf/2/073106DES.pdf

Sivin-Kachala, J., & Bialo, E. (2000). *2000 research report on the effectiveness of technology in schools* (7th ed.). Washington, DC: Software and Information Industry Association.

Stroup, W., Carmona, L., & Davis, S. M. (2005). *Improving on expectations: Preliminary results from using network-supported function based algebra.* Retrieved from http://education.ti.com/sites/US/downloads/pdf/research_stroup_carmona.pdf

Tuttle, H. G. (2007). Digital-age assessment: E-portfolios are the wave of the future. *Technology & Learning, 27*(7), 22.

United States Department of Education. (2008). *Foundations for success: The final report of the National Mathematics Advisory Panel.* Retrieved from http://www.ed.gov/about/bdscomm/list/mathpanel/report/final-report.pdf

Ward, C. R., Reeves, J. H., & Heath, B. P. (2003). *Encouraging active student participation in chemistry classes with a web.* Retrieved from http://www.chem.vt.edu/confchem/2003/a/ward/ConfChem_SRS.htm

Wenglinsky, H. (1998). *Does it compute? The relationship between educational technology and achievement in mathematics.* Retrieved from http://www.ets.org/Media/Research/pdf/PICTECHNOLOG.pdf

Appendix A

The introduction chapter introduced the importance of connecting specific tools to various digital literacy competencies. For mathematics, the connection to digital literacy is as follows:

Technology Tool	Corresponding Digital Literacy				
	Photo-Visual	Reproduction	Branching	Information	Social-Emotional
Wiki	■		■	■	
Podcasting	■	■		■	■
Student Response System	■	■	■	■	■

Appendix B
Glossary

Blog: A Web page containing a series of postings or journal entries. Most of these sites feature easy-to-use interfaces that allow users of all abilities to create their own pages.

Constructivist Learning: A learning theory that suggests that learning is an active process that requires the learner to engage in activities and reflect on what he or she has learned, constructing his or her own understanding.

Discussion Tab: This tab, featured on wiki pages, provide users with access to the wiki with an area to respond to questions as well as to facilitate discussions. Provides similar functionality to an online forum.

History Tab: This tab, featured on wiki pages, provides anyone with access to the wiki the ability to view the history of the page, including any edits that were made to the page as well as who made those changes

Mathcast: A type of screencast that centers on mathematics. They can be made available online for viewing or distributed similarly to podcasts.

Podcasting: A method of publishing digital media files (such as audio or video) to the Internet for playback on mobile devices and personal computers.

RSS (Really Simple Syndication): A syndication format that is popular for aggregating updates to blogs and news sites. An RSS aggregator or reader allows users to see summaries of all of their feeds in one place. Instead of having to visit each Web site to search for new content, the RSS aggregator will pull all of the summaries in and allow the user to choose which content to visit for the full version.

Screencasting: A video screen capture that generally is accompanied by audio narration. These can be extremely useful in education for demonstrations or tutorials.

Student Response System: A set of hardware and software that facilitates teaching activities involving student use of remote controls to respond to teacher-delivered prompts. These also are known as classroom response systems, personal response systems, or audience response systems.

Web 2.0: A term used to describe Web applications that promote greater collaboration among Internet users and other users, content providers, and enterprises. In education, examples of such applications are blogs and wikis.

Wiki: A collaborative Web site that allows users to add and update Web page content through a Web browser. Typically, each wiki is constructed through content added by multiple users.

Appendix C
Resources

Useful Web Sites (Wikis)

WIKIMATRIX
http://www.wikimatrix.org

This site walks you through the process of choosing an appropriate wiki solution for your needs. This includes options for both hosting the wiki on your school's computers and using a wiki-hosting service online.

EDUCATIONAL WIKIS
http://educationalwikis.wikispaces.com

This is a wiki that contains lists of articles and resources that describe how to use wikis in education as well as a comprehensive list of existing educational wikis (many from K–12 classrooms).

MATH CONNECTIONS
https://mathconnections.wikispaces.com

This site is collaborative project for elementary and middle school students to discover real-world math connections.

Useful Web Sites (Podcasting)

THE K–7 MATHCASTS 500 PROJECT
http://math247.pbwiki.com/K-7+Mathcasts+500+Project

The goal of this site is to create a library of more than 500 mathcasts for K–7 mathematics classes. The site contains an excellent tutorial on creating mathcasts.

FREE PODCAST COURSE
http://www.freepodcastcourse.com

This site contains an comprehensive and excellent tutorial on podcasting including detailed information on podcasting and instructions on how to create and publish your own podcasts.

WEB 2.0: COOL TOOLS FOR SCHOOLS AUDIO TOOLS
http://cooltoolsforschools.wikispaces.com/Audio+Tools

This site contains a ton of free Web 2.0 audio tools including podcasting software and audio editors. The Video Tools portion also contains excellent tools for screencasting.

BOB SPRANKLE'S ROOM 208 PODCAST

http://bobsprankle.com/podcasts/0506/rm208vodcast.mov

This is a link to a video that was recorded by Bob Sprankle's fourth-grade class in Wells, ME. It shows the students' podcasting creation process. Truly inspiring!

Useful Web Sites (Student Response Systems)

TI-NAVIGATOR HOME PAGE

http://education.ti.com/educationportal/sites/US/productDetail/us_ti_navigator.html

Home of the TI-Navigator system, this site contains resources to assist teachers in using the TI-Navigator.

PROJECT MATH QUEST

http://mathquest.carroll.edu/resources.html

This site contains a set of resources for classroom voting in mathematics.

CENTER FOR TEACHING: CLASSROOM RESPONSE SYSTEMS

http://www.vanderbilt.edu/cft/resources/teaching_resources/technology/crs.htm

This site contains resources for working with student response systems.

Integrating Technology Into Science Instruction:

Science Learning, Literacy, and the Development of 21st-Century Digital Literacy

Shiang-Kwei Wang, Hui-Yin Hsu, & Todd Campbell

GUIDING QUESTIONS

1. (a) What is the difference between a traditional approach vs. a cognitive tool approach to teaching science? (b) Which approach does my instruction tend to emulate?

2. What technologies are available to enhance science teaching and learning?

Needs Assessment

1. *Keywords*

   Look over the keywords found in this chapter listed below. Rate yourself from one to three on your familiarity with each word. Then use this rating to help you set some goals for reading this chapter.

Word	1 Don't know at all	2 Some familiarity with this word	3 Very familiar with this word
Cognitive Tools			
Simulations			
ICT			
Query			
Geospatial			

2. *Tools*

   Look over the three key technology tools listed below. Rate yourself from one to three on your familiarity with integrating these tools into your science classroom. Then use this rating to help you set some goals for reading this chapter.

Tool	1 Don't know at all	2 Some familiarity with this technology tool	3 Very familiar with this technology tool
Google Earth			
Databases			
Probeware			

3. *Goal(s) for the Chapter*

   Fill in your goals below:

   a. By reading this chapter I hope to _____

      _____ .

   b. By reading this chapter I hope to _____

      _____ .

I n a 10th-grade biology classroom, Mr. Johnson is introducing the topic of study for the next unit—living organisms' interactions with other organisms and the environment. In order to activate students' prior knowledge about organisms, he asks several questions relating to previous biology concepts studied in middle school (i.e., the life functioning of organisms as a compendium of functioning internal structures, the relationship between heritability, and organism survival in an environment). A few students are able to recall some details of the core concepts learned, but for the most part the rest of the students seem to never have studied these concepts before. To assist the students in recalling what they should have learned and will need to understand as a pretext for this unit of study, Mr. Johnson proceeds with a PowerPoint presentation along with a video to provide the students with the concepts needed and how they connect to the new concepts being studied. The presentation and video are followed by a series of questions that Mr. Johnson poses to the students. Students are then given a worksheet with the questions that Mr. Johnson posed and assigned to a group to find answers to these questions. They work in groups at their computers to find answers to the questions through Internet sites provided by Mr. Johnson. He circulates the classroom to make sure that each group is on task and stops to answer questions for clarification as needed. After the group work, Mr. Johnson asks each group to present its answers before holding a whole-group discussion to wrap up the lesson for the day.

As illustrated above, for the most part science teachers are currently integrating technologies to enhance students' science understanding, but this is being done to support instructional strategies that are out-of-step with current science education reform efforts. Reform documents have indicated that "teaching should be consistent with the nature of scientific inquiry" (American Association for the Advancement of Science [AAAS], 1989, p. 147), and that good science teaching would:

- ☼ start with questions about nature,
- ☼ engage students actively,
- ☼ concentrate on the collection and use of evidence, and
- ☼ not separate knowing from finding out. (National Research Council [NRC], 1996, p. 30)

But, as seen in the opening scenario and reported by research nationally (Campbell & Bohn, 2008; NRC, 2005; O'Sullivan & Weiss, 1999;

Windschitl, 2003), for the most part students' experiences in science classrooms are more "inclined to answering questions prescribed in the curriculum using methods also preordained in the curriculum or by the classroom teacher" (Windschitl, 2003, p. 114).

Because there is a rift in what is going on in classrooms and what is supported by research in teaching and learning and national standards documents, it is likely that technology currently is being integrated in ways supportive of traditional methods of teaching. An example of technology integration aligned with traditional methods of teaching will be helpful in illuminating this point. Consider first, a few characteristics of traditional classrooms outlined by Brooks and Brooks (1999):

- Students are viewed as "blank slates" onto which information is etched by the teacher.
- Teachers generally behave in a didactic manner, disseminating information to students.
- Teachers seek the correct answer to validate student learning.
- Assessment of student learning is viewed as separate from teaching and occurs almost entirely through testing. (p. 17)

If classrooms are conceived this way, teachers might seek out presentation technologies such as PowerPoint to enhance their capacity to "etch" learning and disseminate information. This does not mean that PowerPoint should be exclusively grouped with traditional methods of teaching. It is used in this example to exemplify the manner in which technology integration is dependent upon and driven by ideas about teaching and learning. Likewise, in traditional classrooms, when "teachers seek the correct answer to validate student learning" and "assessment of student learning is viewed as separate from teaching and occurs almost entirely through testing," teachers might seek technologies such as computer testing stations to help facilitate students' demonstration of their ability to identify correct answers in a more efficient and manageable format.

Instead of traditional views of teaching and learning, science standards documents (AAAS, 1989; NRC, 1996) were developed considering constructivist principles, "which deem learning as an interpretive process, involving constructions of individuals and social collaborations" (Tobin, Briscoe, & Holman, 1990, p. 411). Brooks and Brooks (1999) offered the following principles of characteristics of constructivist classrooms:

- ☼ Pursuit of student questions is highly valued.
- ☼ Curricular activities rely heavily on primary sources of data and manipulative materials.
- ☼ Teachers seek the students' point of view in order to understand students' present conceptions for use in subsequent lessons.
- ☼ Assessment of student learning is interwoven with teaching and occurs through teacher observations of students' work and through student exhibitions and portfolios. (p. 17)

The American Association for the Advancement of Science (1989) suggested that science teaching "should be consistent with the nature of scientific inquiry" (p. 147) so that students are prepared to engage as a scientifically literate populace. This call also is indicative of the alignment of the standards documents to the constructivist learning theory, whereby it is posited that student learning occurs as students are given space to cultivate understandings of their experiences in the context of their current understandings. Hurd (1998) offered the following for better understanding of what cultivating a scientifically literate populace affords: "a civic competency required for rational thinking about science in relation to personal, social, political, economic problems and issues that one is likely to meet throughout life" (p. 410). The National Research Council (2005) outlined the following five principals of scientific inquiry: (1) framing research questions, (2) designing investigations, (3) conducting investigations, (4) collecting data, and (5) drawing conclusions. As students engage in the scientific inquiry, not only are they developing scientific literacy, but they also are developing specific components of this literacy such as understanding of science (Chang & Mao, 1999; Ertepinar & Geban, 1996; Hakkarainen, 2003), the nature of science (Schwartz, Lederman, & Crawford, 2004), and increasing students' interest and attitudes toward science (Cavallo & Laubach, 2001; Chang & Mao, 1999; Paris, Yambor, & Packard, 1998). With this mission in mind we ask ourselves:

- ☼ What role does technology play in the science learning process?
- ☼ How can teachers integrate technology to support principles of scientific inquiry?

In this chapter we present certain cognitive tools that we believe will extend students' cognitive capacities in the learning process as they articulate, refine, and add to their understandings in science. Using a cognitive tools approach is distinctly different from the traditional approach of using technology. With cognitive tools, the students can access and analyze information, interpret and organize knowledge, and then express the knowledge they have constructed to others. We believe that the tools we present in this chapter are the conduits to the knowledge and literacy that will transfer and/or apply to other settings (within and across disciplines). Cognitive tools will be used to support the transformative learning of science and development of 21st-century digital literacy.

Traditional Approach vs. Cognitive Tool Approach in Science Classrooms

Traditional Approach

Teachers are beginning to use more common technologies in their classroom such as lab equipment, video materials, interactive multimedia programs, open access data sets, and communication tools. Many of these technologies and equipment are indispensable to science learning because science education involves hands-on activities and clear presentation to enable the construction of abstract concepts and complex phenomenon. However, when adopting computer technologies, teachers should consider how the technology can support science learning, and at the same time nurture students' 21st-century digital literacy. Table 3.1 offers a comparison of traditional and cognitive tools approaches in integrating technology into science instruction.

The amazing pace of technological change can be seen as one considers the difference between the world today when compared to just 10 years ago. Ten years ago the Internet was in its infancy with few using or realizing the potential for this revolutionary technology. To date, although there may be technologies currently available to revolutionize the way our students experience science that improves student learning and aligns with the technologies, students are accustomed to using technology in all other aspects of their lives, and for the most part these have not been employed in ways consistent with what we know about teaching and learning.

Table 3.1
Traditional vs. Cognitive Tools Approach
to Technology Integration

Technology	Traditional Approach	Cognitive Tool Approach
Video	A quick search for science videos on the Internet will yield an abundance of options. Most commonly in traditional settings, teachers show videotapes, DVD disks, or YouTube videos related to the learning topics, and then have students answer a set of guided questions as they watch the video.	A teacher in a constructive environment may ask students to complete informational research, before developing a video clip with a simple movie editing tool such as Apple iMovie or Microsoft MovieMaker that encompasses the differences in views about evolution. Through this, the teacher can then facilitate group presentation and discussion, and have students articulate what they understand about the nature of science, what constitutes science, and how they have come to think about evolution as a central theme in understanding biology.
Interactive Programs (Instructional Multimedia and Simulations)	To help ninth graders understand what factors might affect atmospheric pressure, a science teacher uses a simulation program. Students key in variables and observe an animation explaining the influence of mass of molecules on the change of atmospheric pressure. The program also describes the role of temperature on atmospheric pressure, telling the students that lower temperatures lead to higher atmospheric pressures, while higher temperatures lead to lower atmospheric pressures.	An alternative approach to using this applet as a cognitive tool would offer students an opportunity to manipulate the applet prior to any formal discussion. The teacher shows the students how to use the spreadsheet tool provided by Google Docs to document their results and collaboratively share with classmates. After documenting a series of observed data, the teacher asks students to predict how the three variables in the applet (number of molecules, mass of molecules, and ground temperature) affect atmospheric pressure. Students are given a chance to test their predictions through additional applet manipulation. Students then use the presentation tool provided by Google Docs to create an online presentation to communicate their observations and conclusions with peers.
Internet Resources	To help 10th graders understand more about wolves and organism behavior, a science teacher guides students in reading a series of online texts about wolf territories, size of territories, and their habitual behaviors. After the readings, students are required to find pictures and video about wolves online, summarize their findings, and present them with PowerPoint presentations.	A high school science teacher chooses to use an open access data set containing radio telemetry tracking data for wolves available online. In this example, students in a class in Manhattan could explore wolf movement from data provided to them online from wolves at Superior National Forest in Ely, MN. They subsequently complete scientific inquiries where they frame authentic research questions, design investigations, conduct their investigations, collect data, and draw conclusions. The teacher also could guide students to use a 3D satellite mapping engine (Google Earth) to find the locations of these wolves' habitat. Two groups of students can create landmarks with Google Earth, post their landmarks onto a blog, and then discuss their findings through blogs or instant messages.

In order to prepare students to be 21st-century global and digital citizens and revolutionize science teaching, we need to think beyond traditional approaches to technology and instead position students to

> think and act in ways associated with inquiry, including asking questions, planning and conducting investigations, using appropriate [cognitive] tools and techniques to gather data, thinking critically and logically about relationships between evidence and explanations, constructing and analyzing alternative explanations, and communicating scientific arguments. (NRC, 1996, p. 105)

Cognitive Tools Approach

We identified cognitive tools as the catalyst that can make major differences in the traditional and reformed uses of technologies in science teaching and learning. As previously described, a careful examination of traditional technology integration in science teaching and learning reveals that it does not align with research in teaching and learning and the new science standards documents (NRC, 2005). The traditional approach is more didactic and teacher-centered, which confines student learning to the context that limits their learning process to searching for facts and verification of desired results set by the curriculum. To ensure inquiry-based, student-centered learning, we support a cognitive tools approach to encourage student pursuits in scientific inquiry.

What are cognitive tools? Jonassen and Reeves (1996) described cognitive tools as "technologies that can enhance the cognitive powers of human beings during thinking, problem solving and learning" (p. 693). In science education, using technology as cognitive tools supports students' scientific inquiry process, including using technology to facilitate their framing of research questions, design investigations, conduct investigations, collect data, and draw conclusions (NRC, 2005).

Learning with the cognitive tools approach positions technology as an indispensable tool for students to solve problems while developing scientific and digital literacy. In this vein, the tools are used to share their cognitive burden of completing tasks (Salomon, Perkins, & Globerson, 1991). By using cognitive tools in a constructive framework, learners engage in a variety of critical, creative, and complex thinking opportunities, such as evaluating, analyzing, connecting, elaborating, synthesizing, imaging, designing, problem solving, and decision making (Jonassen,

1996). Students become smarter with the use of cognitive tools, just like we became physically stronger with the use of tools such as the hammer (Kim & Reeves, 2007).

To help clarify the notion of the use of cognitive tools in science classrooms, the following integration examples are provided: databases and concept mappings. More cognitive tools will be elaborated upon further in this chapter, however some illustrative examples follow.

DATABASES

In considering an example in a unit focused on volcanoes, teachers can guide students in using a database tool such as Microsoft Access® for data analysis. Teachers can instruct students on the design of tables. These can be used for data input to allow students to more succinctly make comparisons. In our following example, the features of various volcanoes can be collected and displayed (e.g., name of volcano, eruption year, location, volcanic rock type, viscosity, gas content). During this process, students are involved in researching information needed, collecting data, and inputting data in tables for data analysis. By analyzing this data, students can then design additional queries to investigate. Examples may be comparisons of different types of volcanoes, comparisons of volcanoes in different locations, or comparisons of volcanoes with different features. By engaging in these additional queries, students' scientific and digital literacies are cultivated.

CONCEPT MAPPING

Another popular tool used in classrooms is Inspiration®. For example, teachers can guide students in using Inspiration® to create a concept map to represent their understanding about density and buoyancy (Vanides, Yin, Tomita, & Ruiz-Primo, 2003). With Inspiration®, students can easily organize their thoughts by connecting each concept in ways that depict how they have come to understand them. Additionally they can hyperlink information to each component of the concept map to help validate understandings depicted in their maps.

Learning Science With Technology

Although the concept of cognitive tools is relatively new, some educators have facilitated instruction with this model. A cognitive tools approach is aligned with constructivist principles, meaning learning can be enhanced when learners are engaged in "meaning making" experiences (Jonassen, 1999). Therefore, the reason for using cognitive tools in the classroom is to design student-centered and authentic activities; have students research, analyze, and organize information; and present the results to demonstrate their understandings (Iiyoshi, Hannafin, & Wang, 2005; Jonassen & Reeves, 1996; Kim & Reeves, 2007). In addition, by previewing the Changes in Teaching Emphasis (see Table 3.2) outlined in the National Science Education Standards (NRC, 1996), one begins to see the compatibility of the cognitive tools approach with science standards.

TABLE 3.2
Changes in Teaching Emphasis

Less Emphasis On	More Emphasis On
Treating all students alike and responding to the group as a whole	Understanding and responding to individual student's interests, strengths, experiences, and needs
Rigidly following curriculum	Selecting and adapting curriculum
Focusing on student acquisition of information	Focusing on student understanding and use of scientific knowledge, ideas, and inquiry processes
Presenting scientific knowledge through lecture, text, and demonstration	Guiding students in active and extended scientific inquiry
Asking for recitation of acquired knowledge	Providing opportunities for scientific discussion and debate among students
Testing students for factual information at the end of the unit or chapter	Continuously assessing student understanding
Maintaining responsibility and authority	Sharing responsibility for learning with students
Supporting competition	Supporting a classroom community with cooperation, shared responsibility, and respect
Working alone	Working with other teachers to enhance the science program

To best understand these changes, some examples of how technology is being integrated are needed. As an example of a cognitive tools approach improving science learning, Shaw, Baggett, and Salyer (2004) guided fifth graders to use the concept mapping tool Kidspiration® to generate and represent their understanding of scientific concepts, such as

"What affects freezing water?" or "What affects the distance a marble will roll?" The concept mapping tool facilitated the inquiry, investigation, and communication in the process of constructing knowledge. Results from this study indicated that students were engaged in this activity, worked with the desire for independence, and increased their understanding of the science content.

Jones (2003) investigated the effects of a Web site design project on students' motivation and achievement in science learning. He worked with 46 tenth-grade biology students to design an ecology Web site. Compared with the 55 students receiving lecture instruction, students who designed Web sites were highly motivated to learn. Although the cognitive gain of these two groups were similar, the Web site designer group enjoyed the opportunity to use authoring tools, collaborated with peers, and favored the nonlecture format of learning. The results revealed that using computers in a cognitive tools approach did help students learn and improve skills to retrieve and analyze information, produce media content, collaborate with peers, and present and communicate their research results.

In another example, with the support of Information Communications and Technologies (ICT), ChanLin (2008) asked fifth graders to research geographical and ecological information about the areas in which they lived. Students worked in groups, posted the findings on a Web-based journal, interacted with students from other schools to discuss the findings they posted on the Web-based journal, and presented the final results in multimedia formats on the Web. The findings in this study suggested that students improved their conceptual understandings through exchanging views with peers. Additionally, they gained new understandings. The use of the Web design editor sustained students' motivation because they could connect with an audience beyond the classroom walls. In addition to achievement gains, students enhanced their research and organizational skills, ICT literacy, and science literacy.

Schools might already observe that many kids are skilled in computer operation. They are accustomed to using the Internet, posting their own blogs, and chatting through instant messaging. Teaching students how to use computer applications is not enough (Heun, 2006) and with the digital literacy that many of our students already possess, it may not even be necessary.

Educators instead can use computers as cognitive tools to facilitate students' scientific literacy, improve student motivation, and develop

21st-century digital literacy. From these examples, we were able to identify the critical role teachers can play in successfully facilitating science instruction and 21st-century digital literacy to achieve learning gains by using a cognitive tools approach to technology integration. However, this does not mean that teachers or schools have to invest additional monies into expensive computer applications. In fact, there are many free and easy-to-use ICTs or already frequently used applications for teachers to use in the classroom. We will discuss three specific tools teachers can use in the science classroom in the following sections. We also encourage teachers to look for ideas to integrate technology to support science learning from the Partnership for 21st Century Skills Web site (http://www.21stcenturyskills.org/images/stories/matrices/ictmap_science.pdf) to start testing tools in the classroom.

NSES and Technology Alignment

The National Research Council (1996) established the National Science Education Standards (NSES) embracing the philosophy of inquiry-based and student-centered learning. The NESE teaching standards are outlined in Table 3.3.

TABLE 3.3 Science Teaching Standards
Standard A: Teachers of science plan an inquiry-based science program for their students.
Standard B: Teachers of science guide and facilitate learning.
Standard C: Teachers of science engage in ongoing assessment of their teaching and of student learning.
Standard D: Teachers of science design and manage learning environments that provide students with the time, space, and resources needed for learning science.
Standard E: Teachers of science develop communities of science learners that reflect the intellectual rigor of scientific inquiry and the attitudes and social values conducive to science learning.
Standard F: Teachers of science actively participate in the ongoing planning and development of the school science program.

Note. From National Research Council (1996).

ISTE NETS for Students in Science Learning

The International Society for Technology in Education (ISTE, 2007) first established technology integration standards supportive of student learning in 1998 called the National Educational Technology Standards (NETS). More than 90% of the U.S. states have adopted the NETS standards in state department of education documents. The NETS standards provide a strong technology integration framework across curriculum for K–12 teachers and administrators. The NETS standards were updated in 2007 to reflect the need to prepare students to work, live, and contribute to the social and civic fabric of their communities (ISTE, 2007). The new standards focus on preparing students to use technology to solve problems, express creativity, and complete tasks collaboratively.

Let's take a look at the specific indicators of the NETS for Students (NETS·S) standards, and what these indicators mean in science education (see Table 3.4).

Technology Integration Ideas to Enhance Science Teaching

One of the challenges to integrate technology into the classroom is the availability of resources (Norris, Sullivan, Poirot, & Soloway, 2003). Although the computer lab might have enough computers for all students, the cost of purchasing software is still difficult to afford for schools and students. One way to offset the "digital divide" (Norris, 2001, p. 3) is to adopt free ICT tools in teaching and learning. We will list some ideas to enhance science instruction through the use of technology as a cognitive tools approach in this section. These activities align with the cognitive tool approach, NETS standards, and the components of digital literacy. Some technology integration ideas would be:

☀ To guide students in collecting data through probeware, and documenting and analyzing data with Google Docs. Google Docs is a free ICT tool that provides similar functions as Microsoft Word, Excel, and PowerPoint. Google Docs are compatible with other office applications, and can be integrated into Web publishing tools such as blogs and Web pages. Google Docs can be a great tool for students to keep observation journals.

TABLE 3.4
NETS•S Standards and Examples

NETS•S	Meaning	Examples
Creativity and Innovation	Students have the abilities to use technology to express new ideas and develop products to demonstrate the level of their knowledge construction.	Use movie production tools to report a scientific phenomenon observed.
Communication and Collaboration	Students know how to work collaboratively and reach consensus to solve problems through synchronous or asynchronous communication technology.	Use communication tools to report and compare the quality of water samples collected from multiple geographically remote locations.
Research and Information Fluency	Students know how to use technology to support their research process, including designing research, defining problems, retrieving and evaluating information, collecting and analyzing data, and reporting results.	Research factors that affect the speed of glacier retreat.
Critical Thinking, Problem Solving, and Decision Making	Students should be prepared with fundamental cognitive skills in order to more effectively use technology to solve and define problems, plan and manage activities, interpret data through multiple processes and from diverse perspectives, and look for alternative and scientific solutions if the current explanation does not work.	Observe underlying patterns through a simulation tool, define problem, form hypothesis, test hypothesis by using different parameters in the simulation, and find solution.
Digital Citizenship	Students can approach a huge task or project by breaking it down into multiple components. Through the support of technology, people can take responsibilities of each branching task and then complete the major task. In the process, students should know the underlying legal issues and ethical behaviors of using technology, respect diverse opinions, and exhibit leadership to operate in a digital environment.	Possess positive attitudes to collaborate with people in face-to-face environment or virtually by using technology.
Technology Operations and Concepts	Students should possess technology proficiency in a digital environment, such as know how to operate technology systems, select and use the most appropriate technology, and exhibit the attitudes to learn new technologies.	Know when to choose what technology to solve problems and complete tasks, and have the knowledge and skills to operate various applications.

- To guide students in researching information through multiple resources; for example, the use of Google's many search engines (e.g., Web sites search engine, news search engine, image search engine, research paper search engine, and online bibliographic database). Students even can use the Google language tool to access to information offered other than English.
- To help students visualize phenomena that cannot be seen in reality through simulation tools.
- To facilitate students visualizing, analyzing, displaying, and measuring spatial data with a mapping tool, such as Google Earth or Google Astronomy.
- To encourage students collaborating through asynchronous (e.g., Google Docs, blogs) and synchronous (e.g., instant messenger, video conferencing, Second Life 3D environment, and handheld devices) communication tools.
- To give students opportunities to express ideas or present research findings through multimedia format, such as video (e.g., using video editing tools such as MovieMaker, iMovie, or Photo Story), graphics (e.g., using image editing tools such as Photoshop Elements), and concept maps (e.g., using software such as Inspiration®).
- To design a Web-based inquiry activity (e.g., use Google Page to design a WebQuest) to facilitate students' investigation of science problems.
- To guide students to collect, organize, and analyze data through spreadsheets or databases. By tapping information available in open databases, teachers can design a variety of scientific questions to engage students to research authentic problems.

So far, we have shared how technology traditionally has been integrated into science instruction and a vision for how it can be integrated in the future. We noted why this is so important in the science curriculum and began to explain how this could be integrated so that technology could serve as a cognitive tool to strengthen students' learning experiences. In this section we further illuminate ideas for empowering students in science classrooms in ways that will enhance student learning by sharing exemplars of engaging students with technologies as cognitive tools so that teachers can begin to envision and take advantage of these technologies in their classrooms. Google Earth, databases, and probeware each will be introduced separately before the final section focuses on ways to integrate each of these in a manner consistent with the cognitive tools approach adopted.

Google Earth

What Is Google Earth?

Google (http://www.google.com) provides a series of free services that can support ICT integration in educational contexts. Users can access to these services by signing up for a single Google account (link to http://www.google.com, and click "Sign in" to set up a Google account). These services are mutually integrated, making the integration of ICTs more convenient and efficient. One of these services is Google Earth (http://earth.google.com).

Google Earth provides satellite images and 3D terrains to make the geographical virtual field trip feasible and realistic. Due to its visualization and interactivity, more and more educators are looking for ways to integrate Google Earth into their curriculum. For example, science teachers can guide their students in researching population growth of a specific location, and use Google Earth to compare the population growth between locations. Another example uses Google Earth to display the snouts of glaciers (the lowest end of glaciers) from certain periods of time to explain how glaciers have been retreating and what causes this. In addition, Google Earth provides measurement tools so teachers can have students use them to gauge dimension of a 3D building or an area to highlight the mathematical side of scientific investigations. Combined with SMART Board technology, Google Earth adds rich interactivity in the classroom.

How the Uses of Google Earth Can Support Science Learning

Google Earth is more than a 3D mapping tool. It is compatible with multimedia elements, enables hyperlinked features, provides real-time data of the Earth and the sky, and serves as a portal to access geographical documents. Additionally, students have opportunities to contribute content to Google Earth. For example, they can take pictures of water samples, and link the picture to a pacemaker in Google Earth. Combined with Geographic Information System (GIS) software, spreadsheet software, and multimedia presentation applications, Google Earth can become a powerful tool for data collections and presentations. Google Earth can support students' learning and enhance their skills in the following areas:

- spatial thinking;
- map navigation;
- astronomy navigation;
- scientific inquiry; and
- data collection, evaluation, and presentation.

Google Earth Exemplar Activities

BEGINNER: NAVIGATION SKILLS AND VIRTUAL FIELD TRIPS

First, teachers need to download and install Google Earth from http://earth.google.com, and make sure all students have access to Google Earth. First-time Google Earth users will need to launch Google Earth and familiarize themselves with the navigation system. To start with, they need to find a place of interest by locating a landmark. Then they can use the *layers* function to explore related information about the place such as looking at photo images or reading articles about that place posted by *National Geographic* magazine or other users. Each piece of information or material is displayed as one layer in Google Earth. Therefore, users can decide to observe different materials (e.g., image, video, articles) by activating different layers. Once students learn how to navigate Google Earth and are familiar with all features and functions, teachers can guide them to take a geographical virtual visit to places like glaciers and volcanoes.

INTERMEDIATE: DATA COLLECTION AND PRESENTATION

The Advanced Technology Environmental and Energy Center (ATEEC) has designed a thorough video tutorial on how to use Google Earth to share images and video data (http://www.ateec.org/aboutus/ateeczone. htm). Teachers can go through this video tutorial to learn the skills needed for the following sample activity.

Sample Activity: Investigating Water Quality. Students can start working on advanced projects once they are familiar with the Google Earth navigation skills. Teachers can assign a topic for students to research; for example, how water quality has changed in a local river over time. The following steps can be used in completing this activity:

Step 1: Get a Waypoint and Add Content

1. Students can work individually or in groups to take water samples from various locations and take pictures or video clips of the water.
2. With the GPS (Global Positioning System) device, students can log the locations (waypoints) in which they collect the water sample and plug in the data in Google Earth later.
3. Students can upload their pictures and video clips to a free Web server, such as Blogger (http://blogger.com), Google Video (http://video.google.com), or YouTube (http://youtube.com). These multimedia materials will be used later in Google Earth. If students do not have access to the GPS device, they can try to use a nearby address and the zoom function in Google Earth to locate the place.

Step 2: Add Data to Google Earth and Make a Presentation

1. Launch Google Earth, key in the number of waypoints, and then use the search function to locate the waypoints on the spinning globe.
2. Add a new placemark to mark the waypoint in Google Earth. In the placemark window, students have options to input the waypoints data collected with GPS device and write a description in the description window (see Figure 3.1). To attach an image to a placemark, first copy the URL of the image on the Web, and then use a simple HTML language in the description window:

   <img src="URL of the image">
   For example:
   <img src="http://www.sciencebook.net/figure5.jpg">

3. When clicking on the placemark, users can view the image of the water sample and the report written by the students (see Figure 3.2).Students can create a series of placemarks to complete their investigation, and then save the placemarks as a KML Google Earth document. The KML file, a file format

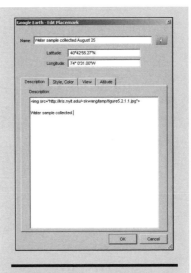

FIGURE 3.1. Placemark editing window in Google Earth.

used to display geographic data in a browser, such as Google Earth, contains all of the information students created and can be distributed to share with anyone who has Google Earth installed on their computers.

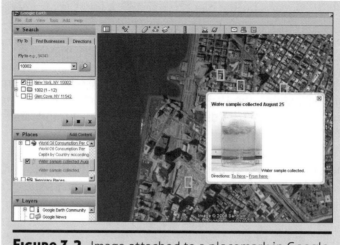

FIGURE 3.2. Image attached to a placemark in Google Earth.

4. When users double click on the KML file to start up Google Earth, they can see these placemarks, read students' research findings, zoom into the sites where samples were collected, visualize the surroundings, and compare other sites. After looking at the presentations of the students' water sample investigations, teachers can follow up with a discussion on what factors affect water samples collected from different locations. Water sample collection can be replaced by any materials according to the topic (e.g., rocks, animals, and insects).

ADVANCED: DATA PRESENTATION

One of the advantages of Google Earth is that it allows data presentation with multiple dimensions. For example, we can present the data of estimated use of water in the U.S. with a table (see Table 3.5), or with a two-dimensional (2D) or three-dimensional (3D) chart. With Google Earth, we can display the data with 3D bars and link the data to a specific location. In this case, the data presented are enhanced with geographical condition and water resource distribution.

Using data described in Table 3.5, we can demonstrate how these data are transformed and displayed with 3D data bars displayed in Google Earth. The following steps show how this can be completed.

Table 3.5
Estimated Use of Water in the United States (Seven States) in 2000

States	Population (in thousands)	Water Consumption (in thousand acre-feet per year)	Water Consumption (acre-feet/per person per year)	Times 43,560 (Convert the unit from acre-feet to cubic feet) (cubic feet/per person per year)	Times 1,000,000 (To make the comparison more obvious)
Alabama	4,450	11,200	2.516853933	109,634	2,516,854
Arizona	5,130	7,540	1.469785575	64,024	1,469,786
Arkansas	2,670	12,200	4.56928839	199,038	4,569,288
California	33,900	57,400	1.693215339	73,756	1,693,215
Colorado	4,300	14,200	3.302325581	143,849	3,302,326
Connecticut	3,410	4,650	1.363636364	59,400	1,363,636
Delaware	784	1,480	1.887755102	82,231	1,887,755
Florida	16,000	22,500	1.40625	61,256	1,406,250

Note. From U.S. Geological Survey (n.d.).

Step 1: Create a 3D shape in Google Earth

1. Launch Google Earth, and use the search tool to locate the state of Alabama. Use the Polygon tool to create a polygon along the Alabama state border (see Figure 3.3).

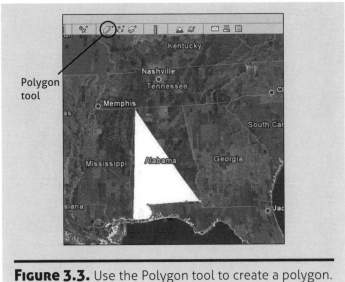

Figure 3.3. Use the Polygon tool to create a polygon.

Step 2: Change the Property of the 3D Shape

1. Click "Style, Color" in the polygon editing window to change the color and opacity of this area. In this case, we changed it to red (see Figure 3.4).

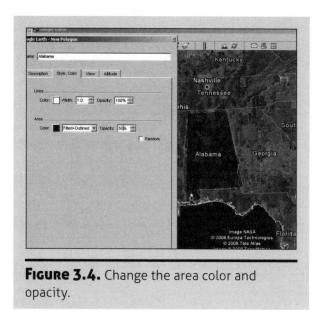

FIGURE 3.4. Change the area color and opacity.

2. Click the "Altitude" tab, and input the number we calculated for Alabama (2,516,854). Check "Extend sides to ground" so the polygon will be extended to the ground and become a 3D shape (see Figure 3.5).

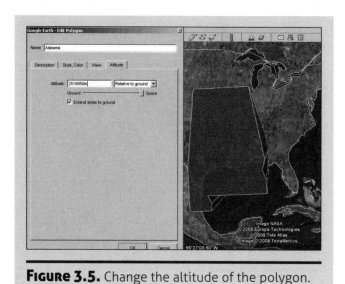

FIGURE 3.5. Change the altitude of the polygon.

Step 3: Use Placemark to Indicate Area

1. We can add a placemark into the 3D shape to indicate the state of Alabama. Then, we can continue to input data of all seven states and create seven 3D bars. The result should be similar to Figure 3.6. The water consumption comparison of these seven states becomes more obvious and easy to interpret. Teachers can facilitate the discussion on how the geographical environment can affect people's water consumption, and how the water resources (ground water and surface water) of different areas may affect people's water consumption behaviors.

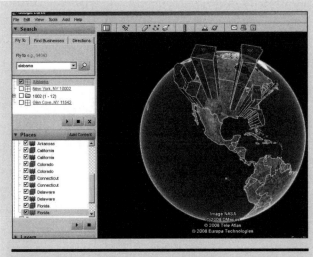

FIGURE 3.6. Estimated use of water in the United States (seven states) in 2000.

Using this activity, teachers can have students explore data on various topics, such as oil consumption of countries. From these activities, we know that Google Earth can facilitate activities addressing the following national science standards:

- ☀ Earth Science
- ☀ Science as Inquiry
- ☀ Science and Technology

These activities also can support all dimensions of digital literacy and all of the ISTE (NET•S) standards. The first time users might not feel comfortable using a new computer application; however, ICT literacy is nurtured through frequent practice. The more students use the applications, the better skilled they will be in using these applications to solve their daily life problems.

EXTENDED ACTIVITY

Google Earth provides a function (Google Sky) to view the planets, stars, constellations, and galaxies in the universe. These real-time images are obtained from observatories around the world including the Hubble Telescope. Google Earth provides a great way to conduct a virtual planetarium field trip (see Figure 3.7). Specifically with the timing dimension added to the Google Sky, users can observe the subtle changes of the planet within a period of time.

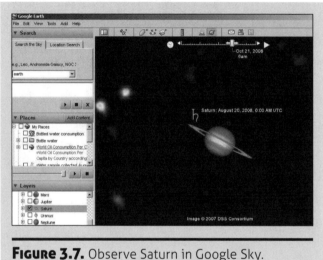

FIGURE 3.7. Observe Saturn in Google Sky.

If the project involves a great amount of placemarks, teachers can guide students to use the free online template provided by Google to manage and maintain these placemarks. This is an advanced application of Google Earth. For teachers who are interested in learning more about this application, please see the complete tutorial at http://earth.google.com/outreach/tutorial_spreadsheet.html. Another online template (http://earth.google.com/outreach/tutorial_time.html) allows students to add time as a fourth dimension in Google Earth to present data. The timing data can be added only with the template. With it, students can display the water consumption per person of each state's data across several years. Other examples include the use Google Earth to present the spread of a virus or the carbon dioxide emitted by a country over several years.

Databases

In this section we will describe how a database tool (Microsoft Access, one of the programs in the Microsoft Office Suite software) can be integrated into science learning. Students can use databases to collect, record, manage, and analyze data. It is an important cognitive tool for understanding scientific concepts.

Databases are systems that help us maintain and manage data; the most important function of databases is to quickly retrieve desired recorded entries according to the questions we ask. Being able to use a database effectively and efficiently will significantly improve our ability to ask questions, conduct investigations, and draw conclusions. The use of databases might be unfamiliar to many teachers; however, with step-by-step instruction, teachers can apply this activity to many topics to help students discover scientific phenomena.

Input Data Into Database

For beginners, teachers should develop a database for students to collect and input data. Students should focus on researching and inputting data into databases, and use the teacher-designed queries to analyze data. To design a simple database, you will need to know the basic components of a database.

We will use Microsoft Access 2007 to design this activity. There are three components you need to know in Microsoft Access:

- *Table:* A table looks like a spreadsheet worksheet. It allows the users to create field names to describe a record. For example, we can describe a car record with the following field names: brand, model, year, and color. We can then create a new record by using the according data, for example: Honda, Element, 2004, Orange. We can continue to establish more records with these field names.
- *Form*: Form is the interface designed for users to view or input new data. We can input data in the table format; however the form provides a friendlier format to input and present data. We can even display a picture in the form.
- *Query*: The query function allows us to ask questions, and then retrieve an answer based on the data within the records we stored in the table. Query is the reason we use a database rather than a spreadsheet tool. To make it relate to our daily life, here we use a

very simple database example: How would the Blockbuster cashier know which customer has which videotape and how much the customer needs to pay? To query further, how could the Blockbuster manager know what types of videos are favored by high school females? Query retrieves the answer according to the questions we ask. For example, after students research and input a list of animals and its habitat, they can use query to find answers to questions such as: "Which animals should be found living in the rain forest?", "What kind of animals will be found in the desert?", or "Can we find elephants in South America?"

How to Set Up a Table, Form, and Simple Query

For students who feel comfortable using technology, teachers can encourage them to set up a table and form, and design simple queries to answer their own research questions. In this activity, we want to prepare students' knowledge of Earth materials by using scientific inquiry and critical thinking skills. Students can research volcano-related information by setting up a table in a database. Teachers should set up keywords for students to research in advance according to the learning objectives. In this case, students are required to locate information regarding volcanoes: name, year of last eruption, country, volcanic rock type, viscosity, and gas content. Teachers can add more keywords depending on the learning objectives and scope such as elevation, prominence, types of volcano (e.g., lava dome, pancake dome), or age of rock. Teachers can provide names of several volcanoes and have students research information pertaining to each volcano. Table 3.6 provides the sample data. The more data the students input, the more clues and findings they will be able to draw.

TABLE 3.6 Sample Data for Database Activity					
Name	Last Eruption	Country	Volcanic Rock Type	Viscosity	Gas Content
Akutan	1992	U.S., Alaska	Basaltic	Low	Low
Krakatoa	2008	Indonesia	Andesite	Intermediate	High
Lassen	1917	U.S., California	Andesite	Intermediate	Intermediate
Mauna Loa	1984	U.S. Hawaii	Basaltic	Low	Low
Myojin	1952	Japan	Basaltic	Low	Intermediate
Pelee	1932	Caribbean Sea	rhyolitic	High	High

Here are the steps for setting up a table in a database.

Step 1: Create a Blank New Database to Store Data
1. Start up Access, create a blank new database, and then create a table. Insert the keyword in the table headings respectively (see Figure 3.8). Close the table and name it "volcano."

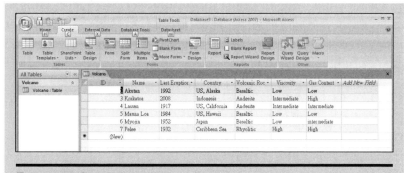

FIGURE 3.8. Create a table in Access.

Step 2: Create a Form to Input Data Students Researched
1. Students need to create a form to input the data they researched. Click "Create," and then click "Form." Access automatically will generate a form template for the students. We are in the template editing mode so we need to close it and save it before we use the form. Close the form and name it "volcano." To use the form, double click the form objective in the left window (see Figure 3.9).

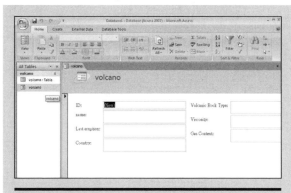

FIGURE 3.9. Double click the form object in the left window to input data through the form format.

2. Now the database is completed. Students can use the database to insert more entries and maintain records. To maximize the cognitive power of the database tool, we need to introduce students to the use of query.

Setting Up Queries in Access

Teachers can guide students to ask various questions depending on the data they found. For example, among the 25 volcanoes they inserted into the database, which volcanoes produce basaltic rock? They also can ask questions combining multiple conditions, such as questioning which volcanoes produce basaltic rock and are located in United States, or which volcanoes producing basaltic rock also produce low density of gas content. The query can help students locate the answers immediately, so they can focus on data analysis and making inferences.

Step 1: Single Query: Which Volcanoes Produce Basaltic Rock?

1. In Access, click "Create," click "Query Wizard," and choose "Simple Query Wizard" (see Figure 3.10).

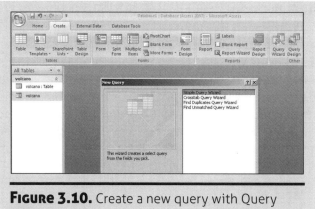

FIGURE 3.10. Create a new query with Query Wizard.

2. In this window, Access needs to know which fields you want to display for the query results. Let's move all fields to the right because when Access displays the results, we want to see the information for all of the fields (see Figure 3.11).

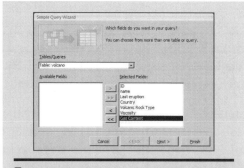

FIGURE 3.11. Select all of the fields for displaying the query results.

3. Type the query in the text field. In this case, input "Which volcanoes produce basaltic rock?" (see Figure 3.12), and then click "Modify the query design." We need to command Access to look for "basaltic" rock from the field "Volcanic Rock Type."

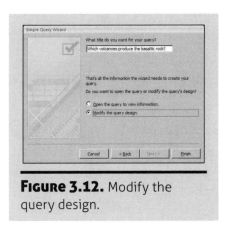

FIGURE 3.12. Modify the query design.

4. Figure 3.13 shows the query design window. Because we chose to display all of the fields for the query results, all of the fields we set up in the table are displayed here. If you do not want to show the information in the "Last eruption" field, simply uncheck the "show" checkbox under the "Last eruption" field.

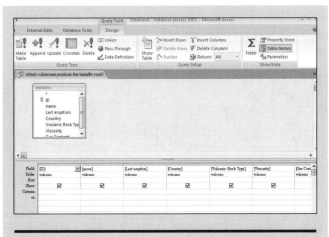

FIGURE 3.13. Query setup window. All of the fields in Show row are selected. This means that when Access displays the query results, all of the fields of the retrieved records will be displayed.

5. How does the Access know we are looking for "basaltic" rock? When we input data into Access, we specify the rock type in the field "Volcanic Rock Type." So, we need to look for "basaltic" in this field. We have to set up a condition in the Criteria field. Use quotation marks to specify the word "basaltic" (see Figure 3.14).

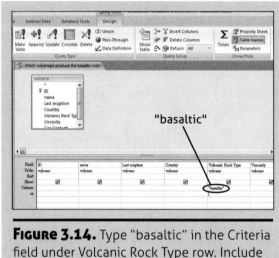

FIGURE 3.14. Type "basaltic" in the Criteria field under Volcanic Rock Type row. Include quotation marks.

6. Close the query window, and save the query settings. Now we're ready to run the query and find out the answer. Double click on the query question "Which volcanoes produce basaltic rock?" from the left object window. Access will retrieve the answer immediately and display the results (see Figure 3.15).

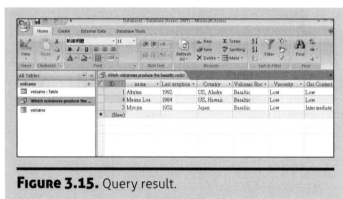

FIGURE 3.15. Query result.

Step 5: Set Up Double Conditions in Queries: Which Volcanoes Producing Basaltic Rock Are Located in the United States?

7. Query 2 includes two conditions. Let's create a new query with the same procedure. In the Query window, specify the query content as "Which

volcanoes producing basaltic rock are located in the United States?" In the Query set up window, set up condition in the Criteria field under Volcanic Rock Type. Use quotation marks to specify the word "basaltic."

8. The second condition is the location "US." However, if we specify "US" in the Criteria field under Country, we cannot retrieve any data because Access will look for the data that contains the exactly two letters "US" in the field of Country. The field "US, Alaska" will not be retrieved because Access does not consider it matches with our criteria "US." To solve the problem, we need to use the magic symbol *. Type "*US*" in the Criteria field under Country (see Figure 3.16). The symbol * is used to represent any letters adjacent to "US." Therefore, Access will retrieve all fields as long as it contains the two letters "US," for example, "US, Alaska."

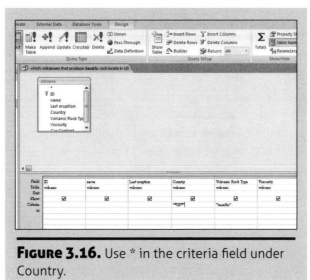

FIGURE 3.16. Use * in the criteria field under Country.

9. Close the query window, and save the query settings. Double click on the query question "Which volcanoes producing basaltic rock are located in the US?" from the left object windows. Access will immediately retrieve the two records that match with the conditions we set up (see Figure 3.17).

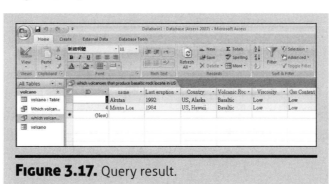

FIGURE 3.17. Query result.

Adding Pictures and Hyperlinks Into a Database

Step 1: Add a Field to Store Graphical Data in Access

1. Access can store pictures and hyperlink information attached to a record. We already set up the table to store keywords we need to use for this activity. To add more fields, we have to revise the table. Right click the "Volcano: Table" object in the left window in Access, and choose "Design View" (see Figure 3.18).

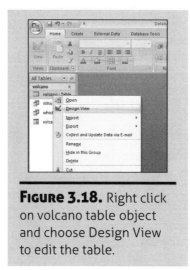

FIGURE 3.18. Right click on volcano table object and choose Design View to edit the table.

2. Access will enter table editing mode. We will see a list of field names we created in the first step. Let's add a new field—"Picture"—under the field name "Gas Content." To store the image in Access, we need to change the property of the field name from Text to OLE object. Click "Text" in the Data Type column next to Picture, and choose "OLE Object" (see Figure 3.19).

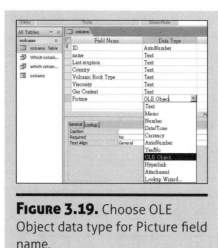

FIGURE 3.19. Choose OLE Object data type for Picture field name.

3. Add a new field name "Web link" under Picture. Change the data type of Web link from "Text" to "Hyperlink." Anything you store in the Web link field will become a hyperlink. Close the table and save the change.
4. Because we edited the table, we also have to change the form design to reflect the change of the table. The good news is that we do not have to reenter data into the form. We have to delete the old form first. Right click on "volcano" form object in the left window and choose Delete (see Figure 3.20).

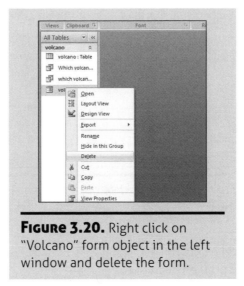

FIGURE 3.20. Right click on "Volcano" form object in the left window and delete the form.

5. Now we have three objects listed in the object window: the volcano table and the two queries we designed (see Figure 3.21).

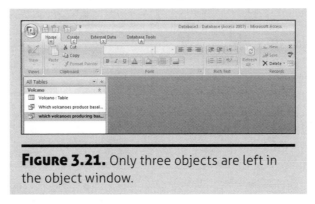

FIGURE 3.21. Only three objects are left in the object window.

6. Make sure you highlight the volcano table object before you create a new form. Click "Create," and then click "Form" to add a new form template. Notice that Access leave some space for Picture and Web link fields. We can change the layout by using the mouse to drag the border

of the field so you can make more space for displaying pictures (see Figure 3.22). Close the form and save the change.

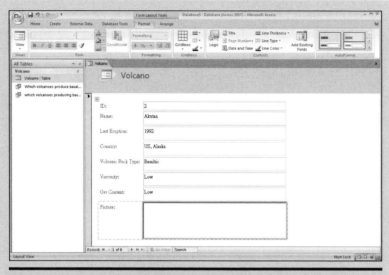

FIGURE 3.22. You can change the space for displaying pictures by dragging the picture box.

Step 2: Research and Locate Volcano-Related Graphical Data

1. Double click on the volcano form object in the left window. The data we entered will be loaded automatically. Now we have to add the picture for each volcano and the Web link. Use a Web browser and go to http://images. google.com. Input "Akutan volcano" into the search field. Google will retrieve a series image of the Akutan volcano. Click the image that we want to add to the record and review the information to make sure this picture is the Akutan volcano, the picture source is credible, and find the copyright information so we can add it to the database (see Figure 3.23).

FIGURE 3.23. Evaluate the picture source. (For example, Image creator: U.S. Geological Survey; Source: http://www. avo.alaska.edu/image.php?id=478.)

2. If you use Internet Explorer, right click on the image and choose "copy" to copy the image; if you use Firefox, right click on the image and choose "Copy Image" to copy the picture. Different Web browsers have different way to allow users to operate copy and paste commands. Usually they are located in the Edit menu in your browser.

Step 3: Input Graphical Data Into Access
1. Go back to Access, right click in the picture field, and choose "paste" to paste the image into the field. Copy the URL of the picture and then paste it into the Web link field (see Figure 3.24).

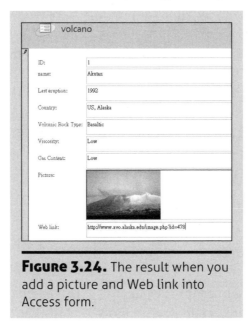

FIGURE 3.24. The result when you add a picture and Web link into Access form.

Design a Unique Database and Query to Test Hypotheses

For students who have the skills to design a database, teachers should encourage them to form research questions and hypotheses, research data, collect data into a self-designed database (they should define their own fields in a database), and design queries to test the hypotheses and answer the research questions.

This database activity is extremely helpful to facilitate students' ICT skills and scientific learning skills. This activity aligns with the following national science standards:

- ☀ Earth Science
- ☀ Science as Inquiry
- ☀ Science and Technology

This activity nurtures all dimensions of digital literacy and all of the ISTE NET•S standards. Students also can apply the use of databases to various fields such as social studies. For example, they could create a database to manage information about all of the world's countries or all of the U.S. presidents, then figure out which countries are dominated by the Communist party or which presidents have led the country during times of crisis.

The key to this activity is to define a good research topic in advance. The topic will affect the research scope and depth, the choices of keywords, and the form of queries. Once students get used to the application of a database tool, it will significantly improve their information processing, data analysis, and evaluation skills, and also support their learning in a particular subject area.

PROBEWARE

What Is Probeware?

Probeware is defined for the purpose of this exemplar, in the manner consistent with Tinker and Krajcik (2001), as the use of probes and sensors in concert with handheld or desktop computers to collect and display real-time measurements of environmental parameters (i.e., temperature, light, motion, force, sound, and electrical power). They afford students the opportunity to engage with real phenomenon, collect and store data, and instantaneously graph data as they are being collected. As an example, Campbell and Neilsen (2009) used a force probe (see Figure 3.25) with students to create a graph (see Figure 3.26) to investigate how friction is related to different surfaces.

Examples of probeware available for use in science classrooms can be found at Vernier Software and Technology (http://www.vernier.com) and PASCO (http://www.pasco.com). Through this type of technology, the focus becomes functional science (science as a way of thinking and problem solving) that empowers students to answer meaningful questions

FIGURE 3.25. Force probe used to investigate surfaces.

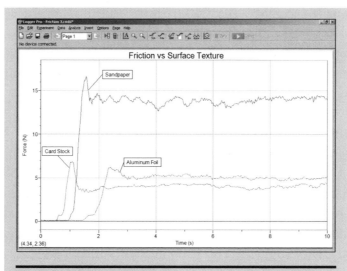

FIGURE 3.26. Examples of graph created with data from probeware.

in their community that are connected to their lives. An example of the empowerment offered by probeware might come as students in Iowa, a state whose economy is dependent on farming, collect water quality data at different locations along the Iowa River and compare the data to the farming practices found along the river. Through this example, students, many of who might become future farmers, are able to collect, analyze, and share data and information with community members to examine the impact of farming practices on water quality, so that informed decisions can be made for improving water quality and sustaining the vitally important focus on farming in the state.

How Can the Uses of Probeware Support Science Learning?

The following, while not exhaustive, is a list of examples of research-supported ways that probeware can enhance science learning:

- ☼ Probeware is supportive of inquiry-based science learning aligned with science standards documents (Vonderwell, Sparrow, & Zachariah, 2005).
- ☼ Probeware supports students interacting with real-time data that assist them in developing understandings of abstract representations (Roschelle & Pea, 2002; Tinker, 2000).
- ☼ Probeware enables the display of concrete actions (i.e., walking in front of a motion detector) in dynamic graphic form that enables students to connect actions with graphs to increase their abilities to interpret graphs (Mokros & Tinker, 1987).

Simple Investigations Using Probeware With Possible Initiatory Questions to Investigate

Hisim (2005) described simple investigations that students can complete involving battery testing using voltage probes, friction studies using force probeware, and UV protection studies using UV sensors. In these examples, Hisim suggested offering students initiatory questions for possible investigation or to initiate students' consideration of their own questions about UV protection. Examples of a few of the questions that Hisim offered for the UV protection investigations are:

- ☼ Can you get a tan or sunburn through a glass window?
- ☼ Which sunglasses really block UV? Are the expensive ones that much better? (p. 40)

In these investigations, students designed a mechanism/procedure for answering one of the above questions or one that they had articulated and used a UV sensor to collect data to inform their study. Hisim (2005) suggested that

> These investigations can be conducted on a sunny day outside or at an open window. Students can measure the percentage reduction in UV intensity as they hold the various objects between the sun and the UV sensor. Unlike UV beads, the measurements can be made instantly, allowing more time for inquiry. (p. 40)

Choosing Their Own Topics to Investigate

As teachers and students become more comfortable completing inquiries in the classroom and using probeware, teachers can consider encouraging students to contemplate this technology as a tool for answering their own authentic questions that emerge as they work to construct understandings grounded in what they have already come to understand (Hisim, 2005).

Forming Collaboratories

Collaboratories are groups of laboratories or, in this case, science classes located at different locations nationally and internationally that are working together to complete investigations. Probeware can be used in collaboratories so that data are collected at different geographic locations and uploaded in a database for classes to "analyze graphical representations of the data, and puzzle over the implications of the findings" (Stanford University School of Education, 2003, para. 6). The School of Education at Stanford University (2003) provided an example of a collaboratory that has formed to involve preservice teachers, their students, and scientists. The preservice teachers collaborated with scientists at Stanford's Jasper Ridge Biological Preserve to study the effects of global warming. They used probeware to measure air temperature, carbon dioxide concentrations, nitrogen levels, and soil temperature. Preservice teachers then used these experiences to teach high school students to collect and analyze temperature data at their school site using probeware. Data collected by students eventually will be posted on a collaborative Web site with Jasper Ridge scientists and become part of a real scientific study.

This example outlines the beginning phase of collaboratories, the formation of partnering groups. In addition to this, it is important that these collaboratories continue as inquiry experiences for students whereby they not only are collecting the data, but they also begin to marshal them—to get answers to questions that they have as they struggle to make sense of the larger consequences of their data or, in the case of the example above, global warming.

Opportunities to engage in a collaboratories can be found at Web sites such as the Center for Innovation in Engineering and Science Education (CIESE) http://www.k12science.org/collabprojs.html. At this resource page, science teachers use discussion boards to explore possible collaboratory projects and initiate contacts with other teachers interested in the same projects. Through this resource, teachers can extend collaboratory projects with other interested teachers involved in CIESE projects. This can begin with suggested probeware data collection, then collaborative planning for additional probeware data collection as needed. Data can be shared so that students from geographically dispersed classes can engage together to investigate issues such as factors contributing to smog. Through projects such as these, science classes can expound upon the studies of smog they may complete in isolation by beginning to consider geospatial factors. Through using data collected in this manner from locations with differing characteristics (i.e., altitude, topography) they can broaden their possible research focuses and develop understandings that might not otherwise be possible.

A Vision for Integrating Google Earth, Databases, and Probeware as an Array of Cognitive Tools for Empowering Students in Science

In the introductory section of this text, the editors painted a picture of the students who are entering classrooms in our schools. These students are characterized as "digital natives" that are immersed in technologies. These technologies are so central to students' lives that they are seen as "invisible technologies" that are seamlessly integrated into everyday experiences to the extent that their use has become second nature. It also is suggested that the prevalence of technology in the lives of students has them processing information in ways that are fundamentally different than students from the past. When these students enter science classrooms, we envision an environment compatible with and equally as engaging for students and teachers and one that has them engaging in scientific inquiry in ways aligned with the science standards documents and one that immerses them in technology in a way that it becomes invisible.

Looking Into the Future

At the beginning of a lesson in a 10th-grade biology classroom, Mr. Johnson was introducing the topic of study for the next unit: living organisms' interactions with other organisms and the environment. He begins this unit by taking his students on a visit to a sagebrush environment adjacent to their school. While at the site, the students are instructed to begin to consider the many organisms that are found in the environment. When the students return to the classroom, Mr. Johnson asks them to develop a concept map detailing what they know about the sagebrush environment. They are instructed to include as many organisms as they can in their concept map and to begin to think about how these organisms might be connected to both other organisms and other materials found in the environment. As they create these maps, Mr. Johnson asks the student to highlight those areas of their concept maps that they are unsure of or have questions about. On the next day, students are asked to share their concept maps with the class and any gaps or uncertainties they have about their maps. After the presentations, students are instructed to identify classmates whose questions or uncertainties mirror their own. Over the next several days of class students work in their groups to develop research questions and procedures that can help answer the questions that they have through Google Docs collaboratively. One group is interested in understanding how soil contributes to the uniqueness of this environment. Remembering their experience from another class where they interacted with a group of students from another school in a state in a different region of the country through a discussion board, they recognize that this state's environment is likely different than their own and invite these students to join them in a comparative study of their environmental soils. They plan to collect data and use Google Earth to create landmarks to document factors characteristic of their environment that might be responsible for the differences identified. Another group's members are interested in how the sunlight in their region contributes to the environment and begins to use probeware to monitor the sunlight from their site so that they can compare it to data found online from a distinctly different environment. As the unit progresses, students articulate objectives for their study, all of which fall within what Mr. Johnson intended (i.e., living organisms' interactions with other organisms and the environment). At the conclusion of this unit of study, each group of students presents the results of their studies, which includes revisiting and presenting their revised concept maps to detail how their work has informed the previous gaps in understanding that were identified. A rubric is used to assess the extent to which what students learned was intended in the unit. The rubric was developed earlier in the process with the help of students who identified what they saw as important indicators of their learning. This rubric was but one measure to help Mr. Johnson and the students better understand what they were learning. Additionally, the students shared their work through a blog with community members in a sagebrush environment symposium held after school where each group shared what they had learned before discussing their findings with community members. Through this process, not only did students gain additional understandings and an appreciation about the environment, they also shared their knowledge with the community at large.

As can be seen in this vignette, the unit of study is starkly different from the one offered at the beginning of the section. Students in this final vignette are experiencing science in a manner consistent with constructive principles, digital literacy, and science education reform documents. They are engaging in scientific inquiry as technology is being employed in the cognitive tools approach framework. In addition, they are engaging in science in a manner consistent with Hurd's (1998) description of scientific literacy where they are developing "a civic competency required for rational thinking about science in relation to personal, social, political, economic problems and issues that one is [they are] likely to meet throughout life" (p. 410).

Reflection

Now that you have read this chapter, reflect on your opening exercise and the information presented to do the following:

1. Write a technology goal:
   a. What skills would you like to acquire?
   b. What hardware/software would you like to acquire?
   c. Identify the resources that you need to make this happen.
2. Set a timeline for achieving your goal.

References

American Association for the Advancement of Science. (1989). *Science for all Americans.* New York: Oxford University Press.

Brooks, J. G., & Brooks, M. G. (1999). *In search of understanding: The case for the constructivist classroom.* Alexandria, VA: Association for Supervision and Curriculum Development.

Campbell, T., & Bohn, C. (2008). Science laboratory experiences of high school students across one state in the US: Descriptive research from the classroom. *Science Educator, 17,* 36–48.

Campbell, T., & Neilsen, D. (2009). Student ideas and inquiries: Investigating friction in the physics classroom. *Science Activities, 46,* 13–16.

Cavallo, A., & Laubach, T. (2001). Students' science perceptions and enrollment decisions in differing learning cycle classrooms. *Journal of Research in Science Teaching, 38,* 1029–1062.

Chang, C., & Mao, S. (1999). Comparison of Taiwan science students' outcomes with inquiry-group versus traditional instruction. *The Journal of Educational Research, 92,* 340–346.

ChanLin, L.-J. (2008). Technology integration applied to project-based learning in science. *Innovations in Education and Teaching International, 45,* 55–65.

Ertepinar, H., & Geban, O. (1996). Effect of instruction supplied with the investigative-oriented laboratory approach on achievement in a science course. *Educational Research, 38,* 333–341.

Heun, C. (2006). Teaching tech literacy in the MySpace generation. *Technology & Learning, 24*(4), 19–20.

Hisim, N. (2005). Technology in the lab: Part II–Practical suggestions for using probeware in the science classroom. *The Science Teacher, 74*(7), 38–41

Hakkarainen, K. (2003). Progressive inquiry in a computer-supported biology class. *Journal of Research in Science Teaching, 40,* 1072–1088.

Hurd, P. D. (1998). Scientific literacy: New minds for a changing world. *Science Education, 82,* 407–416.

Iiyoshi, T., Hannafin, M. J., & Wang, F. (2005). Cognitive tools and student-centered learning: Rethinking tools, functions and applications. *Educational Media International, 42,* 281–296.

International Society for Technology in Education. (2007). *NETS for Students.* Retrieved September 2, 2008, from http://www.iste.org/Content/NavigationMenu/NETS/ForStudents/NETS_for_Students.htm

Jonassen, D. H. (1996). *Computers in the classroom: Mindtools for critical thinking.* Englewood Cliffs, NJ: Prentice Hall.

Jonassen, D. (1999). Designing constructivist learning environments. In C. M. Reigeluth (Series Ed.), *Instructional design theories and models: A new paradigm of instructional theory* (Vol. 2., pp. 215–239). Mahwah, NJ: Lawrence Erlbaum.

Jonassen, D. H., & Reeves, T. C. (1996). Learning with technology: Using computers as cognitive tools. In D. H. Jonassen (Ed.), *Handbook of research for educational communications and technology* (pp. 693–719). New York: Macmillan.

Jones, B. D. (2003). Students as Web site authors: Effects on motivation and achievement. *Journal of Educational Technology Systems, 31,* 441–461.

Kim, B., & Reeves, T. (2007). Reframing research on learning with technology: In search of the meaning of cognitive tools. *Instructional Science, 35,* 207–256.

Mokros, J., & Tinker, R. (1987). The impact of microcomputer-based labs on children's ability to interpret graphs. *Journal of Research in Science Teaching, 24,* 369–383.

National Research Council. (1996). *National science education standards.* Washington, DC: National Academy Press.

National Research Council. (2005). *America's lab report: Investigations in high school science.* Washington, DC: National Academy Press.

Norris, C., Sullivan, T., Poirot, J., & Soloway, E. (2003). No access, no use, no impact: Snapshot surveys of educational technology in K–12. *Journal of Research on Technology in Education, 36*(1), 15–27.

Norris, P. (2001). *Digital divide: Civic engagement, information poverty, and the Internet worldwide.* New York: Cambridge University Press.

O'Sullivan, C. Y., & Weiss, A. R. (1999). *Student work and teacher practices in science* (NCES Publication No. 1999–455). Washington, DC: U.S. Department of Education Office of Educational Research and Improvement and National Center for Education Statistics.

Paris, S., Yambor, K., & Packard, B. (1998). Hands-on biology: A museum-school- partnership for enhancing students' interest and learning in science. *The Elementary School Journal, 98,* 267–289.

Roschelle J., & Pea, R. (2002). A walk on the WILD side: How wireless handhelds may change computer-supported collaborative learning. *International Journal of Cognition and Technology, 1,* 145–168.

Salomon, G., Perkins, D. N., & Globerson, T. (1991). Partners in cognition: Extending human intelligence with intelligent technologies. *Educational Researchers, 20,* 10–16.

Schwartz, R., Lederman, N., & Crawford, B. (2004). Developing views of nature of science in an authentic context: An explicit approach to bridging the gap between nature of science and scientific inquiry. *Science Education, 88,* 610–645.

Shaw, E. L., Baggett, P., & Salyer, B. (2004). Kidspiration for inquiry-centered activities. *Science Activities: Classroom Projects and Curriculum Ideas, 41,* 3–8.

Stanford University School of Education. (2003). *STEP probes science teaching and learning with unique technology.* Retrieved August 23, 2008, from http://ed.stanford.edu/suse/news-bureau/educator/spring2003/pages/article-step.html

Tinker, R. (2000). *A history of probeware.* Retrieved May 12, 2006, from http://makingsens.stanford.edu/pubs/AHistoryOfProbeware.pdf

Tinker, R., & Krajcik, J. (Eds.). (2001). *Portable technologies: Science learning in context.* New York: Kluwer Academic/Plenum.

Tobin, K., Briscoe, C., & Holman, J. R. (1990). Overcoming constraints to effective elementary science teaching. *Science Education, 74,* 409–420.

U.S. Geological Survey. (n.d.). *Estimated use of water in the United States in 2000.* Retrieved July 10, 2009, from http://pubs.usgs.gov/circ/2004/circ1268/htdocs/table01.html

Vanides, J., Yin, Y., Tomita, M., & Ruiz-Primo, M. A. (2003). Using concept maps in the science classroom. *Science Scope, 28,* 27–31.

Vonderwell, S., Sparrow, K., & Zachariah, S. (2005). Using handheld computers and probeware in inquiry-based science education [Electronic version]. *Journal of the Research Center for Educational Technology, 1*(2). Retrieved June 11, 2009, from http://www.rcetj.org/?type=art&id=3383&

Windschitl, M. (2003). Inquiry projects in science teacher education: What can investigative experiences reveal about teacher thinking and eventual classroom practice? *Science Education, 87,* 112–143.

APPENDIX A

The introduction chapter introduced the importance of connecting curriculum to various digital literacy competencies. For science, the connection to digital literacy is as follows:

Technology Tool	Corresponding Digital Literacy				
	Photo-Visual	Reproduction	Branching	Information	Social-Emotional
Google Earth	■		■	■	■
Databases	■	■	■	■	■
Probeware		■	■	■	■

Appendix B
Glossary

Cognitive tools: Cognitive tools refer to computer applications that help support learners with complicated cognitive skills, such as critical thinking and problem-solving activities. Cognitive tools become learning partners to help learners' focus on knowledge construction and representation. For example, learners can design a database to collect data, and then form and test hypotheses with query they designed.

Geospatial: A term used to describe the consideration of global factors (e.g., location, altitude, proximity to oceans) across different locations on Earth. An example may be considering the geospatial differences in human populations' proximity to oceans and the impact of this proximity on human seashore preservation activities.

ICT: ICT stands for Information and Communications Technologies. ICT refers to the computer applications that can facilitate communication and knowledge exchange. E-mail, blog, wikis, and social networking tools are examples of ICT.

Probeware: Probes and sensors used in concert with handheld or desktop computers to collect and display real-time measurements of environmental parameters (i.e., temperature, light, motion, force, sound, electrical power).

Query: Query refers to a powerful function in Microsoft Access database software. It allows users to extract the information they need to answer questions from the data they collected and inserted into the database.

Simulations: Computer generated mediums that represent systems. Students generally are allowed to manipulate variables within the system represented before allowing the system to operate and depict the impact of variable manipulations. An example of this might involve students selecting characteristics of mice before operating the system to determine how these chosen characteristics influence future generations of mice after breeding.

Appendix C
Additional Resources

Useful Web Sites (Learning Standards)

BENCHMARKS ONLINE
http://www.project2061.org/publications/bsl/online

This site contains the full text of the *Benchmarks for Science Literacy* created by the American Academy for the Advancement of Science.

NATIONAL SCIENCE EDUCATION STANDARDS
http://www.nap.edu/openbook.php?record_id=4962

This site provides links to the *National Science Education Standards* developed by the National Research Council.

NATIONAL EDUCATIONAL TECHNOLOGY STANDARDS
http://www.iste.org/AM/Template.cfm?Section=NETS

This site provides free downloadable versions of the most recent NETS standards, developed by the International Society for Technology in Education.

Useful Web Sites (Open Database)

COMPREHENSIVE KNOWLEDGE ARCHIVE NETWORK
http://ckan.net

This is a site that allows users to access data for research purposes. There is a search engine at the site that allows users to find data about topics such as population and climate. Users also can share or upload data to the site.

INFOCHIMPS
http://infochimps.org

This site is described as the "world's best repository for raw data—a sort of giant free almanac, with tables on everything you can put in a table." Data sets range from topics like U.S. and World Census data to emissions of greenhouse gases by type and source data.

Useful Web Sites (Simulation Tools)

EXPERIENCE MATH AND SCIENCE WITH GIZMOS
http://www.explorelearning.com

Gizmos allows students to explore math and science through interactive simulations for grades 3–12.

SCIENCE SIMULATIONS ON THE INTERNET
http://www.kented.org.uk/ngfl/subjects/science/simulations.htm

Computer simulations found at this site can help students better understand real or imaginary events. Elementary and secondary level simulations at this site offer students a chance to study or try things that are not practical or difficult to study physically.

Useful Web Sites (Concept Mapping Tools)

INSPIRATION
http://www.inspiration.com

Inspiration® is a concept mapping tool designed for educational purposes. It is especially for learners in grades 6–12 to express their ideas through graphic organizers.

KIDSPIRATION
http://www.inspiration.com/Kidspiration

Kidspiration is a simplified version of Inspiration designed for students in grades K–5 to build graphic organizers and concept maps.

Useful Web Sites Probeware

VERNIER SOFTWARE AND TECHNOLOGY
http://www.vernier.com

Vernier is a commercial vendor that creates and sells probeware. A virtual product tour is available at the site.

PASCO
http://www.pasco.com

PASCO is another commercial vendor that creates and sells probeware. Information about all of its probeware products and online training for its products is available at this site.

Useful Web Sites (Search Engines)

GOOGLE IMAGE
http://images.google.com

Google image allows users to retrieve and download images.

GOOGLE BOOKS

http://books.google.com

Learners can retrieve information from books digitized by Google.

GOOGLE NEWS

http://news.google.com

Learners can search latest news articles from various news sources.

Useful Web Sites (Web 2.0 Tools)

GOOGLE DOCS

http://docs.google.com

Google Docs provides a set of free, Web-based applications to allow users to edit online documents such as word processing documents, spreadsheets, and presentations. All documents are saved on a Google server so users can collaborate with other users in a real-time format.

BLOGGER

http://blogger.com

Blogger is an online publishing tool that allows users to publish and archive articles online without worrying about complicated HTML code or transferring files to a Web server. Blogger is compatible with multimedia format files so it has been adopted into the education context in many ways, such as e-portfolios, personal journals, newsletters, or multimedia projects demonstrations.

Useful Web Sites (Google Earth)

GOOGLE EARTH

http://earth.google.com

The home page for Google Earth allows you to download this tool for free.

GOOGLE EARTH LESSONS

http://gelessons.com/lessons

This page provides several ready-made lessons for use with the Google Earth tool in the classroom, along with some tutorials on the use of this application.

Useful Web Sites (Multimedia Production Tools)

PHOTO STORY 3 FOR WINDOWS

http://www.microsoft.com/windowsxp/using/digitalphotography/PhotoStory/default.mspx

Photo Story is a free Microsoft application that allows users to create a multimedia slideshow to express their ideas.

IMOVIE

http://www.apple.com/ilife/imovie

iMovie is a Mac-based video editing software that allows users to create a video with titles and background music.

Multiliteracies in Action:

Integrating Technology Into the Literacy Classroom

Grace Enriquez and Stephanie A. Schmier

GUIDING QUESTIONS

1. (a) How can teachers employ traditional and innovative technology applications to enhance student learning? (b) What instructional activities will help me achieve this?

2. What technologies are available to enhance literacy teaching and learning?

Needs Assessment

1. *Keywords*

   Look over the keywords found in this chapter listed below. Rate yourself from one to three on your familiarity with each word. Then use this rating to help you set some goals for reading this chapter.

Word	1 Don't know at all	2 Some familiarity with this word	3 Very familiar with this word
Multimodality			
Hypertexts			
Multiliteracies			
Tags			

2. *Tools*

   Look over the three key technology tools listed below. Rate yourself from one to three on your familiarity with integrating these tools into your literacy classroom. Then use this rating to help you set some goals for reading this chapter.

Tool	1 Don't know at all	2 Some familiarity with this technology tool	3 Very familiar with this technology tool
Blogs			
Wikis			
Video Editing Software			

3. *Goal(s) for the Chapter*

   Fill in your goals below:

   a. By reading this chapter I hope to _____

   _____ .

   b. By reading this chapter I hope to _____

   _____ .

"**L**ine up for the computer lab!"

Upon hearing the familiar direction, Leann stands up, gathers her materials—notebook, pencil case, and writing folder—and tucks in her chair. She follows her teacher, Ms. Barnes, to the computer lab, a bare room with white cinderblock walls and rows of computers atop folding tables. Leann sits in front of one of the computers, logs in with her school ID and password, opens an Internet browser, and types in the Web address that Ms. Barnes has written on the whiteboard at the front of the room. It's a site the class uses often, one full of vocabulary games, word puzzles, and grammar quizzes.

Leann plays a few games and puzzles, checking periodically with classmates seated nearby to see who has the highest scores. Leann glances at Ms. Barnes, who sits at a computer-free table in the center of the lab grading papers, then resumes chatting with her friends and playing games. Occasionally, Ms. Barnes circulates among the students, inquiring about their scores or helping some of them figure out the answer to the puzzle or question on the screen. When Ms. Barnes reaches her, Leann asks for help with a game that challenges her to make as many words as she can from a list of seven randomly chosen letters. At the end of the hour, Ms. Barnes directs students to log off and shut down the computers. Leann picks up her unopened notebook, pencil case, and writing folder, and falls in line to head back to the classroom once more.

In many respects, Leann is one of the fortunate: She attends a school that provides students with access to computers, and she has a teacher who allows students time with technology as part of their literacy learning. However, when we look more closely at Leann's experience, we find ourselves asking a number of questions:

- ☀ What strategies or skills did Leann learn during her time in the computer lab?
- ☀ How did she learn them?
- ☀ What knowledge did she build upon through the activities she engaged in?
- ☀ What role did the technology serve in Leann's learning?
- ☀ How did Ms. Barnes actually use technology as part of her instruction?

We considered these very issues when we took on the challenge of incorporating technology into our own classrooms, and it was only with a long, honest look at our teaching and our goals for students that we began to grasp how wonderful, daunting, and tricky the possibilities of integrating technology into literacy curriculum really are.

Schools are in the midst of a revolution in which the proliferation of educational software, Web sites, and technological tools has provided teachers with an incredible array of materials and opportunities to enhance curriculum and instruction. But simply sitting students down in front of a screen or giving them a tool does not guarantee that the time they spend will be beneficial. More importantly, when we neglect to teach students explicitly how they can draw upon their facility with technology to enrich language and literacy skills in school, we fall short of preparing them to be fully literate citizens of the 21st century.

In this chapter, we address the intimate connection between literacy and technology including both the possibilities and challenges of integrating technological tools into the literacy curriculum. As we draw upon our own experiences to write this chapter, we hope:

- that in sharing our experiences we alleviate some of the concerns you might feel around integrating technology with literacy education;
- that it helps you look critically at current uses of technology in the literacy classroom in order to design instruction that is more meaningful and purposeful for students;
- that it provides you with some valuable tips and knowledge about tools that you can begin implementing in your teaching; and
- most importantly, that it inspires and emboldens you to learn alongside your students with and through technology.

A note about our terminology is necessary before we continue. As we wrote this chapter, we grappled with the question of when to use the term *language arts* and when to use the term *literacy*. The term language arts has been used to include a number of processes involving language that people use for a variety of social purposes, and schools traditionally have emphasized four kinds of language processes—reading, writing, speaking, and listening—in language arts curricula. As globalization and technology advances, the term literacy has begun to supplant language arts, sometimes shifting the focus of curricula and even job titles and responsibilities in schools. Although we also embrace the multiple language skills of reading, writing, speaking, and listening, we prefer to use literacy rather than language arts. Drawing on the work of the New London Group (1996), we believe that the continuing shifts in the global, business, and social scene also have ushered in new forms of communication that go far beyond conventional language-based approaches. To be clear, although we privilege the use of literacy in this chapter, we discuss ways to incorporate technology with instruction about literature, with narrative and essay writing, with storytelling—all of the conventional language arts topics—to help you push your teaching of these subjects forward. Our use of the term literacy, therefore, stems from the understanding that our students need to be adept and flexible with multiple forms of texts and communication.

Scenes From the Past: Traditional Uses of Technology in Literacy Classrooms

We both remember the day technology entered the schools we sat in as young students. For Grace, it was a large, boxy Apple IIe computer that sat in the corner of the classroom. Using it was reserved for students who finished their assignments first or who won the teacher's favor that day. Grace recalls how she and lots of classmates rushed through their regular schoolwork and volunteered to run errands around the school so they could be rewarded with computer access. In Stephanie's school, only the students who were officially identified as gifted could use computers. Thinking that the gifted program sounded like so much fun, she asked her parents if she could be in the program. She was tested, but was not accepted into the program. No computers for young Stephanie.

Thankfully, technology advanced and became affordable and accessible for many more students. By the time we entered the classroom again years later as teachers, it was commonplace for students to type their stories, essays, and reports on word processing software or to use the Internet to research information. But those practices often were reserved for final drafts or major

> Take a moment to recall your first experience with technology as a student in the classroom. What was the technology? Who was allowed to use it? How was it used? Then, think about the kinds of technology you had access to as a first-year classroom teacher. Ask yourself those same questions, and consider how far the role of technology in classrooms has come in your own journey from student to teacher.

projects. VCRs, DVD players, and CD players were the kinds of technology most teachers utilized on a daily basis. Meanwhile, increasingly more sophisticated technology was on its way to our homes and businesses.

A Snapshot of the Current State of Technology Integration in Literacy Classrooms

As literacy researchers and teacher educators ourselves, we constantly are floored by the ways in which literacy teachers conceive of using technology in their classrooms. We know of teachers who have access to LCD projectors, SMART Boards, and video cameras and work consistently to fold these tools into their instruction. On the whole, these remarkable tools are available in relatively few schools because they are quite expensive. The fact that many schools are now seeking professional development in technology for their entire faculty is encouraging. Yet, it can be difficult to fathom how technology can be incorporated into the literacy curriculum in ways that align with the goals of balanced literacy beyond using word processing programs, PowerPoint, online games, or publisher-created software in classrooms that don't have access to specialized equipment.

The good news is that many literacy teachers today acknowledge the significant role that technology plays in contemporary society and are opening up to incorporating advancements in technology into their daily lessons. However, the majority of those teachers are not doing so with the collaborative, systematic support of their colleagues and schools. Instead, they are spending infinite hours of their own time (and usually of their own volition) after school and on weekends attending workshops, gathering professional materials, and learning to use new technology that will enhance their instruction. Integrating technology into their classrooms, it seems, is a goal of many teachers and schools, yet it's primarily up to individual teachers to figure out how to do so. And it's a whole other ball game to figure out how to incorporate these tools in ways that align with proven educational strategies.

Fortunately, some literacy teachers are not discouraged by the challenges of integrating technology into instruction and enjoy the creativity involved in linking technology with literacy education. Some of the most popular and valuable ways teachers and students have found technology useful for literacy instruction are also those that are not tied specifically to literacy, but can be implemented across the curriculum. We list and describe several of those ways below:

- ☼ *Class Web sites*: Recognizing the amount of time students spend online after school hours, as well as the efficacy of the Internet as a means of communication between home and school, many teachers have developed class Web sites. Most of the content posted on these Web sites is informational: announcements and deadlines, assignment instructions, and links to other Web sites as resources for literacy learning.

- ☼ *Online tests and quizzes*: A number of commercial Web sites have been designed to aid teachers in assessing student learning. Sites like Quia (http://www.quia.com) and Discovery Education (http://school.discoveryeducation.com) allow teachers to create online quizzes, tests, surveys, and other assessments for students to complete during or after class time. Such sites are popular with students and teachers because they often provide instantaneous scoring and other features to help teachers manage student records.

- ☼ *Language arts resource Web sites*: A quick search using any Internet search engine will result in dozens of Web sites that provide an abundance of reading materials and literacy-based games and activities for students. Such Web sites often are used in classrooms during free time. Other sites provide resources specifically for teachers. For example, *Read Write Think* (http://www.readwritethink.org) is a popular site maintained by the International Reading Association (IRA) and the National Council of Teachers of English (NCTE) that provides teachers with lesson plans and instructional ideas.

- ☼ *WebQuests*: WebQuests are online teacher-created inquiry assignments designed to guide students through various Internet resources to help them answer questions about a specific topic. Completing a WebQuest typically requires students to read an introduction to the inquiry, follow a specific process to complete a task, utilize a number of online resources, form their own conclusions, and evaluate the experience. Students can complete WebQuests during class or at home.

Table 4.1 provides a detailed resource listing of various Web sites linked to each of these technology uses.

TABLE 4.1 Some Useful Online Resources for Literacy Teachers	
Purpose	**Sites**
For creating class Web sites	☀ http://www.classjump.com ☀ http://www.classnotesonline.com ☀ http://www.classtell.com ☀ http://www.quia.com ☀ http://www.schoolnotes.com ☀ http://www.teacherweb.com
For creating online tests and quizzes	☀ http://quizstar.4teachers.org ☀ http://www.proprofs.com/quiz-school ☀ http://www.quia.com
For language arts resources	☀ http://school.discoveryeducation.com/ schrockguide/arts/artlit.html ☀ http://www.carolhurst.com ☀ http://www.literacyleader.com ☀ http://www.readwritethink.org ☀ http://www.teacherplanet.com ☀ http://www.teachertube.com
For creating WebQuests	☀ http://www.teacherweb.com/twquest.htm ☀ http://www.teach-nology.com/web_tools/ web_quest ☀ http://www.webquest.com

MOVING FORWARD: INCREASING POSSIBILITIES AND OPPORTUNITIES FOR LITERACY STUDENTS

We applaud the innovative and progressive ways in which literacy teachers currently are using technology in their classrooms. What we envision next is a move beyond utilizing technology to support traditional types of print-based curriculum to a more interactive and *multimodal* approach to literacy teaching and learning. Clearly, most of the interactions that literacy teachers and students engage with technology occur online. Moreover, most of these practices and activities are teacher-centered or teacher-designed, perpetuating the notion that technology is not central to students' experiences within the literacy classroom.

Meanwhile, technology advances continue to shape and drive forward the ways we use literacy in just about every other facet of our lives.

We argue that incorporating technology into the classroom can and should take a central role in literacy teaching. Technology offers different modes for constructing texts for different purposes.

> Take a moment to look around and note the technological tools that are within reach right now. Whether you are at home, work, or traveling, think about how you use them, what kinds of texts are involved, and what kinds of literacy skills you call upon as you use those tools.

Technology can aid in the various process stages of constructing and comprehending texts. That is, students can use technology to learn, rather than to present a final product. Furthermore, technology can be used to nurture critical literacy skills and aim toward social justice. With all of these possibilities and more, the integration of literacy and technology can be a truly powerful approach for students' literacy learning.

Why Should Teachers Integrate Technology Into the Literacy Curriculum?

You might still be saying to yourself, "I have so much to teach in order to cover all of the curriculum and content standards. Why should I take on technology on top of everything else?" This question is one that many of the teachers we have worked with bring up when we discuss integrating technology into literacy instruction. In response to this challenge, we ask that you consider how you have integrated technology into your own life. For many of us, technological devices such as cellular smart phones (e.g., Blackberry, iPhone) and laptop computers have become essential components in our everyday lives. Digital mediums such as e-mail, blogs, wikis, and online social networking (e.g., MySpace, Facebook) allow us to stay informed and connected both personally and professionally on a daily basis in ways that are not possible without the use of these interactive tools. Using digital technology, we can quickly locate information, provide feedback, and share our thoughts and ideas with those who have similar interests across the globe. Similarly, integrating digital tools into classroom instruction can facilitate students' abilities to gather information, receive feedback, and publish a variety of texts that showcase their understanding of disciplinary content knowledge.

Still, integrating technology into the literacy curriculum can seem like a daunting task. Before we help with the *how*, we feel it is necessary to discuss the *why*. Thus, in the next section we provide a theoretical perspective that addresses why technology integration is essential to support our students in becoming successful 21st-century citizens. Further, we highlight current educational research documenting the impact of technology integration on student engagement and achievement. Finally, we offer a framework for literacy pedagogy grounded within the National Educational Technology Standards (International Society for Technology in Education [ISTE], 2007, 2008). In doing so, we hope you will feel more determined and prepared as you embark on the exciting opportunity of integrating technology into your curriculum.

INTEGRATING TECHNOLOGY INTO CURRICULUM: A THEORETICAL PERSPECTIVE

We are living in exciting times, where new modes of communication technologies such as the Internet are changing our understandings of literacy. Whereas in the not so distant past, literacy in schools was thought of as reading, writing, listening, and speaking about print-based texts, today literacy includes processing and producing multimodal texts with moving images, sounds, and hyperlinks working together to convey complex meanings (Kress, 2003). Further, the literacy landscape of the 21st-century continues to change as new communication technologies emerge and become integrated into our workplaces and social lives. Consequently, the literacy skills and knowledge that our students will need to participate successfully as members of our local and global communities in the future will continue to change (Anstey & Bull, 2006). This has consequences for literacy teaching and learning, as our students need to be prepared to engage in common literate practices that we cannot yet imagine.

Further, our students are learning digital literacy skills on their own, particularly in online spaces, as detailed in a 2006 report by the Kaiser Foundation documenting the increased use of technology by 3rd-through 12th-grade students. In terms of their digital literacy practices, it is becoming clear that our students are not willing to wait for schools to catch up (Durrant & Green, 2003; Foehr, 2006; Lam, 2000). One way we can begin to address these challenges is to reflect on how our students currently use literacy across classroom, home, and online spaces. For example, a student would probably use different literacy skills when writing an essay for a language arts assignment (e.g., academic language written in complete sentences) than she would when designing a PowerPoint presentation about a science lab project (e.g., charts and graphs, bullet points, animation). Meanwhile, this same student would probably use yet another type of informal language when describing these projects to her family at home or to friends online. Examining how our students use literacy across multiple social spaces can offer a window into their daily flexibility with literacy skills and knowledge. Moreover, it adds insight into how educators can utilize existing literacy skills in order to develop new literacy pedagogical practices that can support students' 21st-century literacy success (Anstey & Bull, 2006).

After considering how central technology is in our everyday literacy lives, you might still have another question on your mind: How can we develop literacy pedagogy that will prepare our students to engage in future common literate practices that we cannot yet imagine? An international consortium of literacy researchers known as the New London Group (1996) came together to tackle this very issue. It was clear to the New London Group that traditional school approaches to literacy teaching and learning, which focus primarily on the reading and writing of print-based texts, do not fully prepare students for the types of communication they likely will be required to engage with based on the increasing cultural, linguistic, and technological diversity of today's workplaces. In response, this team of researchers articulated the concept of *multiliteracies,* which addresses the need for students to consume and design texts in multiple modes (e.g., able to read and design images, video, and hyperlinked texts) for multiple purposes, and to communicate with diverse cultural and linguistic audiences (New London Group, 1996).

Multiliteracies pedagogy includes four components: situated practice, overt instruction, critical framing, and transformed practice (New London Group,

> Take a moment to observe your students using various kinds of technology "on their own turf." That is, what do you see them doing with technology in the few minutes before school starts, as they wait after school for a ride home, or perhaps even during lunch or recess time? Think about what kinds of technology they are using and what kinds of literacy skills are involved. How are those skills similar to what they are expected to do in the classroom?

1996). Through situated practice students become immersed in meaningful literacy practices within a community of learners, which include individuals with a variety of expertise. Experts, which may be teachers, students, or other members of the classroom community (e.g., parents, administrators, community volunteers), serve as mentors and guide learners through the process of designing both print-based and multi-modal texts. By engaging classroom community members as technology experts in the classroom, teachers can overcome their own concerns about technology, and can learn alongside their students while providing guidance and instruction in content knowledge and higher order thinking skills. Overt instruction is a practice that builds on learners' prior knowledge through "active interventions on the part of teachers and other experts that scaffold learning activities" and "that allow the learner to gain explicit information at times when it can most usefully organize and guide practice" (New London Group, 1996, p. 86). Critical framing builds on what students learn through situated practice and overt instruction by supporting them in structuring their emerging knowledge and understandings within social, cultural, political, historical, and institutional systems of knowledge. Finally, transformed practice allows for students to reflect and critique on the practices discovered throughout the learning process, which can facilitate the transfer of meanings to other cultural contexts. In this way, transformed practice serves as an assessment of both the learning processes of students and of the pedagogy itself.

Taken together, the four elements of multiliteracies pedagogy allow for teachers to engage with the unique cultural practices that their students bring to school in the learning process, while building students' abilities to communicate effectively with others from diverse backgrounds across multiple contexts in their lives. In this way, students learn to redesign meaning-making strategies in order to carry them across multiple cultural contexts. From this perspective, multiliteracies pedagogy moves beyond the limitations of traditional approaches to literacy pedagogy, and in turn "creates a different kind of pedagogy, one in which language and other modes of meaning are dynamic representational resources, constantly being remade by their users as they work to achieve their various cultural purposes" (New London Group, 1996, p. 64).

Impact of Technology Integration on Student Engagement and Achievement

Student Engagement With Digital Media for Literacy Learning

As mentioned above, one way to begin understanding how we can integrate technology successfully into the curriculum is to build on the skills that students are developing outside of the classroom. There is a growing body of research documenting the many ways in which youth are developing their literacy skills through engagement with digital media. We have evidence, for example, that students are spending significant amounts of time outside of school, sometimes for several hours a day, writing in online communities (Alvermann, 2006; Chandler-Olcott & Mahar, 2003; Guzzetti & Gamboa, 2005). These youth are drawing on the affordances of interactive online tools such as LiveJournal (Guzzetti & Gamboa, 2005), instant messenger (Lewis & Fabos, 2005), and MySpace (Schmier, 2007) to share their thoughts and ideas through writing for a global audience. A unique advantage to writing in interactive online spaces is the ability for users to receive immediate feedback on their writing from their readers, which provides opportunities for youth to revise and edit their texts in ways that meet the needs of their audiences. Duncan and Leander (2000), for example, documented how adolescents created their own network of Web writing buddies with which they interacted in order to improve as writers for self-expression. Similarly, Chandler-Olcott and Mahar (2003) discovered that through the support of online mentors, participants moved from novice to expert in their digital composing and ultimately became online mentors themselves. Table 4.2 provides a list of common online writing communities.

Table 4.2
Online Writing Communities

There are several sites on the Web where students (and teachers) can post and share their own writing in order to receive feedback from a writing community. Some of the most popular site are:
- LiveJournal (http://www.livejournal.com)
- The Writer's Corner (http://www.writerscorner.com)
- Blogger (http://www.blogger.com)
- Wordpress (http://www.wordpress.com)

Not only do online communities serve as spaces for youth to develop their writing skills, English language learners also have found the Internet to be a productive space in which they can develop their English language skills. For example, Lam (2000) documented how a young English learner took responsibility for his own literacy learning through the creation of an internationally hosted Web site, using the Internet to gain the literacy skills he desired on his own. Similarly, Black (2006) showed how one girl's participation in an online fanfiction community helped her to build facility with a number of literacies, both in English and her native language, Mandarin Chinese. These examples highlight the power that digital media can have to support diverse learners in building literacy skills and knowledge.

Supporting Student Achievement Through Technology Integration in the Classroom

There also is ample evidence that incorporating technology into the writing curriculum can support student achievement. Englert, Manalo, & Zhao (2004) found that the use of computers to support student writing in the traditional language arts curriculum led to increased achievement with at-risk students. Specifically, they discovered that students were motivated by the use of technology and therefore wrote more and demonstrated greater use of conventional writing skills when using a software program designed to support writing than when they used paper and pencil. Nixon (1999) similarly documented how the incorporation of technology into the literacy curriculum through a move from static, typed texts to the design of hyperlinked texts appeared to change the engagement of students who struggled with traditional approaches in the literacy classroom. Finally, there is research that supports the incorporation of technology to move beyond print-based texts to the design of multimedia video productions. Callahan's (2002) work exemplified such efforts of teachers to integrate technology into a critical media literacy curriculum. Specifically, she documented how an innovative high school educator engaged working-class students in the creation of "public radio" documentaries based on their own research into mass media. By providing students opportunities to engage with multimedia as authors and designers for critique of mainstream media messages, Callahan found that students became more savvy readers of the multimodal texts in the world around them, thus exemplifying the necessity to incorporate opportunities for students to critique texts through multimodal design in the literacy classroom.

Literacy Pedagogy and the National Educational Technology Standards

It is clear from the discussion above that integrating technology into literacy instruction can have a powerful impact on student engagement and achievement in the classroom. But what about those content standards that still direct much of your teaching? Implementing technology-integrated multiliteracies pedagogy into your own classroom can be facilitated by utilizing the National Educational Technology Standards (NETS) developed by the International Society of Technology Educators (ISTE, 2007, 2008).

Although the role and power of standards in education are sometimes debatable topics, most literacy educators agree that any list of guidelines or outcomes for student learning must be firmly rooted in current knowledge about literacy and learning. Two prominent professional organizations for literacy education, the International Reading Association (IRA) and the National Council of Teachers of English (NCTE), have issued a joint set of English language arts standards based on a nationwide consensus among literacy educators about literacy and literacy learning. The following list provides those standards for your review with standards referencing technology bolded (International Reading Association and National Council for Teachers of English, 1996, p. 3):

1. Students read a wide range of **print** and **nonprint** texts to build an understanding of texts, of themselves, and of the cultures of the United States and the world; to acquire new information; to respond to the needs and demands of society and the workplace; and for personal fulfillment. Among these texts are fiction and nonfiction, classic and contemporary works.

2. Students read a wide range of literature from many periods in many genres to build an understanding of the many dimensions (e.g., philosophical, ethical, aesthetic) of human experience.

3. Students apply a wide range of strategies to comprehend, interpret, evaluate, and appreciate texts. They draw on their prior

experience, their interactions with other readers and writers, their knowledge of word meaning and of other texts, their word identification strategies, and their understanding of textual features (e.g., sound-letter correspondence, sentence structure, context, graphics).

4. Students adjust their use of spoken, written, and visual language (e.g., conventions, style, vocabulary) to communicate effectively with a variety of audiences and for different purposes.

5. Students employ a wide range of strategies as they write and use different writing process elements appropriately to communicate with different audiences for a variety of purposes.

6. Students apply knowledge of language structure, language conventions (e.g., spelling and punctuation), media techniques, figurative language, and genre to create, critique, and discuss **print** and **nonprint** texts.

7. Students conduct research on issues and interests by generating ideas and questions, and by posing problems. They gather, evaluate, and synthesize data from a variety of sources (e.g., **print** and **nonprint** texts, artifacts, people) to communicate their discoveries in ways that suit their purpose and audience.

8. **Students use a variety of technological and informational resources (e.g., libraries, databases, computer networks, video) to gather and synthesize information and to create and communicate knowledge.**

9. Students develop an understanding of and respect for diversity in language use, patterns, and dialects across cultures, ethnic groups, geographic regions, and social roles.

10. Students whose first language is not English make use of their first language to develop competency in the English language arts and to develop understanding of content across the curriculum.

11. Students participate as knowledgeable, reflective, creative, and critical members of a variety of literacy communities.

12. Students use spoken, written, and visual language to accomplish their own purposes (e.g., for learning, enjoyment, persuasion, and the exchange of information).

As these standards indicate, we as teachers must move beyond traditional forms of text and approaches to literacy instruction to help students develop as fully literate individuals. These standards not only support the integration of technology into literacy curricula, they also call for pedagogical approaches that are flexible and responsive to any future changes in our modes of communication and ways of constructing and comprehending meaning for a variety of purposes. Table 4.3 shows how some of the common learning goals for language arts classrooms tie into various standards.

TABLE 4.3 Aligning Common Learning Topics/Goals With Standards			
Topic/Goal	IRA/NCTE Standard	NETS•S Standard	NETS•T Standard
Communicate effectively	#4, # 5	#2	#2
Read a swath of literature	#2	#3, #4	
Use multiple technological and informational resources	#8	#3, #4	
Conduct research with a variety of sources	#6	#3, #4	
Participate in a number of literacy communities	#11	#5	#4

Note. NETS•S refers to the student version of the ISTE (2007, 2008) standards. NETS•T refers to the teacher version of these standards.

TOOLS AND ACTIVITIES TO ENHANCE YOUR LITERACY CURRICULUM

In this section, we describe some specific technology tools and activities that you can incorporate into your literacy instruction. Although the kinds of technology tools that could be used in literacy classrooms continue to grow in number, we chose to focus on blogs, wikis, and video editing software for several important reasons. First, the tools we selected are ones that many teachers and students alike have used at some point in their lives, or are already using on a daily basis, and have some level of expertise when doing so. Second, many schools and classrooms already provide teachers and students with Internet-connected classroom computers, which is all that is needed to use these tools. Third, the kinds of lessons and activities around these tools that we describe are ones that can be incorporated into the literacy curriculum with relative smoothness and ease. In other words, by focusing on these specific tools, we hope and argue that you can begin integrating some of them into your teaching immediately.

Although we're confident that these tools and activities can be integrated well through various approaches to literacy instruction, we feel that an approach grounded in the pedagogical goals of balanced literacy will provide the most seamless and powerful experiences for students and teachers. Because teachers and researchers may differ in defining and implementing balanced literacy instruction (Freppon & Dahl, 1998; Pressley, Roehrig, Bogner, Raphael, & Dolezal, 2002), we want to clarify our vision and understanding of what balanced literacy means and looks like in classrooms. To us, balanced literacy attempts to fuse the best of direct, skills-based instruction with holistic, student-centered inquiries and experiences with language. It aims to balance skills instruction—such as the teaching of phonics, comprehension strategies, and revision strategies—with reading, writing, speaking, and listening in authentic contexts and for genuine purposes. Balanced literacy also acknowledges that literacy instruction entails both cognitive and affective processes and goals, seeking not only to develop students' academic achievement but also their sense of ownership, engagement, and investment in their literacy work (Pressley et al., 2002). Grounding our teaching in balanced literacy means using a combination of teacher-directed demonstrations, explanations, modeling, and one-to-one conferences, as well as student-led activities such as literature discussion groups, partner reading, personalized process writing in notebooks, and planning of literacy goals (Au, Carroll, & Scheu, 1997; Calkins, 1994, 2000). Because of our own experience with this approach to balanced literacy, the following discussion of technology tools and activities are grounded in this framework for instruction.

Blogs and Wikis

Blogs

Part of the reason that integrating technology into the literacy curriculum seems such a cogent and sensible fit is because of the countless online tools that facilitate writing and self-publishing, as mentioned above. One of the most popular tools advantageous for literacy classroom use is the blog. A blog is an online account of an individual's or group's ideas, reactions, and musings around a particular topic. The name blog is abbreviated from the word Weblog. People all over the world construct blogs about a myriad of topics, from political coverage, to family events, to film and restaurant reviews. Each blog entry is posted chronologically and indexed by date along one of the blog's margins. Sometimes, blog authors add labels or highlight keywords using tags in their entries to create an additional index organized by topic. Aside from written content, bloggers can add pictures, graphs, charts, and audio and video clips to an entry, as well as link to content anywhere on the Web. Each entry also contains a link through which readers can post comments, questions, and reactions to what was posted. Internet sites such as Blogspot (http://www.blogger.com) and Wordpress (http://www.wordpress.com) are popular, user-friendly, free host sites for blogs that are relatively easy to set up and maintain. As always, issues of student privacy must be considered when dealing with any online tool (so make sure to familiarize yourself with your school and school district's Acceptable Use Policy for the Internet).

USING BLOGS TO MEET THE NEEDS OF DEVELOPING LITERACY SKILLS

Blogs provide literacy teachers and students with an appropriate place to nurture and develop a number of discipline-specific skills. Composing what the main content will be requires students to apply writing skills around issues of genre, purpose, and audience. Students also can practice key reading strategies and skills as they read blogs. Watts Taffe and Gwinn (2007) explained that determining what is important, examining text structure, making predictions and inferences, and various other reading skills are in fact essential for reading online text. Furthermore, Godwin-Jones (2006) argued that "blogs by their nature and page structure encourage feedback and represent both a reading and writing activity" (pp. 10–11). If you have a small number of students, you may want to have them create individual blogs. With larger classes, for management purposes, you might find it easier to assign small groups of students to a blog or to use one blog per class. You also could differentiate instruction by assessing students' writing facility and multimodal abilities. That is, if a student finds writing easier to do with pen and paper, then you may want to start him or her there and then scaffold instruction toward using a blog. Conversely, many seemingly resistant writers flourish when technology is incorporated into their literacy instruction (Siegel, Kontovourki, Schmier, & Enriquez, 2008). Ultimately, you as the teacher can best decide how to support students' literacy learning through the incorporation of blogs in the classroom. For all students, we have found that writing responses to others' blogs, particularly those of other class members through discussion threads or comments, can engage students in higher order thinking skills as they develop and articulate ideas about one another's written thoughts.

SAMPLE ACTIVITIES TO TRY IN THE LITERACY CLASSROOM

Digital Writer's Notebooks. Blogs can be incorporated into the literacy classroom as digital writer's notebooks. Digital writer's notebooks capitalize on what we know as teachers about writing instruction and the valuable lessons we've learned as researchers about students' out-of-school interactions with technology. Literacy teachers and researchers have long enjoyed the value of teaching writing with writer's notebooks. A writer's notebook is not a diary or journal in which writers tend to briefly and privately chronicle a day's events, nor is it a language arts notebook in which students take notes from lessons, define vocabulary, or summarize the main event of a reading passage. Rather, writer's notebooks are places where students record quotations, flesh out story ideas, explore haunting memories, experiment with argument, and play with language. Ralph Fletcher (1996) asserted that a writer's notebook is the most important tool a writer can have:

> . . . Writers react. And writers need a place to record those reactions.
> That's what a writer's notebook is for. It gives you a place to write down what makes you angry or sad or amazed, to write down what you noticed and don't want to forget, to record exactly what your grandmother whispered in your ear before she said goodbye for the last time.
> *A writer's notebook gives you a place to live like a writer, not just in school during writing time, but wherever you are, at any time of day.* (italics in original, p. 3)

Writer's notebooks are mainstays in many literacy classrooms because they offer students a personal (but remember not private) place for them to collect the reactions that will then spark a host of other kinds of writing: stories, essays, poems, and so on. The benefits of using this tool are best observed in literacy classrooms that follow a writing workshop structure.

So, why bound this generative kind of writing to the perimeters of a piece of paper or to the pages in a blank book? Much of the online writing we see kids doing on their own, both on- and offline resemble the kind of writing teachers value in writer's notebooks, growing from the ideas, images, and experiences they already have. Online, students write about the music they like, the places they visit, the parties they attend, the people they know—and they weave wonderful stories and arguments around those topics as they do so.

Lesson: Implementing Digital Writer's Notebooks in the Classroom. Mrs. Norris integrated digital writer's notebooks in her ethnically and socio-economically diverse fifth-grade classroom. Students gathered near the front of the room for the start of writing workshop, bringing along the tools they had associated with writing over their years in school—pens and personally decorated black and white marble composition books that served as their writer's notebooks.

"You don't need those today," she told them. "We're going to use the computer for our notebooks." Instead of the large chart paper that many teachers use to model writing during lessons, she directed students' attention to the blog she had created that was projected onto a large white screen via an LCD projector. (You also can gather some students around a computer and introduce the digital writer's notebook through small-group instruction.) She asked the class, "Have any of you seen something like this online before? Could you tell us what this is and what it's used for?"

Some of them knew it was a blog, but others referred more generally to it as a Web site. Immediately, Mrs. Norris knew she had to step back and explain the difference between blogs and informational Web sites. Sammy nodded his head then and announced that his brother kept a blog about his favorite soccer teams. Others nodded, too, and mentioned some of the blogs they were familiar with or had read.

"So, a blog is a personal online space for someone to write her thoughts and ideas about something she's seen or experienced or remembered," Mrs. Norris summarized. "Does that sound like something we use in the classroom when we write?"

After making the connection between blogs and their writer's notebooks, some students predicted what their teacher was going to say next and couldn't hide their grins. But she couldn't just take them to the computer lab and have them start their digital writer's notebooks just then. Along with teaching students what a blog was, Mrs. Norris also felt she needed to explicitly teach them how a blog works. She focused on one blog feature each day as follow-up mini-lessons, teaching students how to add each as part of their digital writer's notebook. Table 4.4 shows some possible mini-lessons for using a blog as a digital writer's notebook.

Table 4.4
Mini-Lessons for Using a Blog as a Digital Writer's Notebook

Note that the procedures for adding pictures, video, audio, and hyperlinks to blog entries are specific to the site you use. We recommend visiting some of the sites we have listed in Table 4.2 and trying them out on your own to determine which is easiest for you to navigate in selecting a blog site for your students.

☀ **Post entries**: Posted entries are the equivalent of writer's notebook entries; that is, what students post are the story ideas, musings, memories, wonderings, and free writing from which they will compose more polished pieces of writing. Posted entries are the meat of a digital writer's notebook. Teach students how to navigate the specific blog they will be using so they can post their entries.

☀ **Insert pictures**: Writers also collect photographs and illustrations to inspire their writing. Blogs allow students to post and share those pictures. Teach students how to post a picture on the blog as part of an entry for their digital writer's notebooks.

☀ **Add audio and video clips**: The digital format of a blog allows writers to include and draw from a variety of multimedia sources for their work. Students can add a video clip from a birthday party or a speech made by a famous politician to serve as a springboard for different types of writing. Teach students how to upload audio and video clips that can enrich their work.

☀ **Insert hyperlinks**: Hyperlinks enable readers to locate similar content in a blog and therefore can be useful for organizing a writer's notebook (e.g., linking all entries that mention a student's pet rabbit). Teach students to reread their posted entries, identify common topics or ideas, and then add hyperlinks to connect the entries that contain them. Students also can insert hyperlinks that direct them to online resources and Web sites that can help them develop their ideas. For example, in Mrs. Norris' class, Gerard inserted a hyperlink into his entry about a recent visit to the emergency room for a broken wrist, linking it to a Web site about the skeletal system so he could refer to it if he needed to look up specific terminology or images that would help him further develop that story.

In addition to adding such features to enrich and organize their writing, Mrs. Norris also taught students how to use the unique features of blogs to help them use their notebook:

- ☀ *labels or keywords*: Including labels or keywords, referred to by bloggers as tags, for each entry allows students to briefly note main details of the entry and catalog them in an index. Students can then quickly use the label or keyword index to find all of their entries about a certain topic or using a certain word, rather than scrolling through each post over and over again. Rosalia, for example, wanted to write an essay persuading readers to preserve a local park. Having tagged her entries with keywords she was able to use the keyword index to find all of her entries about the park—from the neighborhood parties she attended there to the flower garden her school helped plant—and search them for details that might support her main argument for the essay.

- ☀ *blog archive*: Using the entry dates or titles listed in the archive, students can search through their previous entries to help them generate more entries or to select one to develop further into a draft for a particular genre of writing. Using the archive, Caren found an entry about her grandmother from the beginning of the school year and developed a sentence from it into a poem. Ideally, students can continue these blogs as they progress through the grades and revisit entries they had written in previous years.

- ☀ *entry comments*: Students can read and comment on each other's entries as a way of peer sharing or collaboration. Dwann and Carson transferred their partnership in the regular writing workshop online, reading each other's digital writer's notebooks and then writing comments and questions that pushed the other student to improve his writing.

A few weeks later, students were using blogs with as much facility as their traditional writer's notebooks, if not more.

Digital Reader's Notebooks. A blog also can be a fruitful venue for a digital reader's notebook. Like writer's notebooks, reader's notebooks are not places for students to complete prescribed assignments related to reading (e.g., write a letter from one character to another, summarize the main events of Chapter 8, or define vocabulary words from page 14).

Instead, they are spaces where students can write their personal reflections about and responses to what they read:

> The work of keeping a readers notebook should not be a chore. It should reflect a vibrant, vigorous reading and thinking life and a willingness to record that ongoing journey. The writing in a readers notebook should support thinking about books and help scaffold students to write longer about those books. A readers notebook is a place to collect information and take notes, some of which may serve to record their thinking and reading of a text, and some of which may become the basis for longer pieces of writing. (Angelillo, 2003, p. 46)

Although we argue for an expanding definition of text beyond books and the printed page, we value the reading of print literacy as an essential part of 21st-century literacy skills. By keeping a reader's notebook, students track their thoughts about reading in a manner that provides several benefits to them, including helping them make sense of what they are reading and preparing them to actively participate in whole-class or small-group discussions about texts. If students are reading in book clubs or literature circles, they may share their reader's notebooks with each other or even keep a collaborative notebook in which the entire group contributes its reflections about a shared text.

Constructing a digital reader's notebook allows students to collect their thoughts about reading and any other related online research they do into one shared space. A digital reader's notebook also allows students to take advantage of the blog and wiki (which we describe in the following section) features in a way similar to that of a digital writer's notebook. Blogs can be used as individual or group notebooks, with students working collaboratively to compose their responses or to respond to each other's comments. Students can add to, elaborate upon, and question each other's entries at any time during or after school, and teachers can check in on the discussion, extending the conversation that takes place during book club or literature circle time. In addition, students and teachers can use this tool to hold whole-class discussions around shared texts and read-alouds.

Lesson: Using a Digital Reader's Notebook to Extend Your Thinking About Characters. The seventh-grade students in Ms. Ott's class shuffled into the computer lab, which housed 15 computer terminals lining the walls of a large, carpeted room. The class was in the middle of a unit on historical fiction and had been keeping digital reader's notebooks for their novels for about a week by this time. Ms. Ott also had organized them into book clubs of four to five students based on her identification of their reading levels and interests, with each club having its own blog that it collaboratively used for its reader's notebook. Because the computer lab did not have enough computers for each of the 29 students, some of the book clubs sat in circles on the floor to continue reading their novels while the other clubs used the computers first. Halfway through the period, the groups would switch, thus maximizing the class' time and resources.

Before they settled into their work, they turned their attention to Ms. Ott. "Many of you are a good four or five chapters into your books now, so you've already met the main characters and you know the historical setting of the story," she began. "Today, let's focus on thinking more about those characters and getting to know them in deeper ways. We're going to use our digital reader's notebooks to help us do that."

Modeling the process for students, Ms. Ott logged onto the class blog and picked up *Trouble Don't Last* (Pearsall, 2002), the historical novel about the Underground Railroad that she had been using as a demonstration text all week. After scrolling down to the blog archive, she clicked on the label "Samuel," which pulled up every entry she had written about Samuel, the novel's main character. Meanwhile, Grace was helping Ms. Ott coteach the lesson and worked from another computer. She clicked on "Harrison," which brought up all of the entries about another main character. After taking a few minutes to reread the entries, she and Ms. Ott each created a new blog entry, synthesizing the information and reflections from the previous entries to form new conclusions about the characters.

After the mini-lesson, students immediately set to work, dividing the tasks among book club members. One group, which was reading *The Devil's Arithmetic* (Yolen, 1988) about a young girl's experience during the Holocaust, took the lesson a step further. After synthesizing their reflections about Hannah, group members found information about Anne Frank online and wrote another entry comparing her experiences to Hannah's to think even deeper about the character. Another group, which read *The True Confessions of Charlotte Doyle* (Avi, 1990) about a 13-year-old girl's 1832 cross-Atlantic journey on a brig, found pictures and descriptions of sailor's uniforms and living quarters and began pondering how Charlotte must have had to adjust from her upper class upbringing to her new surroundings.

CRITICAL LITERACY WORK WITH BLOGS

Developing students' critical literacy skills is no less important when composing digital texts. Critical literacy stems from a politicized understanding of language, literacy, and texts, requiring readers to consider issues of power, positioning, and perspective in the texts they read and to do so in the name of social justice (Jones, 2006). To nurture their critical literacy skills, students must be text analysts (Freebody & Luke, 1990) who read with questions such as, "Whose voices remain unheard in this text?" and "What does this text imply about what 'normal life' is supposed to be like?" in mind.

Blogs are rich sources of material for practicing critical literacy skills because their author(s) have not necessarily been vetted for any credentials or authority on the matters they discuss. As Albers and Harste (2007) explained, "Today, blogs are used in a variety of ways, to host podcasts, generate a following for political candidates, or to sway opinion" (p. 16). The same can be said of wikis, as we discuss in the following section, and thus, teaching students to be smart users and readers of blogs and wikis requires teaching them to be smart text analysts as well. We have a lot of friends who blog and create wikis, but we also know that some of them still have much to learn about a topic before they spout off and so we read them with a careful, critical eye. Kara-Soteriou (2007) argued that critical literacy benefits students' reading of digital texts in a number of ways:

> It allows students to distinguish between relevant and irrelevant information while searching online; read and interpret the different parts of a website's URL; look at multiple sources of information in order to evaluate the credibility and accuracy of each source; and find out who created a website, what the purpose of it was, and when the information was last updated. (p. 90)

Given that the Internet provides a wealth of texts written from an infinite number of perspectives and positions, students need sharp critical literacy skills to make sense of the texts they come across online.

Lesson: Deconstructing Online Blog Entries. Mr. Colón's fourth graders worked with reading partners during a unit on reading informational texts. Each pair sat before a computer, waiting for the lesson to begin. Responding to student interests and the reality that most of the reading people do on the Internet is with information texts, Mr. Colón and the students had designed the unit to incorporate the reading of blogs. More specifically, they had been practicing strategies for reading informational texts, such as previewing headings, using text features to predict the content of a passage, and setting purposes for reading, with blogs about their favorite pop music bands.

Using Google as their Internet search engine, they typed the names of the bands and "blog" into the search window and found dozens of blogs about each of the music groups that interested them. Students gathered lots of factual information about the bands through their searches: when they formed, how many members were in each, what kinds of music they played, how many albums they had released, and so on. Mr. Colón wanted them to go further—to critically analyze why these bands were popular and what messages their songs conveyed. He began with the Jonas Brothers, a "boy band" that had garnered fame on the Disney Channel and was a hit among his students. A quick search on the Internet by typing "Jonas Brothers blog" into the search box produced lots of blogs devoted to the band, so Mr. Colón assigned one to each pair of students. He asked them to think about and note the following information:

- ☀ Who is the author of this blog?
- ☀ What kinds of information about the band does the author mostly provide? Why do you think that is?
- ☀ What kinds of images are present on the blog? What do you notice about them?
- ☀ If you can listen to any music on the blog, what do you notice about it?
- ☀ If there are any videos of interviews or performances, what do you notice about them?
- ☀ When was this site last updated? How do you know?
- ☀ What kinds of advertisements are on the blog?

The students worked for half an hour, exploring all of the content and features of the blog. Afterward, Mr. Colón reconvened the class to discuss what they had noted. They had discovered that some blogs were written by corporations, such as the Disney Channel and Hollywood Records, and that some were written by individual fans. Most of the written entries were about the band's upcoming performances, but some posted links to newspaper and magazine articles. Much of the advertisements were for fan paraphernalia or other entertainment-related sites. Students also noticed that many of the images were of band members either performing onstage or posing at professional photo shoots. They also noticed that the Jonas Brothers wore trendy outfits and hardly smiled in any of the professional photographs.

"So what do you make of all this?" Mr. Colón asked the class. "What's the purpose of many of these blogs? Are they just there to give you information about the band?"

Some students answered that a lot of what was posted on the blogs was designed to get them to spend money on concert tickets, T-shirts, and CDs, and they noticed that many of those blogs were corporate-generated. Others responded that the photographs made the boys "look cool" so that readers might want to try to dress or act like them. The class had begun to analyze their online reading in terms of power and perspective. Mr. Colón helped them deconstruct the blogs further by asking what voices, opinions, or perspectives were largely missing. And soon, they realized that many of the blogs did not discuss the band's music at all.

Creating and Setting Up a Blog for Use in the Literacy Classroom

Blogs have become an essential part of many classrooms. Thankfully, the technology for creating blogs is generally quite easy to learn and in most cases, free to anyone to use, making it an ideal tool for the classroom. Table 4.5 provides a list of many sites that help educators set up blogs. The following steps will help you and your students create and set up blogs for use in the literacy classroom.

TABLE 4.5 Some Web Sites to Help You Create a Blog
http://www.21classes.com http://www.blogger.com http://www.bravenet.com http://www.livejournal.com http://www.thoughts.com http://www.wordpress.com

Step 1: Create a Blog
  1. Many of the free Web sites that host blogs walk you step-by-step through the process of creating a blog. Because the specific steps depend on which host site you use, the steps below outline the general process

for setting up a blog. Sometimes the order of the steps differs. Make sure to follow the directions and explore the unique options that your particular blog host offers.

2. Choose a host site for your blog. See Table 4.5 for some recommendations.
3. Click on the link to start the process. Usually, the link is a big box that says something like "Create a Blog" or "Sign up for a Blog."
4. Choose a username and password so you can post entries and comments. Make sure you also have an e-mail address where notices can be sent. This is especially useful if you forget your username or password (see Figure 4.1).

FIGURE 4.1. Naming your blog (http://www.blogger.com).

5. Create a title and URL (Web site address) for your blog (see Figure 4.1).
6. Consider how private you want the blog to be, and whom you want to have access to it.

Step 2: Decide How to Use Your Blog in the Classroom

1. Decide if you want to use your blog as a Digital Writer's (see Figure 4.2) or Digital Reader's Notebook (see Figure 4.3).
2. Once you have set up your blog, look for a link that will allow you to post entries.
3. Post your first entry for your students as a demonstration.

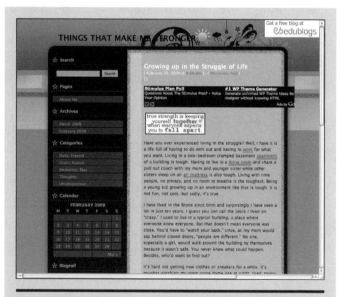

FIGURE 4.2. A digital writer's notebook entry.

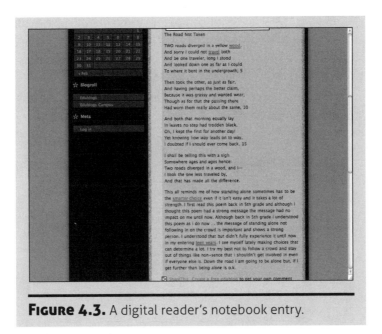

Figure 4.3. A digital reader's notebook entry.

Step 3: Model for the Students How to Use the Blog

1. Explain to students what blogs are. (There is a great YouTube video from Common Craft called "Blogs in Plain English" that explains this clearly. See http://www.youtube.com/watch?v=NN2I1pWXjXI.)

2. Model for your students how to use a blog on an overhead or shared computer.

3. Teach your students about the features of a blog such as:

   a. *Labels or keywords*: Including labels or keywords to tag each entry allows students to briefly note main details of the entry and catalog them in an index. After reading the next chapter in her novel, Monique used the keyword index to find another book club member's entry that predicted what would happen and then commented on what predictions turned out to be right and what had surprised her.

   b. *Hyperlinks*: Students can insert hyperlinks that direct them to online resources and Web sites that could provide further information about their reactions and novels (see Figure 4.4). For example, Seungho linked an entry about his book club's novel, *The Watsons Go to Birmingham—1963* (Curtis, 1995), to some news articles about school desegregation that he referred to in his discussion.

   c. *Entry comments*: Teachers and students can read and comment on each other's entries to extend discussions about their reading (see Figure 4.5). Bridget commented on Rajani's entry about *Journey to Topaz* (Uchida, 1971), encouraging her to read *The Moon Bridge*

(Savin, 1995), another compelling novel about the experience of Japanese American internment camps.

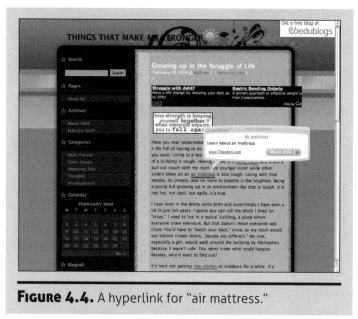

FIGURE 4.4. A hyperlink for "air mattress."

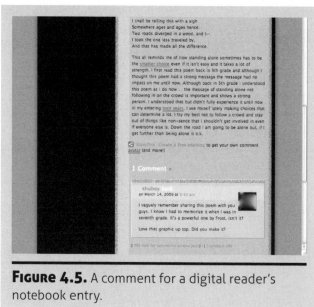

FIGURE 4.5. A comment for a digital reader's notebook entry.

Step 4: Decide How You Will Assess Students' Participation in Classroom Blogs
1. How often do they need to post?
2. How many of their classmates' posts do they need to respond to?
3. How long do their posts need to be?

Wikis

A wiki is an interactive, collaborative Web space that allows users to add to or modify its contents with relatively simple knowledge of the codes and language needed to do so. Most wikis hold a collection of Web pages under an organized framework. Wikipedia (http://www.wikipedia.org) is perhaps the best-known example of a wiki, with thousands of pages full of encyclopedic entries that registered users can contribute to, modify, or update. The pages of a wiki operate and serve specific functions and often are formatted in ways we encounter on many sites on the Web. For example, many wikis contain a home page, a set of main content pages, a discussion page, and a photos page. Additionally, students can create the content of the wiki simultaneously, which is facilitated by the application's ability to track any changes made to its content, thus making students' thought processes more transparent for each other and for teachers as they construct the wiki. Because of these features, groups of people usually work collaboratively to construct and keep a wiki. In classrooms, students can choose and construct what content will be posted in a relatively hassle-free way. Furthermore, wikis can be used for whole-class, small-group, and individual instruction, and each page can contain differentiated activities to meet each student's literacy strengths and needs. Because blogs and wikis are spaces where students can store much of their literacy work over time, these tools also can serve as digital portfolios for assessment.

A number of Web sites provide wikis that are specifically geared for classroom use. They also provide step-by-step instruction for creating a wiki and designing it to meet the needs of teachers and students. Most teachers set up their wikis to include a home page with announcements and general information, a page for online discussions, and several pages for students to add other kinds of content, depending on how the wiki will be used. When creating your wiki, also consider how private you want it to be. Usually, there is an option to limit who has access to the wiki and an option to set up log-in and password information. Don't forget to check whether your school provides access to these Web sites or if they are protected by a firewall.

USING WIKIS TO MEET THE NEEDS OF DEVELOPING LITERACY SKILLS

Like blogs, wikis provide literacy teachers and students with many of the same opportunities to hone essential literacy skills (see Table 4.6 for a comparison of blogs and wikis). Students can apply the same writing and reading skills that they would use with blogs, and because wikis allow their authors more freedom with the Web site's organization and design, a number of other crucial skills rise to the fore. For example, students need to be able to set clear purposes for their reading so they can know which wiki pages will be most helpful. Watts Taffe and Gwinn (2007) emphasized knowing how to navigate text:

> In recent years, the term *navigating* has come to be associated with the Internet, and it requires knowing the difference between browsing and searching and when to use each, how to move within and among websites, and how to save important webpages. It also includes the ability to get the information sources best suited to the reader's purpose as efficiently as possible—knowing when to stop and linger and when to move on quickly. (p. 64)

TABLE 4.6
Understanding the Similarities and Differences Between Blogs and Wikis

	Blogs	Wikis
Features of Written Entries	Entries and comments are posted chronologically, one at a time, on the same page.	Entries and comments are interwoven and continually modifiable, with any changes tracked on another page.
Possibilities for Writing	Only the author(s) of the blog can contribute entries and other content.	Anyone who is a member of the wiki can contribute entries and other content.
Possibilities for Design	Content is posted and uploaded into a standard template.	Any number of pages can be created and added for different purposes.
Possibilities for Collaboration	Students respond to each other's entries by leaving comments at the end.	Students respond to each other's entries by leaving comments at the end or by writing directly in the entry.
Benefits	The format of a blog encourages individual reflection and offers spaces for others to comment on those reflections.	The format of the wiki strongly supports group work and collaboration because anyone can add to or revise its content.

Relatedly, when students create wikis, they must pay attention to audience, text organization, structure, and coherence. Each page of the wiki could feasibly require them to read and write in different genres. Students also can practice speeches and reader's theater, as well as improve their listening and viewing skills with any uploaded audio and video clips.

SAMPLE ACTIVITIES TO TRY WITH WIKIS IN THE LITERACY CLASSROOM: WIKIS FOR INTERACTIVE, COLLABORATIVE WRITING

Once thought of only as a strategy for teaching emergent writers, principles of interactive writing also are useful approaches for developing writers in intermediate and middle school grades. In interactive writing, the teacher and students literally share the pen (or keyboard) to compose a text collaboratively, concentrating on both content and presentation in the process (Tompkins & Collom, 2003). For younger students, the emphasis is on writing words and sentences, using capital letters and punctuation, and teaching phonics and spelling patterns as they compose messages, charts, and other kinds of texts that could be used in the classroom. For older students, the idea can be adapted so that the teacher and groups of students compose a text together, focusing on advanced skills like writing coherent paragraphs, using purposeful grammar and punctuation, and writing for specific genres, such as short fiction, poetry, "how-to" pieces, and personal narratives.

Wikis also allow writers to take this approach a step or two further, encouraging teachers and students to think about complex issues of design while composing. The possibility of composing text across multiple Web pages raises considerations about nonlinear sequence and hypertext (Reinking, 1997). Cohen and Cowen (2008) explained some of the benefits of this kind of writing:

> Writing hypertext allows the writer to digress down a different path to assume that readers will be willing to explore the idea that the author is expanding. With hypertext, a writer can allow the reader to explore a concept or to stay on the straight and narrow path that is developing right on the page. (p. 318)

Thus, composing wikis encourages students to think more holistically about their writing, considering issues of coherence across pages, audience, and purpose. Furthermore, because wikis consist of multiple Web pages about the same general topic, students can work on the wiki simultaneously, tracking the changes each writer makes and collaboratively deciding on the final content and design.

Lesson: Choosing an Idea and Gathering Supporting Information for a Persuasive Essay. Twenty-nine sixth graders sat in the computer lab, each clicking and scrolling through the class wiki they had constructed together for writing. Just a few minutes before, they had learned that writers look through their collections of ideas and think about which one they would like to expand into a draft. They were in the middle of a persuasive essay unit and had spent the last week coming up with possible arguments they wanted to defend in a whole-class essay. The wiki had a few pages devoted to the generation of ideas, and students had eagerly written entries about everything from animal rights to computer-animated movies.

"Read through each entry and think about them carefully," Mr. Tanner guided the students. "Remember what strong persuasive writing looks and sounds like, and ask yourself, 'Is this a topic that we can turn into a strong argument or thesis statement?' and 'Can we gather enough evidence and details to support our thesis?' If you think we can, then vote for it on the wiki."

Mr. Tanner had helped the class design a wiki page that listed all of the topics they had come up with when generating ideas for the persuasive essay and had simple boxes they could check with a click of the mouse to vote for a topic. Midway through the period, he gathered the class together again to tally the votes. The result was a landslide victory for an essay convincing the school to improve its recycling efforts.

"Now that we've voted on the thesis for our essay, we need to start figuring out how to support it. How can we use our wiki to help us do that?" Mr. Tanner asked.

Some students immediately thrust their hands into the air; others pondered the possibilities for a while before volunteering suggestions. After discussing various ideas, students decided to figure out what their main arguments would be, created a wiki page for each, and then added and uploaded any supporting information they could find onto that page. The user-friendly, collaborative nature of the wiki allowed students to conduct research on the Internet and add content to the designated wiki page whenever they found something useful. At the end of writing workshop, students had found information to support each of the main arguments for improving the school's recycling efforts, and they left knowing they could do more research and add to the wiki on their own at home.

Over the next 2 weeks, the class used the wiki in other ways to help them write the persuasive essay:

- ☀ *Drafting, revising, and editing*: Students were divided into five small groups, each in charge of drafting one of the paragraphs for the persuasive essay (introduction, three supporting paragraphs, and conclusion). After all of the drafts were written, students went to the other groups' paragraphs to offer suggestions for revision and editing.
- ☀ *Publishing*: Once the class finished writing, revising, and editing the entire essay, they posted the final product on a separate wiki page for completed publications. That page also contained the final versions of other kinds of writing they had done collaboratively on the wiki throughout the school year.

WIKIS FOR GENRE STUDY

In many literacy classrooms, whole units of study are devoted to particular genres of literature, writing, or speech. Common literary genres that are explored in intermediate and middle school grades are historical fiction, drama, and poetry. When we taught writing in these grades, we focused on the genres of persuasive essay, literary essay, poetry, memoir, and realistic fiction. Lattimer (2003) explained that a genre study is "an inquiry into a text form" and that the objective is "to develop habits of reading and writing [and speaking] that enable students to master the genre itself" (p. 4). Students study a collection of texts within a genre to develop such habits and practice the literacy strategies necessary to use and understand that genre.

For these reasons, wikis are terrific tools to incorporate into a genre study. The various pages of a wiki can be constructed for different purposes, requiring students to engage in different literacy activities related to the genre. For example, students can use the discussion page as they would a collaborative reader's notebook or a dialogue journal in which the students reply to one another's comments. Another page can be used to write book or article reviews, or to upload photos of book covers, video clips of movie trailers that have been made from certain books in the genre, interviews with authors, and other multimedia related to the genre. Still another page can provide students with space to try their hand at writing in the genre they are studying and comment on each other's writing. The possibilities for using wikis in a genre study seem endless.

Lesson: Identifying Essential Genre Characteristics Across Wiki Pages. Mrs. Daniels' eighth-grade students were in the middle of a genre study on gothic fiction, something they had voted on to match the mood of the autumn season. The class had been divided into book clubs that read classic works of gothic fiction, such as *Frankenstein* (Shelley, 1819/2003), *The Strange Case of Dr. Jekyll and Mr. Hyde* (Stevenson, 1886/1982), *The Phantom of the Opera* (Leroux, 1911/1994), and a collection of stories by Edgar Allan Poe. They had constructed a class wiki around this genre at the start of the unit. The wiki contained a home page with general information about gothic fiction, a page for each book club to post information about the novel it was reading, a page with information about famous gothic fiction authors and links to other Web pages about them, and a discussion page where the entire class shared its thoughts and questions about the genre with one another. Each student sat at a computer terminal and logged on to the wiki as the lesson began.

Mrs. Daniels started the lesson by connecting it to the previous day's discussion. "Remember how yesterday, Carla noticed that *Frankenstein* didn't just seem to be about something scary, but that much of the novel seemed to be telling a love story? And then other groups mentioned that they noticed the same thing in their texts, too? That was a fantastic thing to realize, and it's one of the elements that make up the gothic fiction genre. It's not strictly horror, but it mixes elements of horror and romance together into a really thrilling kind of story. We can use our class wiki to identify more of the elements of gothic fiction." Students nodded their heads in understanding, and Mrs. Daniels smiled. She was proud of her students for discovering that characteristic of the genre yesterday.

Mrs. Daniels logged into the wiki and began demonstrating how students could use the wiki to look for similar characteristics and elements across the pages. Grace began reading the wiki pages for *Frankenstein* and *Jekyll and Hyde*. Next, Mrs. Daniels went to the page with information about the authors. There was a clip from a video about Edgar Allan Poe, and she demonstrated how to take notes about his style, inspiration, and works as she watched it. Mrs. Daniels then clicked on the discussion page and began rereading everyone's posts to see what recurring ideas or thoughts about the genre had been written. Finally, she created a new page and began listing some of the characteristics of gothic fiction that she had found. When she had found some information as well, Grace went to the new page and added to the list Mrs. Daniels had started, giving the students a second demonstration of how to complete the comparisons.

After the demonstration, students logged onto the wiki and began reviewing its pages for other features of gothic fiction. Once they found some, they also clicked on the new page and added to the list. Some even revised what Mrs. Daniels and Grace had written. For example, Cheyanne changed "ghosts" to "supernatural beings" and relisted "ghosts" as an example. Other students added "haunted houses," "castles," and "mad scientists" to the list.

In the subsequent weeks, Mrs. Daniels used the wiki again for follow-up lessons and activities, again emphasizing how they could use the particular features of the wiki to further their study of the genre:

- *Connecting reading and writing*: Using the prominent characteristics of the genre, some students created a new wiki page where they could try writing some of their own gothic fiction stories. Because of the interactive nature of the wiki, students could offer suggestions and comment on each other's writing.

- *Intertextual and multimedia explorations*: Students also found clips from some of the movie versions of their novels and posted them on the wiki. This allowed them to begin a conversation on the discussion board about intertextual connections across various gothic fiction media. Moreover, because those clips were added to the wiki, students could easily click back to them to review them if needed.

CRITICAL LITERACY WORK WITH WIKIS

Aside from deconstructing online texts to determine their underlying messages about the world and how one should act within it, critical literacy encourages students to reconstruct texts so that the perspectives that often are not heard in mainstream media are given voice. Reconstructing texts involves rewriting and redesigning them to highlight issues of bias and to show how a story or set of information could be presented in another, equally valid way. Lots of authors already do this. For example, author Gregory Maguire (1995) reconstructed *The Wizard of Oz* to present the wicked witch's side of the story in *Wicked,* and children's book author Jane Yolen (1996) retold the Christopher Columbus story from a native Taino perspective in *Encounter.* Students usually respond enthusiastically when reconstructing texts, as they reread and talk about the ones they plan to rewrite.

Lesson: Reconstructing Marginalized Perspectives of Traditional Tales. Grace sat with a class of fourth graders who had been using wikis to critically read the traditional tales from their childhood, fairy tales that perpetuated the notion that women had to marry in order to live a happy life or subscribe to a narrow definition of beauty and femininity. The students had many of these tales to work with, and had already deconstructed several of them in small groups on their group's wikis. They also had read several reconstructed tales that were available in their classroom and school libraries, such as *The True Story of the Three Little Pigs by A. Wolf* (Scieszka, 1989) and *Cinder Edna* (Jackson, 1998). Now it was the students' turn to try their hand at rewriting a tale.

The following mini-lessons helped them reconstruct the tales with the use of their wikis. You will notice that many of the strategies resemble the kinds of lessons that students are taught when writing with pen and paper. However, because of the increased compositional opportunities that wikis provide, explicit lessons about design also were included.

- ☼ *Brainstorming*: Students learned to create a wiki page where they could brainstorm the many possible ways a tale could be retold to bring forth another perspective. For example, *Snow White* can be rewritten from the point of view of the queen or any of the seven dwarves.

- ☼ *Drafting*: The interactive structure of a wiki allowed students to work collaboratively as they wrote a draft of their reconstructed tale. Students learned to use the discussion page of their wiki to share ideas about the development of the new tale.

- ☼ *Revising and editing*: Because a wiki enables students to track any changes made to the content of a page, students learned to work on their tales simultaneously. Some students concentrated on improving their use of description and dialogue, while others focused on grammar and spelling.

- ☼ *Publishing*: Here, questions about design, format, and presentation arose. Students considered what kind of font they wanted to use, and what imagery a certain font evoked. They also searched the Internet for pictures to help illustrate their stories and thought about where to place them on the page in line with corresponding parts of their tales. Because this project was part of a critical literacy focus, students also carefully scrutinized and deconstructed the pictures they inserted to make sure that the images did not present a contrasting perspective or reinforce mainstream tellings of the tale.

Creating and Setting Up a Wiki for Use in the Literacy Classroom

Before using wikis in your classroom, you'll want to create a wiki specific to your needs. Table 4.7 provides a list of Web sites that offer free or education-geared wikis.

TABLE 4.7
Some Web Sites to Help You Create a Wiki
http://www.pbworks.com/academic.wiki http://www.seedwiki.com http://www.wetpaint.com http://www.wikispaces.com

Step 1: Create a Wiki
1. Many of the Web sites that host wikis walk you step-by-step through the process of creating one. Because the specific steps depend on which host site you use, the bullets below outline the general process for setting up a wiki. Sometimes the order of the steps differs. Make sure to follow the directions and explore the unique options that your particular wiki offers.
2. Choose a host site for your wiki. See Table 4.7 for some recommendations. See Figure 4.6 for a sample starting page.

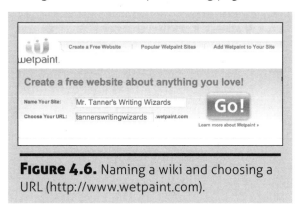

FIGURE 4.6. Naming a wiki and choosing a URL (http://www.wetpaint.com).

3. Choose a username and password so you can access the wiki and post content on it. Make sure you also have an e-mail address where notices can be sent. This is especially useful if you forget your username or password.
4. Click on the link to start the process. Usually, the link is a big box that says something like "Get Started" or "Create Your Wiki."
5. Create a title and a URL (Web site address) for your wiki.
6. Consider how private you want the wiki to be, and whom you want to have access to it. You will need to "invite" others to access the wiki by typing in their e-mail addresses.

Step 2: Decide How to Use Your Wiki in the Classroom
1. Once you have set up your wiki, look for a link that will allow you to create or add pages. It may be helpful to map out the kinds of pages you want to create, as well as the organization and linking of the pages to each other, by first sketching them out in a flow chart.
2. Go to any page and look for a link that allows you to add or edit content.
3. Post your first entry, and explore the other features the wiki has to offer!

Step 3: Model for the Students How to Use the Wiki
1. Explain to students what wikis are. (There is a great You Tube video from Common Craft called "Wikis in Plain English" that explains this clearly. See http://www.youtube.com/watch?v=-dnL0OTdmLY.)
2. Model for your students how to use a wiki on an overhead or shared computer.

Step 4: Decide How You Will Assess Students' Participation in Classroom Wikis
1. How often do they need to post?
2. How many of their classmates' posts do they need to respond to?
3. How long do their posts need to be?

Video Editing Software

Utilizing video editing software in the classroom is an exciting way to incorporate multimodality into a literacy curriculum. At this point you may very well be thinking, "But don't I need cameras, microphones, and tripods? I don't have access to any of that equipment in my school." Although creating digital movies using specialized equipment is a very worthwhile task if one has the resources and time in which to do so, here we offer ways that you can incorporate video editing software into literacy instruction using only your classroom computer(s), allowing students to publish their own videotext productions.

Video editing software is a computer application that allows users to sequence moving or still images as well as add music, voiceover, titles, and transitions. Some of the most popular free video editing software programs are iMovie for Macintosh computers and Windows Movie Maker for PC computers. These software applications are designed to provide users with the ability to create "professional-looking" videos in a simple and user-friendly way. The features and capabilities of these software programs provide opportunities for students to engage in multiliteracies work through the production and reconstruction of multimodal texts in ways that complement a balanced literacy curriculum as we describe below.

Using Video Editing Software to Meet the Needs of Developing Literacy Skills

Working with video editing software can support literacy learners in a variety of ways. First, the timeline feature of the software supports learners in structuring their narratives, and allows them to experiment with different ways of sequencing their stories before final publication. Video editing software also supports learners in understanding how images contribute to the meaning of texts, which can provide insights into their own critical reading of both print-based and multimodal texts. Further, video editing software meets the needs of developing literacy skills by providing an engaging forum through which students can design texts that are relevant to the types of texts they engage with outside of school. The following activities are starting points for you to incorporate digital media into your classroom. We are certain that once you and your students engage in these activities, you will find new and innovative uses for video editing software in your own literacy curriculum.

Sample Activities to Try With Video Editing Software in the Literacy Classroom

CREATING VIDEO USING STILL IMAGES

Even if you plan to have your students use video cameras to produce films as part of your curriculum, we have found that having students create videotexts using still images is a valuable introductory experience. It also is a process that can be used by teachers who never plan to use, or have access to, video cameras in their classroom.

Every year a colleague of ours has his eighth-grade students create local history documentaries of community landmarks such as museums, ballparks, and historical buildings using still images gathered from the Internet. This process of gathering images from the Web facilitates the research process, as students are required to locate Web sites that provide information on local sites. After students select a destination, they search the Internet for information about the history of the location. As they gather information, they document the sites in their writer's notebooks and save the images to folders on the computer. They then engage in the following activities:

- ☼ *Evaluating sources*: Students are taught to evaluate the information they gather from the Web by considering the:
  - source of the content,
  - the purpose of the site, and
  - the authenticity of the information gathered.

Students are encouraged to visit their community landmark location in order to evaluate the authenticity of the information they ascertain from their Web searches. They have to make sure the photographs they choose are either in the public domain or are permissable for use in education, so as to not infringe upon copyright. They also are encouraged to take their own digital photographs (a student can check out the class camera if he does not have his own) to include in their documentaries.

- ☼ *Storyboarding and writing the script:* Using the timeline feature of the video editing software, students sequence the images they have saved (see Figure 4.7). They simultaneously use a word processing program (or their writer's notebooks if they

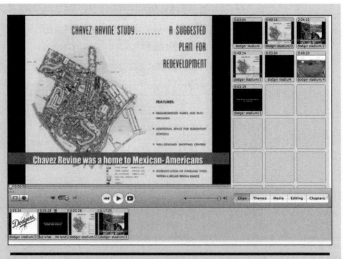

Figure 4.7. Sequencing clips using iMovie software. Students move the images they have downloaded on the right into the space at the bottom where they order and time each clip for their final movie.

choose) to write the narration for their documentaries. After completing the scripts, students record their narratives by speaking into the built-in computer microphone.

- ☼ *Adding title slides, transitions, and effects*: Our colleague has students view different videotexts throughout the unit and note how music, sound effects, title slides, and transitions are used to tell the story. After recording their narratives, students add text, title slides, transitions, and sound effects to their own pieces.

- ☼ *Critique and revision:* Students work in pairs to view each other's documentaries and provide critical feedback. Finally they draw on the affordances of the software, which allows for the easy manipulation of images and rerecording of narratives, in order to redesign their texts incorporating the feedback they receive from their classmates and teacher.

Students who engage in this process create critical texts that highlight their understanding of social issues in their community. One student named Casey created a documentary on the major league baseball ballpark in the city, which was only a few miles away from where she lived. Through her research and with help from her teacher she learned that the team had been the first to allow an African American player to join. She also learned that an entire community of Latino Americans had been forced to move from their homes in order for the stadium to be built. The documentary that she designed and produced articulated the complexity of social justice issues in her community, showing how a team who made history for breaking racial stereotypes displaced an entire community (see Figure 4.8).

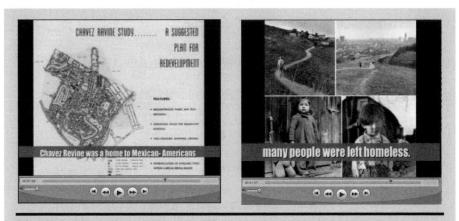

FIGURE 4.8. Local history documentary video clips with text added to images.

ACTIVITY: DECONSTRUCTING AND RECONSTRUCTING VIDEOTEXTS

This activity begins with a genre study of videotexts during which students engage in discussions around the types of videotexts they consume. Students are asked to document the videotexts they watch over a week (e.g., television commercials, YouTube videos, feature films). They then discuss who created the videotexts they consumed and consider for what purposes these texts were created (see this chapter's Appendix C for a template to use in deconstructing videotexts). Further, students compare the videotexts created by professionals such as movie studios and advertising agencies with those created by amateur users and posted to Web sites such as YouTube. Throughout this process students are encouraged to use cinematic vocabulary including terms such as scene, frame, and camera angle. They also are directed to engage in critique of content as well as critique of aesthetic and identification of modes employed (e.g., music, slow motion, writing).

After deconstructing the texts they consume as described above, students then draw on the affordances of the video editing software to reconstruct new videotext. To do so, students, with the help of their teachers if necessary, import a video clip into the software program. Many television shows and commercials are now available on the Internet, which makes this process possible. Students then engage in the types of critical literacy work described earlier in this chapter to redesign the downloaded text from a different perspective, thus taking up the call to social action as described by many literacy leaders, researchers, and educators throughout the last few decades (Bomer & Bomer, 2001; Comber, 1998, 2001; Jones, 2006). Finally, students return to their own videotexts with the critical eye they have developed through deconstructing videos created by others in order to reevaluate their own production.

Introducing Video Editing Software in the Literacy Classroom

Step 1: Document the Videos We Watch
1. Have students keep track of the digital texts they watch over the course of a week in their writer's notebooks (either digital or print-based). Have them record:
    a. What programs they watched (e.g., television sitcom, video made by a friend on YouTube).
    b. Where they viewed each video (e.g., television, computer).
    c. What channel(s) the videos were shown on (e.g., network, cable, YouTube) and at what time.

Step 2: Discuss the Purposes of the Digital Texts We View

1. Ask students to choose a text they recorded in their journal to examine.
2. Have students fill out the template in Appendix C in reference to the video they selected.
3. Engage students in a discussion of the information they provided on their template as they deconstruct and critique their videos.

Step 3: Reconstruct Your Video

1. Model for your students how to add or delete clips, music, text, and sound effects in order to portray the message of the video from a different perspective. (You can find tutorials on how to use the most recent versions of iMovie for Mac at http://www.apple.com/ilife/tutorials/#imovie and Windows Movie Maker for PC at http://www.microsoft.com/windowsxp/using/moviemaker/default.mspx.)
    a. How does the video differ without the music?
    b. What happens when you add slow motion to a scene?
    c. What happens when you reorder the scenes?

2. Have students import their video into the software program you plan to use (e.g., iMovie, Windows Movie Maker) and add their own music, text, and effects in order to tell the story from a different perspective.

Step 4: Reflection on Our Reconstruction Process

1. Have students reflect upon the following:
    a. Which video do you like best, the original text you chose or your redesign? Why?
    b. What did you learn about how music, sound effects, and video effects (e.g., black and white, slow motion) work in a video to portray a message?
    c. How did the process of redesigning a video help you think about the videos you watch on television and the Internet differently?

Conclusion

It is the first day back to school after Memorial Day, and summer vacation is lurking right around the corner. Leann and her classmates are energized from the holiday weekend and the understanding that soon they can sleep in, stay outside, watch TV, and hang out with their friends a little longer each day. Ms. Barnes knows that these last few weeks of school can be tricky as she needs to keep students' attention focused on the remaining lessons she has left to teach.

She is just about to begin the writing workshop when Leann's hand shoots into the air.

"Ms. Barnes, I wrote a poem over the weekend and posted it on the class blog," Leann informs her.

"You did?" Ms. Barnes replies.

"Yeah, I saw Leann's poem last night and wrote a comment about it," Donnie confirms.

"I like Leann's poems," Amanda adds.

Leann smiles. Ms. Barnes does, too. "Well, then we'll start the writing workshop today by reading Leann's poem in the computer lab," she tells the class, "and then we can go through the class blog to see if there are any entries that might inspire us to write more poems."

The children nod enthusiastically. Ms. Barnes starts to think that maybe the last few weeks of school won't be so tricky after all.

Over the last couple of months, Ms. Barnes took a long, honest look at her literacy teaching and her goals for students. She realized that her approach to incorporating technology in the classroom, while enjoyable for all, did not really do much to push students' literacy learning further. Given these tools and the possibilities for integrating technology more fully into the literacy classroom, she envisioned that Leann's computer lab time could actually resemble more of what we have observed and described in the previous section. Perhaps instead of playing games that seem random in purpose and do not necessarily build on the literacy skills students have already mastered, students in Ms. Barnes' class could be designing class wikis, reading and commenting on each other's writing or book reviews, and composing videotexts that tell stories about their lives. Perhaps they could be reading material that is already published online, developing their critical literacy skills by asking questions about the perspectives present and absent in the text. And perhaps instead of wondering how technology helps students' developing literacy needs—or Ms. Barnes realized, wondering what to do as a teacher to support students when they are in the computer lab—teachers can participate in the literacy activities themselves, trusting in the alignment of literacy and technology standards and engaging the technology tools that students are using to raise the level of their skills and challenge them to be fully literate persons in our world. Ms. Barnes decided to rethink and revamp her integration of literacy and technology, and the results were clear. Students were writing and reading more, talking with each other about their work, sharing ideas, and experimenting with multiple ways to use literacy for their communication goals. We are confident that as you implement the instructional tools and strategies that we have provided in this chapter, you too will notice the myriad ways in which your students will benefit from a technology-infused balanced literacy curriculum.

In this chapter, we have shared our rationale and framework for integrating technology into the balanced literacy curriculum and have provided instructional strategies for using blogs, wikis, and video editing software in the classroom. We have found in our work with students and teachers that integrating these tools into the curriculum not only increases student engagement, but provides them with many of the critical literacy skills and knowledge that will help them to be successful 21st-century citizens. Further, we have noticed that our students often carry this knowledge with them into other texts they read and design both in and outside of school. For example, we often overhear our students asking critical questions and making comments about power and positioning in movies they have seen or books they are reading. We also have found that many of our students are writing more outside of school, as they are maintaining their own personal blogs as well as those for class.

REFLECTION

Now that you have read this chapter, reflect on your opening exercise and the information presented to do the following:

1. Write a technology goal:
   a. What skills would you like to acquire?
   b. What hardware/software would you like to acquire?
   c. Identify the resources that you need to make this happen.
2. Set a timeline for achieving your goal.

References

Albers, P., & Harste, J. C. (2007). The arts, new literacies, and multimodality. *English Education, 40,* 6–20.

Alvermann, D. E. (2006). Ned and Kevin: An online discussion that challenges the "not-yet-adult" cultural model. In K. Pahl & J. Roswell (Eds.), *Travel notes from the new literacy studies: Instances of practice* (pp. 39–56). Clevendon, UK: Multilingual Matters.

Angelillo, J. (2003). *Writing about reading: From book talk to literary essays, grades 3–8*. Portsmouth, NH: Heinemann.

Anstey, M., & Bull, G. (2006). *Teaching and learning multiliteracies: Changing times, changing literacies*. Newark, DE: International Reading Association.

Au, K. H., Carroll, J. H., & Scheu, J. A. (1997). *Balanced literacy instruction: A teacher's resource book*. Norwood, MA: Christopher-Gordon.

Avi. (1990). *The true confessions of Charlotte Doyle*. New York: Avon.

Black, R. W. (2006). Language, culture, and identity in online fanfiction. *E-Learning, 3,* 170–184.

Bomer, R., & Bomer, K. (2001). *For a better world: Reading and writing for social action*. Portsmouth, NH: Heinemann.

Calkins, L. M. (1994). *The art of teaching writing*. Portsmouth, NH: Heinemann.

Calkins, L. M. (2000). *The art of teaching reading*. Boston: Allyn & Bacon.

Callahan, M. (2002). Intertextual composition: The power of the digital pen. *English Education, 32,* 46–65.

Chandler-Olcott, K., & Mahar, D. (2003). "Tech-savyiness" meets multiliteracies: Exploring adolescent girls' technology-mediated literacy practices. *Reading Research Quarterly, 38,* 356–385.

Cohen, V. L., & Cowen, J. E. (2008). *Literacy for children in an information age: Teaching reading, writing, and thinking*. Belmont, CA: Thompson Wadsworth.

Comber, B. (1998). Critical literacy: What's it all about? *Education Matters, 3*(3), 9–14.

Comber, B. (2001). Critical literacies and local action: Teacher knowledge and a "new" research agenda. In B. Comber & A. Simpson (Eds.), *Negotiating critical literacies in classrooms* (pp. 271–282). Mahwah, NJ: Lawrence Erlbaum.

Curtis, C. P. (1995). *The Watsons go to Birmingham—1963*. New York: Yearling.

Duncan, B., & Leander, K. (2000). *Girls just wanna have fun: Literacy, consumerism, and paradoxes of position on gURL.com*. Retrieved June 1, 2009, from doi:http://www.readingonline.org/electronic/elec_index.asp?HREF=/electronic/duncan/index.html

Durrant, C., & Green, B. (2003). Literacy and the new technologies in school education: Meeting the l(IT)eracy challenge? In H. Fehring & P. Green (Eds.), *Critical literacy: A collection of articles from the Australia Literacy Educators' Association* (pp. 142–164). Newark, DE: International Reading Association.

Englert, C. S., Manalo, M., & Zhao, Y. (2004). I can do it better on the computer: The effects of technology-enabled scaffolding on young writers' composition. *Journal of Special Education Technology, 19,* 5–21.

Fletcher, R. (1996). *A writer's notebook: Unlocking the writer within you*. New York: Avon Camelot.

Foehr, U. G. (2006, December). *Media multitasking among American youth: Prevalence, predictors and pairings* (Report No. 7592). Washington, DC: The Henry J. Kaiser Family Foundation.

Freebody, P., & Luke, A. (1990). Literacies programs: Debates and demands in cultural context. *Prospect: Australian Journal of TESOL, 5*(7), 7–16.

Freppon, P. A., & Dahl, K. L. (1998). Balanced instruction: Insights and considerations. *Reading Research Quarterly, 32,* 240–251.

Godwin-Jones, R. (2006). Tag clouds in the blogosphere: Electronic literacy and social networking. *Language Learning & Technology, 10*(2), 8–15.

Guzzetti, B., & Gamboa, M. (2005). Online journaling: The informal writings of two adolescent girls. *Research in the Teaching of English, 40,* 168–206.

International Reading Association, & National Council for Teachers of English. (1996). *Standards for the English language arts.* Newark, DE: Author.

International Society for Technology in Education. (2007). *National educational technology standards for students* (2nd ed.). Washington, DC: Author.

International Society for Technology in Education. (2008). *National educational technology standards for teachers* (2nd ed.). Washington, DC: Author.

Jackson, E. (1998). *Cinder Edna.* New York: HarperCollins.

Jones, S. (2006). *Girls, literacy, and social class: What teachers can do to make a difference.* Portsmouth, NH: Heinemann.

Kara-Soteriou, J. (2007). Computers in the classroom: The Internet as a resource for critical literacy learning and applications. *The New England Reading Association Journal, 43,* 90–96.

Kress, G. (2003). *Literacy in the new media age.* New York: Routledge.

Lam, W. S. E. (2000). L2 literacy and the design of the self: A case study of a teenager writing on the internet. *TESOL Quarterly, 34,* 457–492.

Lattimer, H. (2003). *Thinking through genre: Units of study in reading and writing workshops.* Portland, ME: Stenhouse.

Leroux, G. (1994). *The phantom of the opera.* New York: Puffin Classics. (Original work published 1911)

Lewis, C., & Fabos, B. (2005). Instant messaging, literacies, and social identities. *Reading Research Quarterly, 40,* 470–501.

Maguire, G. (1995). *Wicked: The life and times of the Wicked Witch of the West.* New York: ReganBooks.

New London Group. (1996). A pedagogy of multiliteracies: Designing social futures. *Harvard Educational Review, 66*(1), 60–92.

Nixon, H., (1999). Towards a (cyber)pedagogy for multimedia multiliteracies. *Teaching Educational Theory, 10,* 87–99.

Pearsall, S. (2002). *Trouble don't last.* New York: Dell.

Pressley, M., Roehrig, A., Bogner, K., Raphael, L. M., & Dolezal, S. (2002). Balanced literacy instruction. *Focus on Exceptional Children, 34*(5), 1–14.

Reinking, D. (1997). Me and my hypertext:): A multiple digression and analysis of technology and literacy. *The Reading Teacher, 50,* 626–642.

Savin, M. (1995). *The moon bridge.* New York: Scholastic.

Schmier, S. A. (2007, April). *Spatial design: Shaping social spaces for possibilities through the design of multimodal texts.* Paper presented at the annual meeting of the American Educational Research Association, Chicago.

Scieszka, J. (1989). *The true story of the three little pigs by A. Wolf.* New York: Viking Press.

Shelley, M. (2003). *Frankenstein, or the Modern Prometheus.* New York: Penguin. (Original work published 1819)

Siegel, M., Kontovourki, S., Schmier, S., & Enriquez, G. (2008). Literacy in motion: A case study of a shape-shifting kindergartner. *Language Arts, 86,* 89–98.

Stevenson, R. L. (1982). *The strange case of Dr. Jeykll and Mr. Hyde.* New York: Bantam. (Original work published 1886)

Tompkins, G. E., & Collom, S. (2003). *Sharing the pen: Interactive writing with young children.* Upper Saddle River, NJ: Prentice Hall.

Uchida, Y. (1971). *Journey to Topaz.* Berkeley, CA: Heyday Books.

Watts Taffe, S., & Gwinn, C. B. (2007). *Integrating literacy and technology: Effective practice for grades K–6*. New York: Guilford Press.

Yolen, J. (1988). *The devil's arithmetic*. New York: Puffin.

Yolen, J. (1996). *Encounter*. New York: Harcourt.

Appendix A

The introduction chapter introduced the importance of connecting curriculum to various digital literacy competencies. For literacy, the connection to digital literacy is as follows:

Technology Tool	Corresponding Digital Literacy				
	Photo-Visual	Reproduction	Branching	Information	Social-Emotional
Blogs	■		■	■	■
Wikis	■	■	■	■	■
Video Editing Software	■	■	■	■	■

Appendix B
Glossary

Blog: An abbreviation of the term *Weblog*, it is an online journal maintained by one author or a single group of authors.

Language arts: Traditionally, the skills and processes involving language—such as reading, writing, listening, and speaking—that students learn in school.

Literacy: Traditionally, it is the ability to read and write. Given the diverse, global, and technological world in which we live, many educators now conceive of literacy as the ability to use a variety of language and communication processes—including speaking, listening, computing, texting, drawing, and designing—to convey and interpret ideas.

Multiliteracies: A pedagogy put forth by The New London Group that addresses the need for students to consume and design texts in multiple modes (e.g., able to read and design images, video, hyperlinked texts), for multiple purposes, and to communicate with diverse cultural and linguistic audiences.

Multimodality: The use of multiple modes such as image, sound, and animation in the construction of a text.

Online social networking site: A Web site primarily designed for users to communicate with each other for social purposes.

Reader's notebook: A notebook or space where one can write down personal responses to reading and to inspire further discussion and thinking about a text. Unlike a traditional notebook, a reader's notebook is not meant for responses to given prompts, but a place where readers can record their vast range of individual thoughts, questions, and reactions to a text.

Tags: Keywords, phrases, or images associated with online content. To "tag" something is to identify it as a keyword, phrase, or image and then link it as a reference in another text.

Video editing software: A computer application that allows users to sequence moving or still images, as well as add music, voiceover, titles, and transitions.

Wiki: A Web site comprised of a collection of Web pages that can be edited by anyone who has access to it.

Writer's notebook: A notebook or space where one can collect and write down thoughts, ideas, questions, memories, and so forth to inspire more polished pieces of writing. Unlike a journal or diary, a writer's notebook is not solely meant for recording events, but is a place where writers can play with language and writing.

Appendix C
Additional Resources

Template for Deconstructing Videotexts

Narration	Images	Music	Author
☼ Whose voice is telling the story? ☼ Is there anyone who doesn't speak? What does that tell you? ☼ What types of information is being given?	☼ What types of shots are used (e.g., close up, wide angle)? ☼ How does the camera move to create the images (e.g., zoom, pan)? ☼ Whose point of view is the camera portraying? ☼ Are any special effects used? If so, why do you think they were used?	☼ What types of music are playing in the video? ☼ What do you notice about the music (e.g., when it is playing, volume)?	☼ Who created this video? ☼ For what purpose was it created? ☼ Who do you think is the intended audience?

Useful Web Sites (Blogs)

21CLASSES
http://www.21classes.com

21Classes is a blog site that promotes student blogging. Its customizable and user-friendly design allows teachers to work with students to learn about the process of blogging while encouraging them to create stimulating Web content.

BLOGGER
http://www.blogger.com

Blogger is an easy-to-use blog community that provides free Web space where users can post videos and photos to customized blog pages.

LIVE JOURNAL
http://www.livejournal.com

This is a free, customizable blogging service predicated upon classic notions of journaling. Each personalized "journal" includes multimedia features and RSS feeds to other blogs and can be accessed remotely.

THOUGHTS.COM

http://www.thoughts.com

This free host site provides unlimited bandwidth to allow for continuous image, video, and podcast sharing on each blog space.

WORDPRESS

http://www.wordpress.com

Wordpress is another free blog site where teachers can choose from dozens of themes to create blogs that can be edited by multiple users and include sidebar widgets that link to Flickr, Meebo, and other multimedia sites.

THE WRITER'S CORNER

http://www.writerscorner.com

This blogger community relies upon collaboration to encourage and develop effective writing skills for all ages and ability/experience ranges. Using this same approach, The Writer's Corner has created a special group for children ages 8–18 called the Kids Writing Center.

Useful Web Sites (Curriculum)

CAROL HURST'S CHILDREN'S LITERATURE SITE

http://www.carolhurst.com

This site is a valuable classroom resource addressing children's literature through book reviews, curriculum suggestions, and subject association.

DISCOVERY EDUCATION

http://school.discoveryeducation.com

Hosted by the Discovery Channel, this site includes a number of features for use in K–12 classrooms. Free lesson plans, videos, puzzles, and more can be used to teach students about global warming, fuel economy, and the weather.

DISCOVERY EDUCATION: KATHY SCHROCK'S GUIDE FOR EDUCATORS

http://school.discoveryeducation.com/schrockguide

Kathy Schrock has created an index that categorizes curriculum-enhancing Web sites addressing a wide-range of subject matter including literature, history, and music.

READ WRITE THINK

http://www.readwritethink.org

Sponsored by the National Council of Teachers of English and the International Reading Association, this Web site combines lesson plans, Web resources, and student materials that satisfy 12 standards established to direct successful literacy education.

TEACHNOLOGY
http://www.teach-nology.com/web_tools

This Web site offers free access to more than 30,000 lesson plans, 7,500 printable worksheets, teaching tips, and WebQuests. In addition, TeAchnology reviews more than 250,000 educational sites, providing links to sites that deal with at-risk and multicultural education, funding, literacy, and more.

Useful Web Sites (Evaluation Tools)

PROPROFS QUIZ SCHOOL
http://www.proprofs.com/quiz-school

ProProfs allows educators and laymen alike to create, share, and review quizzes. This free resource allows quizzes to be circulated via e-mail, blogs, and Web links and generates analytical grade reports for teacher evaluation.

QUIA
http://www.quia.com

This Web site combines three educational resources: Quia Books, Quia Web, and IXL Math. Teachers can browse and use workbooks and textbooks using Quia Books and create games, quizzes, Web pages, and more on Quia Web. IXL focuses specifically on developing math skills, helping educators by making math practice fun!

QUIZSTAR
http://quizstar.4teachers.org

Teachers can upload multimedia files to create interactive quizzes using QuizStar. Students can access these quizzes from any location and review their answers once the quiz has been completed.

Useful Web Sites (Instructional Videos)

TEACHERTUBE
http://www.teachertube.com

TeacherTube features instructional videos that employ character acting, group discussion, and demonstrations to address historic and scientific topics as well as those dealing with classroom instruction.

Useful Web Sites (Social Networking)

LITERACY LEADER
http://www.literacyleader.com

Literacy Leader is a social networking site that allows teachers and students worldwide to share and discuss research, resources, ideas, and issues in literacy education.

Useful Web Sites (Website Design, Maintenance, and Posting)

BRAVENET
http://www.bravenet.com

This site offers Web hosting and domain name services in addition to providing Web tools including message forums, guestbooks, photo albums, blogs, and online calendars to create a comprehensive Web site.

CLASSJUMP.COM
http://www.classjump.com

ClassJump is a free Web site provider allowing teachers to manage more than one class by employing its user-friendly interface to communicate with parents and post homework information and other documents for students.

CLASSNOTESONLINE.COM
http://www.classnotesonline.com

This user-friendly classroom interface allows teachers to communicate with students and parents about homework, daily assignments, and other important class-related activities.

CLASSTELL.COM
http://www.classtell.com

Designed to maximize efficiency in both development and use, ClassTell helps educators create easy-to-use Web sites with blog, homework, calendar, and other features to maximize use in the classroom.

SCHOOLNOTES.COM
http://www.schoolnotes.com

Teachers can post notes, homework, and class information for student and parent access using this free Web resource.

TEACHERWEB
http://www.teacherweb.com

TeacherWeb is an easy-to-use Web site development interface providing teachers with the tools necessary to create navigable and multifunctional Web sites and WebQuests as quickly and effectively as possible.

Useful Web Sites (Wikis)

PBWORKS: EDUCATIONAL
http://pbworks.com/academic.wiki

PBWorks offers educational wiki solutions that allow teachers to create workspaces that include RSS feeds, tags, multimedia plug-ins, and more in a matter of seconds.

WIKISPACES
http://www.wikispaces.com

This wiki host site offers free wiki development for educational purposes. Features include simple page linking, image and file uploads, widgets, WYSIWYG Page Editor, and more.

CHAPTER

5

Tradition and Innovation:

The Intersections of Technology in the Social Studies

Elizabeth K. Wilson, Vivian H. Wright, and Chris Inman

GUIDING QUESTIONS

1. (a) How can teachers employ traditional and innovative technology applications to enhance student learning? (b) What instructional activities will help me achieve this?

2. What technologies are available to enhance social studies teaching and learning?

Needs Assessment

1. *Keywords*

   Look over the keywords found in this chapter listed below. Rate yourself from one to three on your familiarity with each word. Then use this rating to help you set some goals for reading this chapter.

Word	1 Don't know at all	2 Some familiarity with this word	3 Very familiar with this word
Technology Application			
TPCK			
Virtual Worlds			
Traditional Integration			
Innovative Integration			

2. *Tools*

   Look over the five key technology tools listed below. Rate yourself from one to three on your familiarity with integrating these tools into your social studies classroom. Then use this rating to help you set some goals for reading this chapter.

Tool	1 Don't know at all	2 Some familiarity with this technology tool	3 Very familiar with this technology tool
Specific Software Programs			
Digital Media Sharing			
Digital Photo Story			
Wikis			
Virtual Worlds			

3. *Goal(s) for the Chapter*

   Fill in your goals below:

   a. By reading this chapter I hope to _____

   _____ .

   b. By reading this chapter I hope to _____

   _____ .

Recently, when one of the authors was discussing technology in her teacher education classes, one of her students asked, "Whatever happened to the Oregon Trail software?" The classroom was filled with "Oohs," "Aahs," and "Oh yeahs," as many of the preservice teachers shared their recollections of the impact this software had on their experiences in K–12 social studies. This prompted the teacher educator to investigate software's current value and application in the classroom. She realized that, although she now considered this a "traditional" technology, software does not carry that label nor has it lost its "value" in the teaching classroom. In discussing this chapter, this prompted us to ask ourselves, "Do we prompt such labeling?" and "Why can't the convergence of traditional and innovative technologies be better recognized?"

As educators, we must realize that our future students will continue to expand and to grow in their technological repertoire; we cannot predict the technologies they will use in their everyday lives 5 years from now. As a result, we must seek ways to meet the changes that their expectations will demand. Yet, we should not forego pedagogical tools that have proven successful. In working with preservice and in-service social studies teachers, we have observed a dichotomy between teachers' understanding of traditional technologies and innovative technologies. As teacher educators, we have noted that a PowerPoint presentation may be considered innovative by one teacher and very traditional (if not archaic), by another. However, what many teacher educators and classroom teachers do not acknowledge is that tradition can "meet" innovation, intersecting contextually to enhance teaching and learning.

This chapter presents an overview of technology integration and the uses of three applications (software, digital media sharing, and virtual worlds) in teaching and learning. We present a view that transcends both traditional and innovative uses. We draw upon recent Technological Pedagogical Content Knowledge (TPCK) research throughout this chapter, while emphasizing how the intersection of traditional and innovative can occur (and quite painlessly!).

Tradition Meets Innovation

We hope to present both traditional and innovative methods that teachers may utilize and draw upon. We firmly believe that both method types are important and essential in a teacher's knowledge of how and when to use technology. The purpose is not to label a teacher as being traditional or innovative, but to raise awareness of how a teacher can recognize any technology that engages students and enhances learning.

In our own teaching, each of the authors utilizes very different technology integration models and methods. For example, while only one of the three authors routinely integrates virtual worlds into his classroom, the other authors recognize the potential of using virtual worlds in teaching, learning, and research. In fact, one of the remaining authors is conducting an extensive research project utilizing Second Life's (http://www.secondlife.com) potential for engaging students in meaningful social studies instruction. Finally, the third author routinely visits a virtual world targeted to elementary children (Club Penguin; http://www.clubpenguin.com) with her 10-year-old son so that they can maintain care of the family virtual pet. Sometimes, the two of them visit another virtual world (Wizard 101; http://www.wizard101.com) where they navigate their way through Wizard City, earn points that are used to strengthen their wizard, and try to save their world. These are some examples of how innovative technologies are being used routinely by our current and future students in everyday life and play.

Digital technologies have changed the way we read, communicate, learn, and explore. Contextually, we have new definitions of literacy as they relate to digital technologies. Prensky (2009) even noted that it is no longer enough to just teach students digital literacy (e.g., information literacy on how to conduct and evaluate online research resources), but that we, as educators, must develop and offer guidance toward *digital wisdom*. Prensky indicated that

> Parents and educators are digitally wise when they recognize this imperative and prepare the children in their care for the future—educators by letting students learn by using new technologies, putting themselves in the role of guides, context providers, and quality controllers, and parents by recognizing the extent to which the future will be mediated by technology and encouraging their children to use digital technology wisely. (p. 29)

These ideas are applicable to the social studies, a discipline often viewed as irrelevant and boring by students. Social studies teachers should recognize that their digitally wise students can enhance social studies learning with their knowledge and skills through the various digital media they use on a daily basis. This may require teachers to change the ways they teach and facilitate student learning. Providing students with the avenue to think and learn while using different tools to which they already are accustomed may change students' perceptions of social studies.

Technology Integration in the Social Studies

Although social studies educators have been slow to integrate technology (Whitworth & Berson, 2002), recent initiatives (e.g., National Council for the Social Studies [NCSS], 2006) have helped in the effort. With an emphasis on standards, assessment, and data-driven decision making in today's educational climate, it appears to be even more important to utilize technology efficiently and effectively. Social studies educators suggest that teacher educators should be at the forefront of this effort (Bolick, Berson, Coutts, & Heinecke, 2003; Diem, 2000). Diem (2000) stressed the need to address technology to ensure that preservice teachers develop their appropriate comfort zone for gaining technology skills and integrating technology to enhance teaching and learning. However, the reality is that once novice teachers are teaching in their own classrooms, they often experience difficulty in integrating technology in the teaching of content (Wright & Wilson, 2005–2006) and may question the authenticity of technology integration (Swan et al., 2007).

Traditional Technology

Although intensive instructional technology initiatives have been implemented, technology capacity has increased, teacher training has improved, and technology policies have changed, many of the traditional barriers in integrating technology remain for in-service social studies teachers (Wright & Wilson, 2005–2006). We have recognized that isolated teacher training does not develop effective technology integration in social studies classrooms. Instead, social studies teachers must be creative and self-reliant in seeking resources and tools to meet the pedagogical needs of their tech-savvy students. This will not be accomplished by just using a computer or some other technological tool; meaningful teaching and learning must take place. As Doolittle and Hicks (2003) cautioned:

> If integrating technology means nothing more than enhancing the traditional delivery system of social studies content, where laptops replace notebooks, where PowerPoint slides replace handwritten overheads, where e-textbooks replace hard copy textbooks, then we will be no closer to the NCSS vision of transformative, powerful social studies instruction. (p. 75)

Not surprisingly, there has been much debate about the quality and outcomes of instruction provided through technology integration in the social studies. Although the debate continues, the possible power of technology in the field of social studies has been well established. Crocco (2001) discussed the *leverage* provided by technology, stating that it has the capability to make passive social studies instruction into a more active, student-centered discipline.

Innovative Technology

As we consider technology integration in social studies classrooms, we must think of it as a cohesive piece of a puzzle that includes content and pedagogy. The technology should not stand alone, but instead should complement the content and pedagogy to facilitate student learning that helps equip students with the necessary 21st-century learning skills. Supporting this notion is the framework, TPCK, which "argues against teaching technology skills in isolation and supports integrated and design-based approaches as being appropriate techniques for teaching teachers to use technology" (Mishra & Koehler, 2006, p. 1045). In social studies education, TPCK can make the content more "democratic and meaningful" for students by "utilizing the technology habits and experiences which frame their lives" (Lee, 2008, p. 141). Taking this idea a step further to emphasize the interconnectedness of the content, pedagogy, and technology, educators in social studies and other disciplines who have examined the concept of TPCK have reconceptualized it as *TPACK*. Due to this reconceptualization, the subsequent definition of TPACK is:

> Effective use of technology, we have learned, involves the ability to make informed decisions on how to take advantage of the affordances of technology (with a sensitivity to the concomitant constraints technologies

bring to the table) to support specific pedagogies within a particular content area. Thus, teachers need the Total PACKage: the knowledge that lies at the intersection of knowledge of Content, Pedagogy And Technology (i.e., TPACK). (Thompson & Mishra, 2007–2008, p. 35)

With today's multiple technologies being seamlessly integrated into our daily lives, teachers and students are finding a growing number of opportunities to use technology (NCSS, 2006). As such, social studies teachers must capitalize on their students' everyday uses of technology to enrich social studies content and pedagogy that, just a few years ago were not possible without technology. The basic economics of supply and demand dictate that we supply the type of educational system that society demands.

Today's social studies students use technology in every facet of their lives: (a) communicating with friends and family (e.g., text messaging, social networking), (b) seeking information outside of school (e.g., automobile GPSs, Wikipedia, Web sites), and (c) in their workplaces (e.g., computerized cash registers). As social studies teachers present social studies content, they should address the NCSS standards while incorporating the National Educational Technology Standards (NETS), which retool and prepare our students with 21st-century skills and focus on six core competencies: (a) creative thinking; (b) communication and collaboration; (c) research and information fluency; (d) problem-solving; (e) digital citizenship; and (f) technology applications as they take the skills and knowledge obtained through use of "traditional" technologies (e.g., PowerPoint, word processing, software) and move to successful use of "innovative" tools (e.g., Web 2.0, virtual worlds). Social studies teachers demonstrate an understanding of TPACK when they prepare instruction to meet NCSS standards and reflect, while simultaneously infusing instruction with technology to address the NETS standards. Ensuring that both sets of standards are met concurrently with each supporting the other demonstrates TPACK as described above.

The Future: How Tradition and Innovation Converge

We do not want to deemphasize the importance of any technology, but rather emphasize the use of the technology to enhance social studies teaching and learning. As described earlier, various barriers may prevent teachers from using one technology or another (e.g., time, accessibility, comfort). However, we emphasize the importance of being aware of innovations students are using at any given time (i.e., Twitter, Facebook, text messaging, YouTube) and the understanding of how such technologies may engage and motivate the learners.

The integration of any technology tool should take place with careful preparation by teachers and students. In addition, the tool should be introduced in context, extend learning, encourage inquiry, and make learning meaningful (Mason et al., 2000). Weis, Benmayor, O'Leary, and Eynon (2002) claimed that advances in multimedia and digital technologies have the ability to change teaching and learning because they enable students to become researchers, storytellers, and historians. Manfra and Hammond (2008–2009) noted that the use of digital media in the classrooms is relatively new; they found evidence in their qualitative study that teachers did reconfigure technology, pedagogy, and content knowledge (as noted in TPACK by Mishra & Koehler, 2006) as digital documentaries were completed by their students, writing:

> Both the teachers and their students reconceived the content in a new form—as a digital documentary—which required narrating history in a visual and oral presentation. The pedagogy also adapted to the technology. The teachers turned to collaborative student groupings, one-on-one instruction, and extended class time to facilitate student production of the digital documentaries. (p. 238)

In this chapter, we present different scenarios in which we illustrate how teachers and students can demonstrate their digital wisdom with the intersection of both traditional and innovative approaches for three applications (software, digital media sharing, and virtual worlds), illustrating ways in which social studies content, pedagogy, and technology connect to provide meaningful learning opportunities for students. Each section will include a chart that will provide a definition of the application and illustrate how the technology, content, and pedagogy presented can meet NCSS and NETS standards. We also provide resources that can be helpful in developing social studies instruction. Then, in the end, we introduce you to a "virtual" student, Buzz Social (see Figure 5.1). Buzz will illustrate the

FIGURE 5.1. Buzz Social in a virtual world.

possible innovations future students will see in their classroom. Buzz goes to school in a virtual environment and has history at his fingertips—virtually! Although many of us do not totally understand what a virtual classroom may look like, reality is that someday we may *need* to understand. Therefore, we hope the information in this chapter better prepares us all for developing our digital literacies in and out of the social studies classroom.

Software

More than 20 years ago, using software in a social studies classroom was considered innovative for a variety of reasons. Although a teacher with a computer in the classroom was a rarity, software was one of the few technological tools available for classroom use. Rooze (1983) noted the potential of social studies software to "revolutionize" social studies instruction by providing drill and practice, tutorials, computerized databases, and simulations.

Today, educational software seems to have taken a backseat to other technologies in the social studies. One reason can be attributed to a lack of modeling provided in teacher education programs (Bolick et al., 2003). Without participating in or seeing innovative software uses, new teachers select technologies that appear to be more readily accessible or easier to use. Some software may be considered expensive when compared to other technological resources. Another issue may be that social studies software has not reflected "best practice" in social studies research (van Hover, Berson, Bolick, & Swan, 2004). Furthermore, some may view software as static, while tools utilized via the Internet are viewed to be more current because they can be updated and shared more easily.

During the previous two decades, interactive software programs like Where in the World Is Carmen San Diego, Oregon Trail, and Decisions Decisions! often were used to promote social studies teaching and learning. Today, a wide array of software types exist and include graphic organizers (e.g., Inspiration®; see http://www.inspiration.com), photo and movie editing (e.g., Photo Story, Windows Movie Maker, iMovie), and Web development (e.g., FrontPage, Dreamweaver, GoLive). Other software resources range from word processing to collaborative blogging programs.

There are many benefits to using software programs in the social studies classroom. Regardless of the type, today's software applications are interactive and most are inquiry-based. Software programs can address many learning needs (e.g., drill and practice, content instruction, research) and usually are easy to use. In addition, most software is reasonably priced. Aside from the software, only a computer is needed and the software is easily accessed—it can be downloaded from the Internet onto a computer or uploaded from a CD-ROM to a computer. With either, set-up takes only minutes.

This section will illustrate how to employ traditional and innovative technologies and pedagogies in the social studies classroom. We will discuss how to implement the software Oregon Trail and a digital media sharing tool, Photo Story 3, to develop digital diaries.

Oregon Trail

This computer simulation is one of the most well-known pieces of educational software. Even though it was designed more than 30 years ago, it is interactive and inquiry-based. Although Oregon Trail is remembered fondly by college students and adults, as evidenced in our college classrooms, some may question using a piece of computer software in today's classroom. After all, students are visiting virtual worlds and using so many other forms of technology every day. In this section we discuss ways in which Oregon Trail, produced by the Learning Company, can make social studies learning come alive for students.

The Oregon Trail software program engages the social studies learner in a simulation of a trip across a new territory in 1848. This software program provides opportunities for students to engage in decision making, critical thinking, and problem solving. As they travel the Oregon Trail, social studies students employ history, geography, and economic thinking skills. The teacher may choose to use Oregon Trail as an introduction to or conclusion for a unit that includes study of the historical, geographic, and economic concepts related to travel on the Oregon Trail. To view a definition of software and to find some resources for the Oregon Trail, see Table 5.1. Table 5.1 also lists the NCSS and ISTE standards that may be addressed in using this software in the classroom.

TABLE 5.1
The Oregon Trail and Software in the Social Studies Classroom

Definition	Software is a form of technology that can facilitate teaching and learning. It can be loaded onto a computer or other piece of hardware from a storage device or it may be downloaded from the Internet. Software comes in a variety of forms (e.g., tutorials, simulations).
NCSS Standards	☀ Time, Continuity, and Change ☀ People, Places, and Environments ☀ Individuals, Groups, and Institutions ☀ Production, Distribution, and Consumption of Goods and Services
ISTE Standards	NETS for Students: ☀ Communication and Collaboration ☀ Research and Information Fluency ☀ Critical Thinking, Problem Solving, and Decision Making NETS for Teachers: ☀ Facilitate and Inspire Student Learning and Creativity ☀ Design and Develop Digital-Age Learning Experiences and Assessments ☀ Model Digital-Age Work and Learning
Resources	*Digital Editing Resources* Photo Story: http://www.microsoft.com/windowsxp/using/digitalphotography/photostory/default.mspx iMovie: http://www.apple.com/ilife/imovie *Podcasting Resources* iTunes: http://www.apple.com/itunes/whatson/podcasts *Digital Historical Resources for the Oregon Trail* Go West: Imagining the Oregon Trail: http://edsitement.neh.gov/view_lesson_plan.asp?id=277 All About the Oregon Trail: http://www.isu.edu/~trinmich/Allabout.html Learning Experience: Westward Ho: http://www.connected-learning.org/Products/cphipple2.htm Trail Archive: http://www.isu.edu/~trinmich/00.n.trailarchive.html *Books* Levine, E. (1992). *If you traveled west in a covered wagon*. New York: Scholastic Paperbacks. Levine, E. (2002). *The journal of Jedediah Barstow: An emigrant on the Oregon trail*. New York: Scholastic.

Some ideas for implementing the Oregon Trail software in the classroom include:

- ☼ The Oregon Trail software can be utilized in the more traditional sense individually, with small groups on desktop or laptop computers, or even as a whole-class activity by using an LCD projector to project the program from a computer to a screen for the entire class to view and discuss together.

- ☼ As students study the unit, they may read books (see Table 5.1 for suggested books) and conduct outside research to develop an understanding of the time period; this will provide important background knowledge needed while participating in the computer simulation. Once students have a context for the time period, they are ready to travel the trail.

- ☼ Oregon Trail (5th edition; The Learning Company, 2001) follows the experiences of the Montgomery family as they travel across new territories. Using journals, a guidebook, and a map, the students become travelers with the Montgomery children and their guide Captain Jed. As travelers on the trail, the students will confront challenges and make decisions regarding provisions to buy, routes to take, and food and medical situations to address.

- ☼ During the software simulation, the teacher can ask the students to engage in a simulated journal activity as they contemplate the dilemmas they encounter during the trip. Journal writing allows for reinforcement of the content studied and presented via the software. If the teacher does not have anything more than a computer and an LCD projector, the lesson can stop there.

SCENARIO: DIGITAL DIARIES FROM THE OREGON TRAIL

What we have discussed thus far is a more traditional approach to incorporating Oregon Trail into social studies instruction. Here, we demonstrate the convergence of traditional and innovative technologies to further the social studies learning. A teacher may decide to extend the social studies content presented in the software by asking students to develop digital diaries that represent the experiences of the trip they took with the Montgomery family during the Oregon Trail simulation. Digital diaries can encourage students to use critical thinking skills as they examine the Oregon Trail, to write/construct captions and journal entries that emphasize knowledge acquisition, and to use technology skills to present the information through digital images.

Before students employ digital images, they need to develop a method of assessing the quality and the appropriateness of the images they choose to use. Bull and Thompson's (2004) Framework for Using Digital Images is a tool that teachers can present to their students before they locate images for their digital diaries. In this approach, the students learn to: (a) acquire images, (b) analyze images, (c) create products, and (d) communicate and disseminate products. Through this process, students develop a better understanding of how to locate images and how to analyze their quality and appropriateness for the final product. With these skills, students can begin their search of digital collections (e.g., The National Archives, Library of Congress) for digital images that represent their journey on the Oregon Trail. Then, students can begin to develop their digital diaries through the use of the free photo-editing program, Photo Story 3 (a link can be found in the steps below). Photo Story 3 is a free Microsoft program that gives the user step-by-step procedures to connect pictures, effects, text, and music (music may be created within the program or imported) into a digital story.

Developing a Digital Diary for the Oregon Trail in Photo Story 3. Photo Story 3 can be downloaded for free from http://www.microsoft.com/windowsxp/using/digitalphotography/PhotoStory/default.mspx. The computers also must have Windows Media Player 10 (this may be downloaded from http://www.microsoft.com). The following steps should be used in this project:

Step 1: Beginning the Digital Diary
1. Load Media Player 10 and Photo Story 3 onto the computer.
2. Open the Photo Story 3 program.
3. On the page that says "Welcome to Photo Story 3," click "Begin a new story," and then click "Next." (See Figure 5.2; please note that once a photo story has been created, "Play a Story" can be selected.)

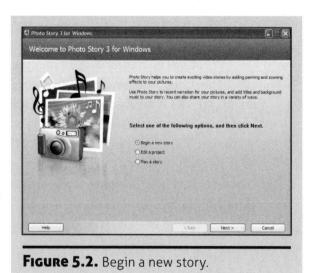

FIGURE 5.2. Begin a new story.

Step 2: Inserting Digital Images

1. After researching digital collections (e.g., National Archives) for appropriate photographs, artwork, or images illustrating the Oregon Trail (students should save the images to an external storage device such as a flash drive), students will insert images in their stories.
2. On the "Import and arrange your pictures" page, students will click "Import pictures . . . " to insert their saved images into the project.
3. Students should import all of the images they want to use in their digital diary before moving on to the next step.

Step 3: Editing Pictures

1. Some of the pictures will have black space around them. If the students do not want this space, they should click "Remove black borders . . . " and Photo Story 3 will run through all of your pictures, removing the black space. After this process is complete click "Next."

Step 4: Adding Text

1. Now students can add text to their digital diaries. Font and font color may be changed at this screen. Students should click on the font icon that looks like this and then click on "OK" after they have chosen the font, font size, and color.

Step 5: Inserting Transitions

1. Now, the students will choose the transitions for the pictures. A transition effect is how one photo transitions to the next when the presentation is playing.
2. At the "Narrate your pictures and customize motion" page, click on the "Customize motion . . ." button.
3. At the "Customize motion" page click the "Transition tab" at the top of the page. Choose the transition and click "Save"; then, choose "Close."

Step 6: Adding Music

1. In this step the students can add music to their projects.
2. At the "Add background music" students can click on the first picture and then click the "Create Music . . . " button. Once on the "Create Music" page, students can decide which music is most appropriate for the timeline. There are several options and students also can import music they have downloaded.
3. Click "Next" to move to the last step of creating a project in Photo Story 3.

Step 7: Saving Your Story

1. In this step students will save their digital diaries. On the "Save your story page" click on the first option "Save your story for playback on your computer."
2. Under "File name" click "Browse" and from the "Save As" window click on the down arrow next to the "Save in:" window. Choose "Removable disk" as the location for saving your file. Type in a file name that describes your project and then click "Save."
3. Now, at the bottom of the page, click the "Save Project . . . " button to save your project. Should you decide to make any changes at a later time, you can open the project, make the changes, and produce the corrected diary/movie.
4. Click "Next" and a window that says "Building Your Story" will appear. When that screen clears, the window "Completing Photo Story 3 for Windows" will appear. In this window, students will click "View your story" to watch the finalized projects.

Using this program, students can search for and evaluate representations that reflect the travels on the trail. Students can even create their own visual representations (e.g., drawings, paintings) that can be scanned and included in their storyboard (see Figure 5.3). Once the pictures for the digital diary are selected and arranged, the students may write captions, insert their narration, and/or insert music into the slides representative of their experiences. Although we only discussed Photo Story 3, other programs (e.g., Picasa, Smilebox), which allow users to publish photo "stories," are available. However, not all photo publishing programs allow users to include voiceovers, music, and movie features into the final product.

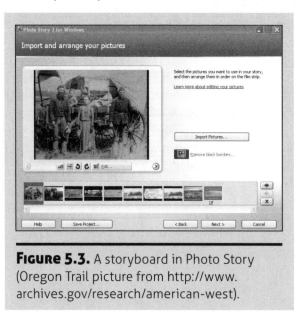

FIGURE 5.3. A storyboard in Photo Story (Oregon Trail picture from http://www. archives.gov/research/american-west).

Digital Media Sharing

Digital media sharing is a collaborative technology process that allows teachers to utilize multiple technologies. For example, students might create a soundtrack for an historical event using new or downloaded music, then share that soundtrack as an audio podcast. Digital media sharing allows teachers to move beyond the traditional product, utilizing technology to encourage students to publish and share their creations and implementing Web 2.0 technologies. To view a definition of digital media sharing and to find some resources, see Table 5.2. Table 5.2 also lists the NCSS and ISTE standards that may be addressed in digital media sharing.

This section will talk about two ways in which digital media sharing can be used: the creation of and sharing of a pictorial history using Web interfaces such as TeacherTube and YouTube and the creation of a wiki to share text and pictorial information. By using a study of the effects of the Vietnam War, teachers may even create an extended project that encourages students to develop pictorial histories, post them, then expand upon those histories in textual form, providing background information and then links to their videos in wikis.

Storytelling and Digital Pictorial Histories

Storytelling is not new; students have been capturing family histories, memories, and events for decades as a valuable instructional tool for social studies instruction. Until the 1990s, most of those "stories" were captured on analog storage devices such as cassette deck tape machines or videocassette recorders and later "told" to students, friends, and families in a face-to-face session. Although businesses, government, television, and radio have had access to more expensive digital technologies for years, the affordability and accessibility of digital media have, only recently, made the technologies available in schools and homes, leading to new ways to create digital media.

Typically at each National Educational Computing Conference (NECC), there is a "hot" technology. At the 2005 conference in Philadelphia, it was certainly podcasting. That year the NECC attendees had to arrive early if they wanted a seat in a podcasting session, where they learned more about podcasting and how, as educators, they could use the technology in their classrooms. Although podcasting had been possible before the

TABLE 5.2
Digital Media Sharing

Definition	Digital media sharing is collaborative and sharable media.
NCSS Standards	☀ Time, Continuity, and Change ☀ Civic Ideals and Practices ☀ People, Places, and Environment ☀ Production, Distribution, and Consumption
ISTE Standards	NETS for Students: ☀ Creativity and Innovation ☀ Communication and Collaboration ☀ Research and Information Fluency NETS for Teachers: ☀ Facilitate and Inspire Student Learning and Creativity ☀ Design and Develop Digital-Age Learning Experiences and Assessments
Resources	*Digital Editing Resources:* Photo Story: http://www.microsoft.com/windowsxp/using/digitalphotography/photostory/default.mspx Movie Maker: http://www.microsoft.com/windowsxp/downloads/updates/moviemaker2.mspx iMovie: http://www.apple.com/ilife/imovie *Audio Resources/Podcasting:* Audacity: http://www.audacity.sourceforge.net GarageBand: http://www.apple.com/ilife/garageband iTunes: http://www.apple.com/itunes Odeo: http://www.odeo.com *Photo Editing/Sharing* Flickr: http://www.flickr.com iPhoto: http://www.apple.com/ilife/iphoto *Digital Video Sharing* TeacherTube: http://www.teachertube.com YouTube: http://www.youtube.com *Wikis and Blogs* PBworks: http://www.pbworks.com Wikispaces: http://www.wikispaces.com Blogger: http://www.blogger.com *Other Resources* The Library of Congress American Memory: http://lcweb2.loc.gov/ammem/index.html

Philadelphia NECC conference, 2005 was certainly a "growth" year for educators to begin incorporating podcasting in their classrooms.

Since that conference, podcasting has remained a popular technology for educators and now, in addition to digital audio, educators are incorporating digital video in lesson plans. The digital editing of audio and video has been made easier with simple-to-use editing programs, many of which now come preinstalled on computers. We feel that these programs can easily be integrated into the social studies classroom.

For example, GarageBand is a program developed by Apple and is bundled with the iLife software suite on Macintosh computers. With GarageBand, the user can work with multiple audio tracks, construct songs, synthesize music, and add audio effects. Windows Movie Maker is another software application; included on Microsoft Windows computers, it allows for editing of both audio and video. Another program that the authors of this chapter have often used for digital storytelling is Photo Story 3, which was described earlier. Any of these programs, along with many other options (e.g., iPhoto, iMovie, Audacity, QuickTime) have tutorials and help screens to aid educators in their use.

Additionally, educators can consider using Atomic Learning (http://movies.atomiclearning.com/k12/home), a software tutorial resource that features short, Web-based tutorial movies on more than 120 applications. Social networking sites (e.g., Facebook, MySpace), collaborative Web 2.0 online tools such as blogs and wikis, photo-sharing sites (http://www.flickr.com), and music sharing sites (http://www.odeo.com and http://www.apple.com/itunes/store/podcasts.html) are just a few examples of where you can share digital media easily and quickly. Furthermore, you can download media that may be helpful to you in the classroom from these sites.

Although many teachers may utilize digital media solely within their classrooms, sharing digital media has become very popular and is just a few clicks away. There are many Web-based tools that make digital file sharing easy. For example, educators can upload digital media to communities such as the educationally focused TeacherTube, while students may opt for sharing digital files via the popular media sharing site YouTube. However, although school content filtering systems will most likely ban YouTube, TeacherTube access generally is allowed.

Teachers can sign up for free accounts at http://teachertube.com. TeacherTube is designed to share educational media; content cannot contain advertisements or anything inappropriate. The site accepts media files in several formats including those files rendered in Windows Media Player (.wmv or .avi), QuickTime (.mov), and the popular .MPEG files. Many of today's digital cameras make this even easier by containing the software in the camera itself. For example, the Flip Video camera comes with a pop-out USB connection. After the user shoots the video, the camera can be inserted into an USB port; the software automatically pulls up the video and gives the user an opportunity to edit and to save the video in a format for Internet uploads. For the social studies teacher, an excellent way to utilize these resources is to implement an assignment that requires a "digital story."

Today, if you wanted your class to research, write, and record a historical field trip, you may still use traditional tools to present the final account such as a cassette tape recorder, camera, scanner, and PowerPoint presentation software. All of these tools still work, they are accessible in the school, and most teachers are very comfortable with these technologies. However, making all of these traditional tools work together *and* be shareable may prove difficult.

Imagine, instead, if you were to use a digital video (or still) camera to record a field trip, access digital editing software (already loaded on your computer), and then upload the finished story and video about the historical field trip to TeacherTube so that others around the world could share in the history. As discussed previously, TeacherTube is an online community for educators to upload, tag, and share content with others. Users can make content public or private, but there are specific rules to follow and content may be rejected or can be reported as inappropriate.

Using digital media in the classroom provides multiple ways to integrate technology in the social studies. The versatility of using digital storytelling methods by teacher educators and classroom teachers has been demonstrated through use of

IDEAS FOR IMPLEMENTING DIGITAL STORYTELLING

* For the classroom teacher, digital media can be used to examine cultural identity (Carroll & Carney, 2005) such as telling the story of a family member's participation in an historical event (e.g., D-day invasion at Normandy).

* Digital stories also may illustrate a teaching concept (Dupain & Maguire, 2007) others can adapt for their classrooms (this is the focus of the many instructional videos posted on TeacherTube).

* They also can present personal responses to debates (Theodore & Afolayan, 2008) such as those associated with a political campaign and share narratives of teaching and learning experiences (Tendero, 2006).

historical, instructional, personal, and reflective stories (Wright, 2008). It is a great way to engage your students in engaging and meaningful instruction.

There are many opportunities to experience such versatility in the social studies through both traditional and innovative methods. Next, we give one short example of how to use digital stories (and also share the digital media!). In addition, we will offer many different tools that may be used in the classroom implementation of digital media sharing.

SCENARIO: USING DIGITAL MEDIA AS COLLABORATIVE AND COMMUNICATIVE TOOLS TO DEVELOP A PICTORIAL HISTORY

Our example is one that includes the study of public opinion over the course of the Vietnam War during one social studies classroom unit plan.

Step 1: Preparing Your Students
1. You should begin the unit by showing a poignant PowerPoint presentation featuring full-screen photographs of both the war and the anti-war protests that occurred (therefore, a traditional technology—PowerPoint with photographs—is used). Short clips of popular music, born from the events of the war, are heard as the photos are projected.

Step 2: Developing Pictorial Histories
1. After you have modeled how pictures and music help depict the events associated with the war, your students will then begin developing their own pictorial history, to be presented in video format.
2. Students research and develop a pictorial history of the war that can be edited.
3. Students can use a variety of software programs such as Photo Story 3, Movie Maker, iPhoto, or iMovie to accomplish this task; the important note to teachers is that students will accomplish this task! Steps for actually creating the videos will vary according to the software program used. You need to remember to observe and take part in this technology learning curve if you have not done so already.
4. Students will present their videos to the class and upload them to file sharing sites such as YouTube or TeacherTube.

Step 3: Extension: Creating Written Narratives
1. Your students also can develop a written narrative to share on a private class blog (http://www.blogger.com or http://edublogs.org). This extension is a good way to synthesize what they have learned. Blogs are Web sites that, while primarily text-based, may include other media such as pictures and audio. Blogs often are used as a method to produce reflective journals, online diaries, and written narratives.

2. Through their research using multiple online resources of primary documents, students can examine cultural differences. For example, Gallup Polls taken during the Vietnam War could be analyzed, and changes could be reported in the student narratives.
3. Timelines of significant events of the war may even be developed and included on the blog. (A great online resource for timeline development is called Timetoast, found at http://www.timetoast.com).

Wikis

A similar type of project can utilize Web 2.0 technologies by allowing students to develop a collaborative class wiki. The potential for increasing student engagement and enhancing teaching and learning is great with so many Web 2.0 technologies currently available and even more becoming accessible as technology continues to evolve. One such Web 2.0 tool is a wiki to share research, notes, and presentation materials. A wiki may even serve as a cumulative activity for a project such as the one outlined in the following section.

For example, if you assign your students to collaborate on the creation of a media conglomerate that has a newspaper, a radio station, and a television station, you could utilize a wiki. Your students are to work together to create the content for the media conglomerate, and the content they create will reflect how public opinion about the Vietnam War changed over time. By using a wiki, the class will be able to create an online newspaper that tracks public opinion of the Vietnam War.

Before we go any further, let's fully describe what a wiki is and how a teacher can utilize a wiki in his or her classroom. First, the word wiki in Hawaiian translates to "quick." In a word, that is what makes wiki creation for classroom instruction so appealing—wikis can be created quickly and may be edited or changed just as quickly. (The most popular wiki most of us use is Wikipedia.) Wikis are included in the Web 2.0 toolbox as they are easily created, easily changed, and collaboration-encouraged and collaboration-engaged tools. Online resources available to education-minded wiki users include http://pbworks.com and http://wikispaces.com. At either of these sites, educators are encouraged to explore wiki page creation and to develop different pages and files.

In our example, students are reflecting on how public opinion about the Vietnam War changed over time. Using a wiki, the class will create an online newspaper that tracks public opinion of the war. In the previous project, students used digital media creation software such as Windows Movie Maker or Photo Story 3 to make videos regarding the Vietnam War, and they then posted the created content on TeacherTube. You can link that project with a wiki project by embedding the videos in the wiki. However, an even easier method to connect technology projects is to link to TeacherTube or another file sharing site within the wiki. There are multiple ways to learn and to utilize technologies in collaboration with one another. The ultimate teaching and learning goal is to learn and to share in the knowledge gained. A collaborative wiki, which shows links to other student projects posted on iTunes and YouTube, is presented in Figure 5.4.

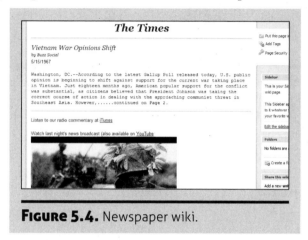

FIGURE 5.4. Newspaper wiki.

Scenario: Creating a Wiki Using PBworks. The steps below will help you get started in setting up your first wiki. There are several wiki creation sites available, but we will use PBworks.

Step 1: Finding PBworks and Creating Your Account
1. Go to http://www.pbworks.com.
2. Click on the "Get Started" button (see Figure 5.5).

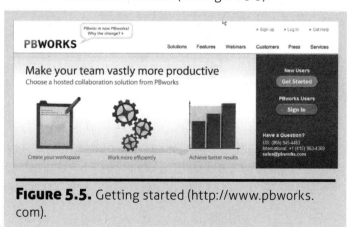

FIGURE 5.5. Getting started (http://www.pbworks. com).

Step 2: Selecting Educational Option

1. Among your choices, select the "Educational" link (see Figure 5.6).

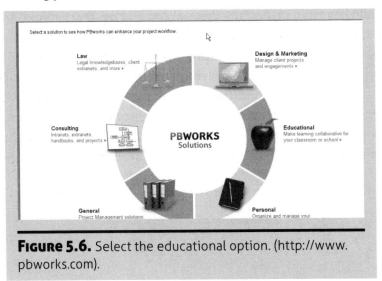

FIGURE 5.6. Select the educational option. (http://www.pbworks.com).

Step 3: Selecting Try It Now!

1. On the right side of the page, select the "Try it Now!" button (see Figure 5.7).

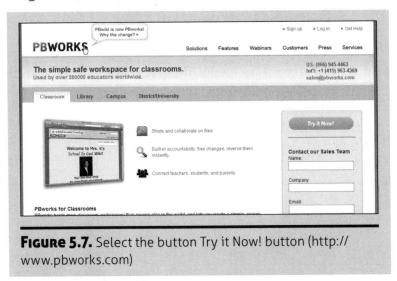

FIGURE 5.7. Select the button Try it Now! button (http://www.pbworks.com)

Step 4: Choosing Your Plan

1. You can choose from three plans: Campus, Classroom, or Basic (see Figure 5.8). Basic is the free account, so select the "Select" button in the "Basic" column. You can upgrade your free account at any time.

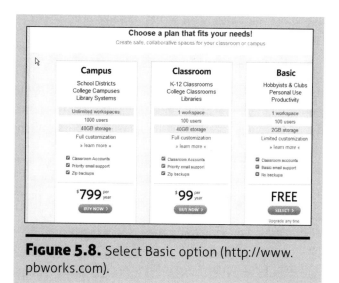

FIGURE 5.8. Select Basic option (http://www.
pbworks.com).

Step 5: Setting Up Your Wiki
1. Beside "Choose your address," give your wiki an appropriate Web address (see Figure 5.9).

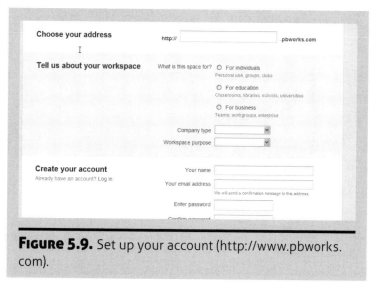

FIGURE 5.9. Set up your account (http://www.pbworks.
com).

2. Beside "Tell us about your workspace," and under "What is this space for?", select "For education." Next the "Company type," select an option that best describes your situation. Next to "Workspace purpose," select an option that best fits how you plan on using the wiki.
3. Beside "Create your account," provide your name and your e-mail address. A confirmation e-mail will be sent to your e-mail address that will allow you to activate your wiki. Then, create a password. (You have

now created a PBworks account, so remember your password.) Select the "Next" button.

Step 6: Establishing Parameters
1. First, check your e-mail to find the confirmation e-mail. Click on the link provided in your e-mail. Once you have selected the link, you will be taken to a wiki page that will allow you to establish the security parameters of your wiki.
2. Under "Who can view this workspace?" select "Only people I invite or approve."
3. Under "Who can edit this workspace?" select "Only people I invite or approve."
4. Select the checkbox indicating that you agree to the PBworks terms of service.
5. Click on the "Take me to my workspace" button.

Step 7: Editing Your Wiki Page
1. You'll now be on the FrontPage of your wiki. Click on the "Edit" tab at the top of the page (see Figure 5.10).

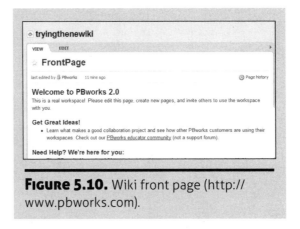

FIGURE 5.10. Wiki front page (http://www.pbworks.com).

2. Once in the edit screen, you can see that the interface is much like Microsoft Word.
3. To add words, simply click where you want to type and begin typing.
4. You can change the font color and size, and make other format changes by using the format bar at the top of the page.

Step 8: Attaching a Document or Image to Your Wiki Page
1. Locate the "Page Tools" navigation menu on the right side of the page.
2. Click on "Images and files." Click on the "Upload files" link, and then find the file or image you would like to upload, and click on the "Open" button.

3. The file/image automatically uploads. Next, take your mouse and click on the place inside your wiki where you would like to place your file/image.
4. Now, go back and click on the file/image that you previously uploaded and it will appear in the wiki.

Step 9: Embedding a Movie From YouTube
1. Go to the format bar at the top of the page, and click on "Insert Plugin."
2. Scroll your mouse over "Video" and select "YouTube Video."
3. Now, if you have not already done so, open another Internet tab and go to http://www.youtube.com to find a movie clip you want to embed in your wiki.
4. Copy the embed code, and go back to your wiki (see Figure 5.11).
5. Paste the embed code into the "Configure: YouTube video (Step 2 of 3)" box and click on the "Preview" button.
6. Then click on "Ok."

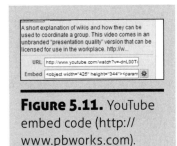

FIGURE 5.11. YouTube embed code (http://www.pbworks.com).

Step 10: Embedding a Movie That You or a Student Create and Produce
1. Go to the format bar at the top of the page, and click on "Insert Plugin."
2. Scroll your mouse over "Video" and select "Upload a video."
3. Select the "Browse" button, find your movie file, and select the "Open" button.
4. Select the "Submit" button.

Step 11: Uploading a Movie From TeacherTube
1. Go to http://www.teachertube.com. Find a movie at TeacherTube, and copy the Web address.
2. Go back to your wiki page, and paste the Web address into the page. You have now created a link to the movie at TeacherTube.

Step 12: Finalizing Your Page
1. At the bottom of page, click on the "Save" button.
2. Always remember to save your work.

Virtual Worlds

In this section, you will be introduced to virtual worlds and environments, which are quickly becoming a hot topic in education. Some of the strategies discussed in this section are not, as of this writing, completely possible for K–12 educators to fully implement. However, all educators should be aware of what students can do, or are currently doing in various virtual environments. It is important for educators to be informed about the current and future possibilities for social studies education in virtual environments.

Why is this so important? The answer is that the concept of digital literacy is becoming an increasingly important part of educating our students for the world they will eventually inherit and lead, and therefore educators should take the lead in offering students "guidance in developing digital wisdom" (Prensky, 2009, para. 29). Educators offer digital guidance by "letting students learn by using new technologies, putting themselves in the role of guides, context providers, and quality controllers" (Prensky, 2009, para. 29). Likewise, parents can provide digital guidance by "recognizing the extent to which the future will be mediated by technology and encouraging children to use digital technology wisely" (Prensky, 2009, para. 29). Social studies teachers have a unique opportunity to take the lead in providing this guidance, and in using these tools to teach students about both social studies content and digital wisdom.

What is a virtual world? A virtual world can be defined as a "persistent, synthetic, online environment that can be accessed by many users at the same time" (Castronova, 2008). Sarah Robbins-Bell (2008) said that virtual worlds have four characteristics:

- ☀ they are persistent in that they exist regardless of whether a user is logged on;
- ☀ they are multiuser environments populated by many individuals;
- ☀ they allow users to create avatars that represent the user visually in the virtual world; and
- ☀ they are hosted over wide area networks that allow for a virtual environment available on a global scale. (p. 26)

In this section we also discuss games; although online gaming may not meet all these characteristics, online gamers are involved in a virtual environment. To view a definition of virtual worlds and to find virtual world resources, see Table 5.3. Table 5.3 also lists the NCSS and ISTE standards that may be addressed.

	TABLE 5.3 Virtual Worlds
Definition	A virtual world is a "persistent, synthetic, online environment that can be accessed by many users at the same time" (Castronova, 2008).
NCSS Standards	☼ Culture ☼ Time, Continuity, and Change ☼ People, Places, and Environment ☼ Individual Development and Identity ☼ Individuals, Groups, and Institutions ☼ Power, Authority, and Governance ☼ Production, Distribution, and Consumption ☼ Science, Technology, and Society ☼ Global Connections ☼ Civic Ideals and Practices
ISTE Standards	NETS for Students: ☼ Creativity and Innovation ☼ Communication and Collaboration ☼ Research and Information Fluency ☼ Critical Thinking, Problem Solving, and Decision Making ☼ Digital Citizenship ☼ Technology Operations and Concepts NETS for Teachers: ☼ Facilitate and Inspire Student Learning and Creativity ☼ Design and Develop Digital-Age Learning Experiences and Assessments. ☼ Model Digital-Age Work and Learning ☼ Promote and Model Digital Citizenship and Responsibility ☼ Engage in Professional Growth and Leadership
Resources	*Elementary to Middle School:* Webkinz: http://www.webkinz.com Club Penguin: http://www.clubpenguin.com Whyville: http://www.whyville.net Quest Atlantis: http://atlantis.crlt.indiana.edu *High School:* Active Worlds: http://www.activeworlds.com Second Life: http://www.secondlife.com Teen Second Life: http://www.teen.secondlife.com

Avatars

In a virtual world, users move about an artificial environment with an avatar, an in-world representation of themselves. The actual avatar can resemble how the person looks in the real world, or it can look very different. Depending on the virtual world, avatars can engage in activities unique to that particular world. For instance, Webkinz (http://www.webkinz.com) allows children to use an avatar that represents a stuffed animal. The child must then take care of the animal as they would care for a real pet. The child can also interact with other children who are represented by their pet avatar, answer trivia, and play games. For students in middle school grades, sites such as OurWorld (http://www.ourworld.com) and Dizzywood (http://www.dizzywood.com) offer safe virtual environments where students can interact and communicate with each other socially and play games.

In contrast, the virtual world of Second Life (http://www.secondlife.com) offers a very different experience for individuals age 18 and up. (Teen Second Life, which can be found at http://www.teen.secondlife.com, can be used with students ages 13–17.) Second Life operates much like the real world; there are no objectives and achievements to attempt to reach. In Second Life, individuals can actually live a second, virtual life, complete with owning virtual property, running virtual businesses, and living in virtual marriages.

MMORPGs

Virtual worlds are not new to young people. Students spend much free time playing a version of a virtual world called a massively multi-player online role-playing game (MMORPG). Examples of currently popular MMORPGs include World of Warcraft, Final Fantasy, and Phantasy Star Online. MMORPGs typically have a main storyline in which players engage, but there are countless other smaller missions that have little to do with the main storyline. While playing a MMORPG, young people choose a character with unique attributes, and then meet up with other players to go on quests and complete missions. During these quests/missions, players must work together and share their unique abilities to help each other reach their identified goal.

Students also, very recently, have visited and explored online virtual communities, which are more directly tied to educational pursuits. Since 1999, students have been visiting and interacting with each other inside the virtual community of Whyville (http://www.whyville.net). In Whyville, students play educational games and in so doing they earn "clams," the virtual currency inside Whyville. With clams, students can purchase other virtual items to improve their virtual life. Students also design their own face in Whyville, and they have the ability to go to events or to start a business as well.

Another similar environment is called Club Penguin (http://www. clubpenguin. com). Club Penguin is similar to both Whyville and Webkinz in that kids choose an avatar, meet other kids from around the world, participate in activities in-world, and play educational games. Club Penguin, however, is unique in that currency earned in-world (inside Club Penguin) can be used to help real people in the real world through a program called "Coins for Change." How does this work? First, kids earn virtual currency, called "coins," by playing games. Then, they donate the virtual coins they have earned to a cause of their choice. Club Penguin then donates a million dollar prize to three different charities that represent how the children chose to donate their earned virtual coins. Kids can choose between helping other kids in developing countries, supporting the environment, or promoting children's health.

These process skills connect to social studies in that students can directly see how their actions in a virtual world/environment can impact the real world around them. These activities also may lead to further classroom discussion and activities that address several thematic strands as set forth by the NCSS, such as: (a) culture; (b) people, places, and environments; (c) production, distribution, and consumption; (d) global connections; and (e) civic ideals and practices.

Educators at all levels (K–12, higher education) are venturing into virtual worlds and using them in a variety of ways. For example, Castronova (2008) found that users in a virtual environment follow the Law of Demand in economics as they would in the real world. Therefore, a virtual environment could theoretically be used as a platform in which students could engage in authentic economic decision-making situations. For example, the for-profit institution, University of Phoenix, has created a virtual city called Kelsey, in which "virtual schools and businesses function like case studies" and "students use them to diagnose and solve typical problems of organizations" (Wasley, 2008, para. 3).

A software program, available to schools only, called Quest Atlantis (QA) provides a virtual 3D environment whereby students ages 9–15 (grades 4–8) must complete various quests (Tan, Seah, Yeo, & Hung, 2008). During these quests students participate in both real-world and simulated situations, such as conducting environmental studies and developing action plans. QA also provides resources for teachers, including a teacher's manual, a teacher's toolkit guide, lesson plan units for specific content areas, and other tools. The social studies unit plan can be found at http://atlantis.crlt.indiana.edu/site/view/Educators#13. In this unit, students visit the ancestral Puebloan people of the American Southwest to see and experience their culture and way of life.

Due to the fact that QA is funded by grants from the National Science Foundation, NASA, Food Lion, and the MacArthur Foundation, the program is not yet available in all U.S. states. Currently, there are QA centers in California, Florida, Indiana, Massachusetts, New Jersey, and North Carolina, as well as centers in other countries, but there are plans for expansion. QA also doubles as a professional development opportunity, as it requires a leadership team consisting of teachers, administrators, and librarians to work together to implement the program in the school. A professional development workshop to learn the system/software also is required. If you are interested in using QA, visit http://atlantis.crlt.indiana.edu/site/view/Educators#11. From the site, you can submit a teacher/facilitator form.

Certainly, social studies teachers today can use a variety of traditional methods to teach students about history, government, economics, and all of the different disciplines under the social sciences banner. For example, while a student in high school economics, one of the authors recalls an individual from Junior Achievement visiting his classroom one-day-a-week throughout an academic semester. During this time, the guest teacher from Junior Achievement would bring a computer software program to class; the program simulated a business and students would use the software to run a business, learn about economic concepts, and compete on the open market against other companies (i.e., other students) in the same industry. No doubt, software programs such as this still exist and are valuable learning tools. However, there is a significant limitation to the software program: When the guest teacher left at the end of class, so did the software program! Students only had access to the software program on a very limited basis.

What if a time limit did not exist? What if an environment existed in which students could enter at any time, from any computer with an Internet connection, and run a business while learning valuable economic concepts and principles? The reality is that environments such as the one described already exist, in the virtual world. Theoretically, what could social studies education look like in a virtual world? Consider the following scenario.

SCENARIO: RUNNING A BUSINESS IN A VIRTUAL WORLD

The following scenario is a snapshot of what economics *could* look like in the virtual world of Second Life. Our goal is to increase awareness of teachers and educators to the future possibilities of virtual worlds in social studies education.

As an economics teacher you want to teach your students about concepts such as elasticity, supply, and demand. Again, you can use any number of traditional methods to teach your students about these concepts. You also could use a virtual environment. In this virtual environment, students must take the concepts they have learned in the classroom and apply them to running a virtual business. Students must choose the business to run, design a business plan, create the products to sell or services to provide, and then proceed to run the business. For example, a student could decide to open a virtual clothing store inside the virtual environment. The student would create the business from the ground up, like one would in the real world. This would entail raising virtual capital, selecting the right virtual location for the store, setting the layout of the store, designing and constructing the virtual clothing (see Figure 5.12), placing advertisements for the store at key locations in the virtual world, encouraging advertisers to place ads in the store, and completing virtual transactions.

FIGURE 5.12. Clothing store models in Second Life.

Such an activity would not be easy, and would require a significant amount of instructional time to introduce the virtual environment and to learn how to build and design basic buildings and objects. Lab time would need to be scheduled throughout the semester in order to give students enough time and opportunity to learn and develop these skills. Ideally, this type of activity would be best delivered as a semester-long scaffolding project meant to culminate at the end of a semester. Then, at the end of the semester, students would present their business in class and discuss the various economic concepts and principles used to aid them in their business decisions. The student could realistically answer whether the business plan was successful or not, as well as discuss potential changes to the business model that would improve the success of the business.

Again, these are examples of what social studies education could theoretically look like in a virtual environment. Some of the capabilities described already exist, while others have yet to be constructed. The beauty, however, of virtual worlds, such as Second Life and Active Worlds, is that content inside the virtual environment is user-designed, user-created, and user-generated. It is waiting for you to get started.

The steps below will help you begin your investigation of virtual worlds. We will visit Second Life first, then provide the steps for getting started in Teen Second Life.

Step 1: Getting Started With Second Life
1. Go to http://www.secondlife.com.
2. Click on the "Get Started Free Download Button" on the Second Life front page (see Figure 5.13).

FIGURE 5.13. Second Life front page (http://www.secondlife.com).

Step 2: Setting Your Avatar and Personal Settings

1. Select a starting look (This is your avatar. You can change your avatar once you are inside Second Life.) See Figure 5.14 for a screen shot showing the starting screen.

FIGURE 5.14. Create your Second Life account (http://www.secondlife.com).

2. Choose "Create a First Name" to give yourself a first name. For the sake of privacy and security, you may not want to use your real-life first name for your Second Life first name.
3. Click on "Select a Last Name," select the "Get Available Last Names" button, and then choose from a limited selection of last names.
4. Type your e-mail address in the "Email Address" box and the "Confirm Email Address" box.
5. Select the country in which you reside from the dropdown menu.
6. Indicate the day, the month, and the year in which you were born.
7. Type your actual first name in the "Real-Life First Name" box and type your last name in the "Real-Life Last Name" box.
8. Indicate whether you are a male or female.
9. Type in a password, which you create, in the "Password" box as well as in the "Confirm Password" box.
10. Select a security question and type the answer in the "Security Answer" box.
11. Indicate that you are not a robot by retyping the captcha (the fuzzy words you see on the screen) in the "Verify You Are Not a Robot" box.
12. Mark the checkbox next to the "Terms of Service" and select the "Create Account" button.

Step 3: Downloading Second Life
1. On the next page you will download the Second Life client. The client will download directly onto your computer. You will use the client to access Second Life (see Figure 5.15).

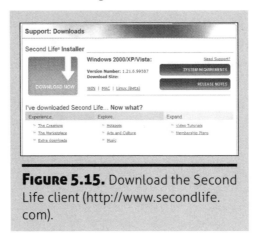

FIGURE 5.15. Download the Second Life client (http://www.secondlife. com).

2. To operate effectively, the Second Life client requires your computer to have certain requirements, so before you download, select the "System Requirements" button and check to see that your computer meets the requirements.
3. Once you have checked your system requirements, download the client by choosing the client that represents your computer operating system by selecting Windows (WIN), Mac (MAC), or Linux (Linux Beta).

Step 4: Starting the Program
1. Once you have downloaded the client to your desktop, open the client and log in (see Figure 5.16).

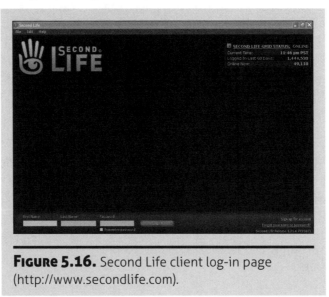

FIGURE 5.16. Second Life client log-in page (http://www.secondlife.com).

Step 5: Practice Moving in Your New World
  1. Take some time to familiarize yourself with the controls.

Step 6: Navigating to Specific Places
  1. Visit a specific place, such as the United States Holocaust Museum. Select the "Search" button at the bottom of your screen. Select the "All" tab.
  2. In the search box, type "U.S. Holocaust Museum." When you see the list of results appear, select the first link called "US Holocaust Museum1 Region."
  3. Finally, select the "Teleport" button. You should now see the U.S. Holocaust Museum. Go inside the museum to begin your experience.

The steps below will help your students (ages 13 to 17) get started in Teen Second Life. The steps are similar to the steps taken to join Second Life.

Step 1: Getting Your Teen Started With Second Life
  1. Go to http://www.teen.secondlife.com
  2. In the middle of the page, click on "Free Basic Account."

Step 2: Setting Your Avatar and Personal Settings
  1. Select a starting look. (This is your avatar. You can change your avatar once you are inside Teen Second Life.) Choose "Create a First Name" to give yourself a first name. For the sake of privacy and security, you may not want to use your real-life first name for your Teen Second Life first name.
  2. Click on "Select a Last Name," select the "Get Available Last Names" button, and then choose from a limited selection of last names.
  3. Type your e-mail address in the "Email Address" box and the "Confirm Email Address" box.
  4. Select the country in which you reside from the dropdown menu.
  5. Indicate the day, the month, and the year in which you were born.
  6. Type your actual first name in the "Real-Life First Name" box and type your last name in the "Real-Life Last Name" box.
  7. Indicate whether you are a male or female.
  8. Type in a password, which you create, in the "Password" box as well as in the "Confirm Password" box.
  9. Select a security question and type the answer in the "Security Answer" box.
  10. Indicate that you are not a robot by retyping the captcha (the fuzzy words you see on the screen) in the "Verify You Are Not a Robot" box.
  11. Mark the checkbox next to the "Terms of Service" and select the "Create Account" button.

12. Steps 3 through 7 for Second Life are the same as, or are similar to, Teen Second Life.

Although access to Teen Second Life for adults is difficult, it is possible for educators to enter on a restricted basis. Linden Lab allows educators, nonprofit organizations, and businesses the option to purchase private, adult islands in Teen Second Life. All islands owned by adults are located to the south of the teen mainland and all of the teen-owned islands. Adults are not allowed to leave the private, adult island but teens have the ability to visit the island and interact with adults, including teachers. Educational and nonprofit groups receive educational discounts. Any adult requesting access must also go through a screening process. Keep in mind that any student age 18 and up also must go through the screening process. More detailed and in-depth information about entering Teen Second Life can be found by visiting the Second Life: Educators Working with Teens wiki at http://www.simteach.com/wiki/index.php?title=Second_Life:_Educators_Working_with_Teens. A list of educational projects currently taking place in Teen Second Life also can be found by visiting this site.

Although building, creating, and scripting in Second Life is beyond the scope of this chapter, there are several books available that can assist educators in getting started, and becoming familiar with, Second Life and Teen Second Life. These resources include the following:

- *Second Life: The Official Guide* by Michael Rymaszewski, Wagner James Au, Cory Ondrejka, Richard Platel, Sara Van Gorden, Jeanette Cézanne, Paul Cézanne, Ben Batstone-Cunningham, Aleks Krotoski, Celebrity Trollop, Jim Rossignol, and Second Life residents from around the world;
- *How to Do Everything With Second Life* by Richard Mansfield;
- *Scripting Your World: The Official Guide to Second Life Scripting* by Dana Moore, Michael Thome, and Karen Zita Haigh; and
- *Second Life for Dummies* by Sarah Robbins and Mark Bell.

LOOKING INTO THE FUTURE

We turn now to our student, Buzz Social. Buzz has been very busy. His social studies teacher has given him and his fellow students a virtual field trip project and report assignment. Each student will individually present the project and paper report at the end of the semester. Buzz's teacher has asked him and each of his classmates to begin their virtual field trip by entering the virtual world of Second Life. The teacher has already spent a significant amount of time inside Second Life, is familiar with the environment, and has preselected a large number of historical destinations of which students can choose to visit. Before Buzz can begin his semester-long project, however, the teacher takes Buzz and his classmates to a computer lab inside the school. In the lab, Buzz is introduced to Second Life and he is taught how to move around and interact with the environment and with other avatars. Throughout the semester, Buzz's teacher has provided opportunities for the class to go the computer lab to work on the project in Second Life. While in the computer lab, Buzz looks at the teacher's list of selected historical destinations, and decides he will visit and research the American Old West. Inside Second Life, Buzz visits a virtually recreated Dodge City in the American Old West (see Figure 5.17).

FIGURE 5.17. Dodge City, 1875 (http://www.secondlife.com).

He walks about the town, looks in the shops, and visits local ranches. Fortunately, Buzz's teacher also has the Oregon Trail game software, and Buzz uses the game to give him even more detailed experiences in the Old American West. Throughout Buzz's experiences in Second Life and with Oregon Trail, he has been taking pictures of his adventures using screen-capturing technology.

With the information he has gathered, Buzz searches through encyclopedias and other resources in the classroom and in the school's library to help him finish collecting all the data he needs. Now Buzz has all of the data ready to create his presentation. Using a screen capturing program, Buzz creates a digital story with images, text, music, and narration and creates a movie in QuickTime format. Buzz then goes inside Second Life, and uploads his movie presentation into a movie display already created for him and his fellow classmates by his social studies teacher. Now, Buzz, his classmates, and his teacher can watch the historical documentary/movie he has created. Additionally, other students from around the world can see the documentary/movie and leave notes, comments, and suggestions for Buzz. In fact, a student inside Second Life from South Korea sees the documentary/movie and is fascinated because he has always wanted to know about the American Old West. He sends Buzz a note on Second Life, and Buzz responds. They then begin to converse and speak to each other on Second Life because Second Life has language translation software.

While completing this presentation, Buzz has taken on many roles and demonstrated his digital wisdom. He has been a learner, a historical researcher, a reporter, a tour guide, and a creator. In the process, Buzz's experiences also were broadened because he met someone from another country and culture who has helped open his mind to different people with different lifestyles and experiences.

The above vignette is a snapshot of what social studies *could* look like in the virtual world of Second Life. Again, our goal is to increase awareness of teachers and educators to the future possibilities of virtual worlds in social studies education. Technology offers social studies students many possibilities (as demonstrated through Buzz Social's experiences) and opportunities (as outlined with our three applications) to make social studies content and pedagogy engaging and meaningful. As social studies students evolve as learners, technology consumers, and citizens, social studies teachers must teach social studies by using technology to offer "a way to authentically represent American society in students' lived school experiences" (Lee, 2008, p. 140). No matter what social studies content is taught, what pedagogies are used, or what technologies are employed, teachers must recognize that today's students use technology to navigate and negotiate all aspects of their lives. When seizing these opportunities, it is vital that, as social studies educators, we seek ways to intersect traditional and innovative methods as we continue to seek powerful, challenging, meaningful instruction that engages our students in active social studies learning.

REFLECTION

Now that you have read this chapter, reflect on your opening exercise and the information presented to do the following:

1. Write a technology goal:
   a. What skills would you like to acquire?
   b. What hardware/software would you like to acquire?
   c. Identify the resources that you need to make this happen.
2. Set a timeline for achieving your goal.

References

Bolick, C., Berson, M., Coutts, C., & Heinecke, W. (2003). Technology applications in social studies teacher education: A survey of social studies methods faculty. *Contemporary Issues in Technology and Teacher Education, 3.* Retrieved from http://www.citejournal.org/vol3/iss3/socialstudies/article1.cfm

Bull, G., & Thompson, A. (2004). Establishing a framework for digital images in the school curriculum. *Learning and Leading With Technology, 31*(8), 14–17.

Carroll, D., & Carney, J. (2005). Personal perspectives: Using multimedia to express cultural identity. *Contemporary Issues in Technology and Teacher Education, 4,* 465–488.

Castronova, E. (2008). *A test of the law of demand in a virtual world: Exploring the petri dish approach to social science.* (CESIFO Working Paper No. 2355, Category 10: Empirical and Theoretical Methods). Retrieved from http://www.ifo.de/pls/guestci/download/CESifo%20Working%20Papers%202008/CESifo%20Working%20Papers%20July%202008/cesifo_wp2355.pdf

Crocco, M. S. (2001). Leveraging constructivist learning in the social studies classroom: A response to Mason, Berson, Diem, Hicks, Lee, and Dralle. *Contemporary Issues in Technology and Teacher Education, 3.* Retrieved from http://www.citejournal.org/vol1/iss3/currentissues/socialstudies/article2.htm

Diem, R. (2000). Can it make a difference? Technology and the social studies. *Theory and Research in Social Education, 28,* 493–501.

Doolittle, P. E., & Hicks, D. (2003). Constructivism as a theoretical foundation for the use of technology in social studies. *Theory and Research in Social Education, 31,* 72–104.

Dupain, M., & Maguire, L. (2007). Health digital storytelling projects. *American Journal of Health Education, 38,* 41–43.

Lee, J. K. (2008). Toward democracy: Social studies and TPCK. In AACTE Committee on Innovation and Technology (Ed.), *The handbook of technological pedagogical content knowledge (TPCK) for educators* (pp. 129–144). Mahwah, NJ: Lawrence Erlbaum.

Manfra, M., & Hammond, T. (2008–2009). Teachers' instructional choices with student-created digital documentaries: Case studies. *Journal of Research on Technology in Education, 41,* 223–243.

Mason, C., Berson, M., Diem, R., Hicks, D., Lee, J., & Dralle, T. (2000). Guidelines for using technology to prepare social studies teachers. *Contemporary Issues in Technology and Teacher Education, 1*. Retrieved February 1, 2009, from http://www.citejournal.org/vol1/currentissues/socialstudies/article1.htm

Mishra, P., & Koehler, M. J. (2006). Technological pedagogical content knowledge: A framework for teacher knowledge. *Teachers' College Record, 108*, 1017–1054.

National Council for the Social Studies. (2006). NCSS technology position statement and guidelines. *Social Education, 70,* 329–332.

Prensky, M. (2009). H. sapiens digital: From digital immigrants and digital natives to digital wisdom. *Innovate,* 5(3). Retrieved February 1, 2009, from http://www.innovateonline.info/index.php?view=article&id=705

Robbins-Bell, S. (2008). Higher education in virtual conversation. *EDUCAUSE, 43*(5), 24–34.

Rooze, G. (1983, November). *Integrating computer software into social studies instruction.* Paper presented at the annual meeting of the National Council of the Social Studies, San Francisco. (ERIC Document Reproduction Service No. ED239586)

Swan, K., Mazur, J., Trullinger, L., Brock, D., Ross, A., Holman, A., et al. (2007). The voice of reason: Social studies pre-service teachers debrief their initial experiences with technology integration. *Social Studies Research and Practice, 2,* 261–279. Retrieved from http://www.socstrp.org/issues/PDF/2.2.11.pdf

Tan, S. C., Seah, L. H., Yeo, J., & Hung, D. (2008). Online learning communities in K–12 settings. In J. Voogt & G. Knezek (Eds.), *International handbook of information technology in primary and secondary education* (Vol. 20, pp. 249–266). Dordrecht, The Netherlands: Springer.

Tendero, A. (2006). Facing versions of the self: The effects of digital storytelling on English education. *Contemporary Issues in Technology and Teacher Education, 6,* 174–194.

The Learning Company. (2001). *The Oregon Trail* (5th ed.) [Computer Software]. Novato, CA: Broderbund.

Theodore, P., & Afolayan, M. (2008, March). *Using digital storytelling to increase cultural competence in teacher education students.* Paper presented at the annual meeting of the American Educational Research Association, New York City.

Thompson, A. D., & Mishra, P. (2007–2008). Breaking news: TPCK becomes TPACK! *Journal of Computing in Teacher Education, 24*(2), 38.

van Hover, S. D., Berson, M. J., Bolick, C. M., & Swan, K. O. (2004). Implications of ubiquitous computing for the social studies curriculum. *Journal of Computing in Teacher Education, 20,* 107–111.

Wasley, P. (2008). U. of Phoenix lets students find answers virtually. *The Chronicle of Higher Education, 54*(48), A1–A10.

Weis, T., Benmayor, R., O'Leary, C., & Eynon, B. (2002). Digital technologies and pedagogies. *Social Justice, 29,* 153–167.

Whitworth, S., & Berson, M. (2002, April). *Computer technology in the social studies: An examination of the effectiveness literature (1996–2001).* Paper presented at the annual meeting of the American Educational Research Association, New Orleans, LA.

Wright, V. (2008). Digital storytelling in teacher education. In L. Tomei (Ed.), *Encyclopedia of information technology curriculum integration* (pp. 235–237). Hershey, NY: Information Science Reference.

Wright, V., & Wilson, E. (2005–2006). From preservice to inservice teaching: A study of technology integration. *Journal of Computing in Teacher Education, 22*(2), 49–55.

Appendix A

The introduction chapter introduced the importance of connecting specific tools to various digital literacy competencies. For social studies, the connection to digital literacy is as follows:

Technology Tool	Corresponding Digital Literacy				
	Photo-Visual	Reproduction	Branching	Information	Social-Emotional
Software Programs	■		■	■	■
Digital Media Sharing	■	■		■	■
Digital Photo Story	■	■	■	■	■
Wikis		■	■	■	■
Virtual Worlds	■		■	■	■

Appendix B
Glossary

Digital media sharing: Media that is produced using various digital hardware and software products and later shared with others through collaborative and interactive digital communities, including online and cell phone communities, such as YouTube, TeacherTube, Facebook, text messaging, and other similar outlets. Multiple digital media may be shared and can include music, images, video, presentations, games, and a combination of media.

Pedagogy: Pedagogy generally refers to the art and science of teaching and is an umbrella term used to describe teaching strategies and methods.

Software: A general term to describe computer programs that allow for the user to perform various tasks such as to communicate, analyze, create, and produce, and other tasks. Software can encompass games, online resources, and more.

Technological Pedagogical Content Knowledge (TPCK): TPCK is the practice of interweaving the technology, pedagogy, and content for meaningful and purposeful teaching and learning; TPCK emphasizes the interconnectedness of the technology in presenting the content.

Technology application: The practice of integrating technology in teaching and learning.

Virtual worlds: A computer-based simulation of reality, or the real world, but one that is synthetic and representational. Virtual worlds can simulate work, play, and educational environments.

Appendix C
Additional Resources

Useful Web Sites (Digital Editing Resources)

PHOTO STORY
http://www.microsoft.com/windowsxp/using/digitalphotography/photostory/default.mspx

This software allows you to connect pictures with text, video, and music in a multimedia presentation.

MOVIE MAKER
http://www.microsoft.com/windowsxp/downloads/updates/moviemaker2.mspx

Movie Maker allows you to create, edit, and share home movies on your PC.

IMOVIE
http://www.apple.com/ilife/imovie

This software, which comes bundled with the Apple iLife software, allows you to create movies using video, still images, music, text, and other multimedia materials.

Useful Web Sites (Audio Resources/Podcasting)

AUDACITY
http://www.audacity.sourceforge.net

This is a free, open software source for editing audio files.

GARAGEBAND
http://www.apple.com/ilife/garageband

This application, which is bundled in Apple's iLife software, allows you to record, manipulate, and publish audio files.

ITUNES
http://www.apple.com/itunes

iTunes is a free hosting site for podcasts. Students also can find and listen to podcasts on a variety of informative topics.

ODEO
http://www.odeo.com

Odeo makes it easy for students to find and play music off the Internet.

Useful Web Sites (Photo Editing/Sharing)

IPHOTO
http://www.apple.com/ilife/iphoto

This application, preloaded on every Macintosh computer, allows you to edit, share, and store your photos.

FLICKR
http://www.flickr.com

Flickr is a photo storage and editing Web site. Students also can browse photos in the public domain here.

Useful Web Sites (Digital Video Sharing)

TEACHERTUBE
http://www.teachertube.com

TeacherTube features instructional videos that employ character acting, group discussion, and demonstrations to address historic and scientific topics as well as those dealing with classroom instruction.

YOUTUBE
http://www.youtube.com

YouTube is the Web's largest collection of videos. Teachers can sort through the videos for informational clips on specific topics or post student-created videos.

Useful Web Sites (Wikis and Blogs)

PBWORKS
http://www.pbworks.com

PBworks, also known as PBwiki, is a blog hosting site with a special option for teachers wishing to create blogs in their classrooms.

WIKISPACES
http://www.wikispaces.com

Wikispaces has free, K–12 specific blogs for teachers.

BLOGGER
http://www.blogger.com

Blogger is an easy-to-use blog community that provides free Web space where users can post videos and photos to customized blog pages.

Useful Web Sites (Other Resources)

THE LIBRARY OF CONGRESS AMERICAN MEMORY
http://memory.loc.gov/ammem/index.html

The American Memory is a special collection of archives at the Library of Congress. They have special section of this site for teachers that includes lesson plans and activities.

Conclusion:

Why Teach With Technology?

*Kevin D. Besnoy, Lane W. Clarke, John Thieken,
and Tirupalavanam G. Ganesh*

I find myself, as I do at Christmas every year, in a room full of my wife's colleagues from the bank at which she works. (I hate this holiday party.) It's not that I dislike my wife's colleagues, it has more to do with the one conversation I am doomed to repeat every year. You see, I teach middle school, and every year someone has to complain about how much schools are spending on technology and how little return there is. I can tell before it even happens; the conversation will start off pleasantly enough and then he or she will list their reasons why the money for technology is being wasted: "Technology is an excuse for teachers not to do their jobs; students should be learning academics, not playing on computers; these new calculators do all the work for the students; and kids today have enough time to play with technologies on their own." It's about this time that I smile and politely excuse myself. As I walk to the opposite side of the room I think to myself, "They just don't understand."

If you are going to devote your life to education then you are going to run into those who know best without that overrated thing called experience. Experience notwithstanding, is there a point to the party patron's testament? What is our obligation to teach with technology—aren't children immersed enough with technology at home? Are we spending too much money on technology—does just putting a computer in a classroom increase student achievement? Is technology an excuse for teachers to delegate instructional responsibilities to the technological tool? As with any type of tool, technology can be used in a positive or a negative manner. As with any type of instruction, the manner in which a teacher integrates technology will influence who gains access to the knowledge presented. Technology's educational strength comes from its flexible and tireless nature. As seen in the previous chapters, each author painstakingly explained how thoughtful and strategic integration could answer some of these skeptical questions and strengthen the claim that technology has the ability to enhance education for all students. These enhancements take the form of interactive lesson plans and engaging students to become an active part of the learning process. However, it is important that we have answers to the skeptics' questions so that we do not have to slink away from conversations such as the one described.

What Is Our Obligation to Teach With Technology?

Is the purpose of school to teach students about technology or to enhance academic achievement through the use of technology? Our answer is all too simple: Why not both? Technologies in the United States are being created and improved at a startling pace. Devices are becoming so user "friendly" that most citizens are unaware of how such devices work or even what specific technologies go into making and operating them.

The understanding associated with how technology works is referred to as technological literacy, while one's ability to manipulate a technology is referred to as technological competency. In fact, the National Academy of Engineering (Pearson & Young, 2002) defined technological literacy as the capacity to understand the broader technical world, and technological competency as the ability to work with specific pieces of technology. The relationship between technological literacy and technological competency is not a dichotomous one. In order to use technology as a tool capable of enhancing the educational experiences of each student, the students must be able to manipulate the technologies in efficient and effective ways. Whether you are designing lessons with specific technology objectives in mind or lessons that incorporate technology as a learning tool, always remember to include activities and discussions geared toward technological literacy and competency.

Each chapter in this book addresses both technology competencies (how to use technology) as well as how students can develop the broader skills of digital literacy. If students are left alone with technology there is little doubt that they would easily master technology competency (this is readily displayed by most teenagers), but it is unclear if they would develop the technological literacy that their futures may now depend upon in today's globalized economy. Therefore it is up to the schools to bridge the competency-literacy gap. In the introduction chapter we explored the many dimensions of digital literacy: photo-visual, reproduction, branching, information, and socioemotional. Throughout each chapter we explored how these facets of digital literacy are met through the use of various technological tools. However, we believe that developing digital literacy goes beyond just using technology but also requires deliberate attention to supporting a new type of literacy in the classroom.

Schools also have an obligation to meaningfully integrate technology in ways that compensate for differential technology access. The discrepancy between the *haves* and the *have nots* is referred to as the digital divide. In the last 10 years, the digital divide has been shrinking in terms of the number of fixed phone lines, mobile subscribers, and Internet users. In 2004, 18.8% of world inhabitants had a fixed phone line, up from 1.54% in 1994; 27.4% had mobile phones, up from 1% in 1994; and 13.8% had Internet access, up from .46% in 1994 (World Summit on the Information Society, 2005). Although this divide does seem to be shrinking, it does still exist. Theoretically speaking, the digital divide should cease to exist in schools. The only problem with such a claim is the assumption that access to technology is equitable for all schools and all students. Where we are outside a major metropolitan city, the discrepancies between schools and districts can be stark. Some schools we work with have multiple computers in the classroom, SMART Boards, document projectors, and projection systems, while other schools—sometimes in the same district—might have one outdated computer and a television on a cart. Some older schools have difficulty providing the cables for hook-ups or may have limited outlets in the classrooms—while others have wifi for each student. Despite these differences, schools provide an opportunity for those students who do not have access to technology at home to engage with and learn about technology. If students do not have the opportunity to engage with and learn about technology at home, then it is imperative that the schools provide such an opportunity. The American economy will not survive if we self-select the few who have access to technology to be the future technological class.

Are We Spending Too Much Money on Technology? Does Just Putting a Computer in a Classroom Increase Student Achievement?

A common myth that seems to be prevalent suggests that simply putting technology into schools will directly improve student achievement; in other words, more technology will result in more achievement (Kleiman, 2000). Certainly when used appropriately, technology is a flexible and powerful tool that can potentially increase depth of understanding and overall student achievement.

Unfortunately, as with any educational tool, technology can be used ineffectively and inefficiently. Reasons for this include: little to no support for technology integration by both administrators and technicians; limited access to appropriate technologies; a poor understanding of educational practices; a limited knowledge of how to use the technology; or a misunderstanding of why the technology is being used. Whether teaching at a school with the best technology and support or at a school that is lucky to have books and pencils, the basic criteria for using technology effectively remains the same.

Recall that digital technologies and instructional technologies can be different. If your school is short on digital technologies, then take it upon yourself to use the resources at hand. Remember, it's not the technology that makes a lesson great; it's how the teacher uses the technology. Take care to avoid inappropriate uses of digital technologies; good teaching is the key to an effective classroom (Zucker, 2008). Using technology without an educational purpose can discourage students, while reinforcing negative conceptions of technology. It is inaccurate to think that students will be successful simply by making contact with technology. So how can educators design lessons that effectively integrate technology? There are two approaches to follow:

- ☼ select a technology that best fits your lesson, or
- ☼ design the lesson to fit the technology.

In the first approach, technology is used as a tool that requires you to adapt the technology to fit the lesson. For many teachers, this is more appealing because they are simply using technology to enhance lessons that they have previously taught. In essence, they are building upon the work that they have already completed.

The second approach focuses on the technology, requiring you to adapt the lesson to fit the technology. Teachers are a little less motivated to follow this path because it requires that they completely revamp their lessons. As such, there is less certainty that students will be able to meet stated objectives. However, over time, the second approach tends to yield better results because it requires teachers to update lessons that are intended to take advantage of new technologies.

There is a need for both approaches and it is important that you practice them both. Whether you choose technology as a tool or technology as the focus, your pedagogical content knowledge and pedagogical technical knowledge will have the greatest influence on the lesson. Make no mistake, when technology is integrated into classroom practices, there will be a radical shift in your teaching style and your vision of the classroom. Initially, the lesson and/or the technology might not be completely successful. This potential result is worrisome, but necessary if pedagogical change is to occur. Changes may include less focus on lectures, increased awareness of student problems and achievement, improved physical orientation of the classroom, and more effective evaluation (Dede, 1998). This is exactly why the one-size-fits-all approach to lesson plans and technology integration is unrealistic.

If you plan on having your students interact with the technology, the following criteria are necessary for positive educational experiences:

1. Assess technical knowledge before implementing the technology (don't assume).
2. Utilize technology in a way that requires students to interact and think. Do not use the technology as a means of mimicking procedures. A good question to ask is: Who is doing the thinking, the student or the technology?
3. Utilize the technology to provide multiple representations of the content.
4. Provide a means for students to self-monitor progress.

The previous chapters highlight ways that technology can be used as both a tool and a focus. By having readers blog about the books that they have read, interact in Second Life as part of a social studies unit, or create databases and queries on volcanoes, teachers are not just putting technology in their classroom but using it thoughtfully to support good teaching and enhance student learning.

One Size Does Not Fit All

Over the past century, many have seen technology as the cure-all that will lead education into greatness. Even though the advancements in technologies have become almost unrealistic and the application of technologies almost limitless, always remember that technology is an instructional tool. In fact, technology is your tool and you are the classroom expert. As such, the particular tool should be used in a manner that enhances the educational experiences of your students. If the tool has no instructional value, then it should not be integrated into the curriculum.

Unfortunately technology is not a one-size-fits-all solution to education. Without the proper guidance, technology can do as much harm as it can good. It is unreasonable to think that providing every student access to technology is sufficient enough to enhance their understanding and motivation. Access to technology is only part of the equation. In order to implement any technology tool in way that promotes digital literacy, teachers must be trained in how to design effective activities and lessons.

Teaching is a dynamic profession that employs insightful and imaginative professionals. These experts attempt to provide every student a relevant education that prepares them to meet the demands of contemporary society. The first step in becoming the type of teacher who embraces technology—not just delegates technology—is to educate yourself. Hopefully, reading the chapters in this book has contributed to your knowledge base and exposed you to new and innovative instructional possibilities around technology. However, this is just a first step. In order to move forward you need to take this new knowledge and apply this to your classroom, your school, and your content.

Next Steps: Moving Forward by Creating Your Own Personal Technology Improvement Plan

One way to avoid the one-size-fits-all approach is for you to create a Personal Technology Improvement Plan (PTIP; Besnoy, 2007). You cannot sit by and wait for school districts to implement instructional technology (IT) focused professional development activities. Rather, you must take the opportunity to independently identify your technology needs, locate resources that meet those needs, and participate in learning sessions. Creating a PTIP allows you to personalize your professional development around your particular instructional needs (see Appendix A for a blank PTIP).

This multistep process requires that you conduct a needs assessment, establish short- and long-term goals, identify and participate in professional development opportunities, implement your new skills, and evaluate progress. According to Besnoy (2007), PTIPs serve three basic purposes.

  ☼ First, they allow you to create and implement a continuous professional improvement plan.

- ☀ Second, due to the personalized aspect, they are intrinsically motivating and allow you to develop skills at a comfortable pace.
- ☀ Third, they demonstrate a commitment on your part to meet the needs of the 21st-century student.

Needs Assessment

The first step in creating a PTIP is for you to conduct a needs assessment and determine which resources/skills you want to develop. The basic purpose of this step is to provide you with a direction as you navigate your plan. The easiest way to complete this step is to fill out a needs assessment survey. There are several that can provide you the necessary information, however, it is important to make sure that the one you use is current. Due to the rapid changing nature of technology, it would not be advisable to complete one that is more that 3 years old. It is important to conduct an annual needs assessment to measure progress and reevaluate specific needs.

WHAT SKILLS DO I ADDRESS IF I AM A NOVICE?

As with any project, figuring out where to begin is the most daunting task, especially if after completing the assessment you determine that you need help with everything. There are two solutions to this dilemma. First, pick a skill, any skill, and begin from there. In reality, you have so much to work on that it really does not matter where you begin, as long as you start developing a new technology skill set. Second, you should find an individual in the school building or district who can act as an IT skill set partner. Much like a workout partner, the two of you can learn and practice together. This external motivating factor will encourage you to continue with your plan and allow you to share resources, frustrations, and successful experiences.

Writing Goals

Goals are a common element of all professional development plans, and your PTIP must have both short- and long-term goals. However, how do you distinguish between short- and long-term goals? It is important for you to remember that short-term goals are those that can be accomplished in a short period of time. Furthermore, your collection of short-term goals should have a common theme and lead you to accomplishing a long-term goal. According to Besnoy (2007), short-tem goals should be accomplished within a 4–5 month time frame. On the other hand, you should write long-term goals with the mindset that they can be accomplished by the end of your PTIP.

SHORT-TERM GOALS

When writing short-term goals, you should consider two types. First, there are skill acquisition goals, which focus on your ability to implement new technologies in ways that promote the digital literacies. Second, there are hardware/software acquisition goals, which enable you to acquire the necessary IT to implement in your classroom. In some instances, you will not be able to complete a skill acquisition goal without first acquiring the necessary hardware/software. Examples of short-term skill acquisition goals include:

- I plan to integrate blogs into my curriculum (literacy chapter).
- I plan to integrate student response systems in my classroom (math chapter).
- I plan to create an avatar in Second Life (social studies chapter).

Each of these goals is specifically stated and easily can be achieved in a brief time period.

Additionally, a teacher should set goals that include acquiring newer and more robust hardware/software. Examples of short-term hardware/software acquisition goals include:

- I want to attain a projection system so I can model how to use a blog as a digital writer's notebook (literacy chapter).
- I want set of graphing calculators (math chapter).
- I want to download Photo Story (social studies chapter).

Although achieving these goals might seem costly, there are several technology grants available for teachers that provide funding to make these aspirations attainable.

Depending on your comfort level, as determined by the needs assessment, each of these goals can be achieved within a few months. Remember that it is important for you to be realistic about your comfort level, skill level, available resources, support, and student proficiency. For instance, a novice might not be able to create a Web page for the entire school within a short time frame. However, a novice can learn how to set up a basic Web page and post classroom information in just a few weeks.

LONG-TERM GOALS

The best way to establish and maintain an effective PTIP is to establish one or two long-term goals that are extensions of your short-term goals. As with your short-term goals, your long-term goals should reflect skill and hardware/software acquisition goals that will transform your classroom into an environment that promotes digital literacy skills. Examples of long-term skill acquisition goals include:

- ☼ I want to learn how to teach my students to create a series of math podcasts (math chapter).
- ☼ I want to learn how to integrate digital story telling into my classroom (social studies chapter).
- ☼ I want to learn how to incorporate Google Earth into the teaching of volcanic activity (science chapter).

Attaining these achievable goals requires you to create and commit to a sustained PTIP.

Many of these goals cannot be achieved without acquiring new hardware. As such, you should consult an IT specialist as to the specific hardware/software required to complete the long-term goals. Examples of hardware/software acquisition goals include:

- ☼ I want to expand the number of unidirectional microphones available so that I can create mathcasts (math chapter).
- ☼ I want to have the school district's Internet filter modified to allow my students access to virtual worlds (social studies chapter).
- ☼ I want a pod of classroom computers so that my students can publish their writings to a blog (literacy chapter).

Although the goal(s) can be lofty or small scale, they should be consistent with your other stated PTIP goals.

Identify and Access Resources

After conducting a needs assessment and writing goals, you need to implement the PTIP. It is important to for you to identify a number of professional development opportunities and select the ones that match your interests and needs. There are several resources available that can aid in this step. Many universities offer courses in instructional technology. Another resource is professional organizations such as the International Society for Technology in Education (ISTE; http://www.iste.org). Each year it hosts the National Educational Computing Conference (NECC) where experts in the field of instructional technology present the latest strategies. Finally, many local educational agencies and state educational agencies offer IT workshops to develop skills that easily can be implemented into current lesson plans.

Identifying resources is just half the battle. You will not successfully complete your PTIP if you do not access the identified resources. Take the time and register for professional development opportunities. For novices, it is best to first dip your toe in the water (take one opportunity at a time) and then progressively get yourself more involved (Thurlow, 1999). If you are more advanced, you should take this opportunity to push yourself to expand your expertise.

Implement Learned Skills

This section of the PTIP is exciting because it represents the culmination of a lot of hard work. According to Kelly and McDairmid (2002), teachers should implement new strategies as they are learned. Don't wait until the end of a staff development to integrate new skills; rather, use them as you learn them. This will increase the value of the staff development sessions because you will understand what works and what does not work. It also provides you an opportunity to ask the instructor tangible questions about specific strategies.

Another benefit of implementing the new skills is that your students will immediately see your dedication to improving your craft. This realization helps to improve learning and teacher/student relationships. Moreover, you will be giving your students an opportunity to utilize computers in their learning.

Evaluation

It is important to constantly evaluate your progress. As a new skill is learned and implemented, you should evaluate how effectively you integrated your new skill/resource into the classroom. According to Thurlow

(1999), evaluation informs you what worked and how to improve upon what did not work. Moreover, it provides you with necessary feedback as to which skills need to be learned to further progress through the PTIP. There are two forms of evaluation that you should conduct: student feedback and personal reflection.

The easiest method for gauging student opinions about implemented IT skills is to ask them directly. You should survey your students to determine if the implemented IT tools were successful. Generally speaking, you will not have to pry this information from students, especially if they are allowed to respond anonymously.

Furthermore, you should participate in the reflective teaching process. You need to reflect on the effectiveness of the implemented skills and how to improve them the next time. Implementing new skills is always difficult, but practicing them in authentic situations makes for more efficient instruction.

Conclusion

When Mr. Goodman began teaching fourth grade in 1996, he never thought that he would need to know how to incorporate educational technology into his classroom. He thought, "My students are too young to know how to use a computer and they are not sophisticated enough to make it worth my time to teach them." That all changed 10 years ago, after watching his kindergarten-aged son sit down at a computer and create a presentation about poisonous dart frogs. It was at that moment he recognized the instructional importance of becoming more technology savvy. So Mr. Goodman began to set goals for himself that would provide him with the skill set to become technologically literate. Ultimately he wanted to become comfortable enough with computers so that he would be able to seamlessly integrate them into his classroom. However, he knew that he would have to start small, so his first goal was to learn how to do what his son was doing.

After 10 years of slowly learning new skills and implementing them into his classroom, he is much more comfortable. He acknowledges that he is not as savvy as he wants to be, or as his students, but he is able to integrate computers into his classroom. He is amazed as how quickly the time has passed and commented, "It was scary at first, not knowing if my new skills would work or not. However, the more goals I set for myself, the more I accomplished. I took on the mindset that I would learn one skill at a time and then move on to the next one. There are moments that I still feel like I am behind the times, but I just try to learn one new skill a year. By taking this approach, I have learned so many new skills and found new, interesting ways to engage my students in meaningful instruction."

References

Besnoy, K. (2007). Creating a personal technology improvement plan for teachers of the gifted. *Gifted Child Today, 30*(4), 44–49.

Dede, C. (Ed.). (1998). *ASCD yearbook.* Reston, VA: Association for Supervision and Curriculum Development.

Kelly, P. P., & McDairmid, G. W. (2002, April). *Professional development under KERA: Teacher's decisions and dilemmas.* Paper presented at the annual meeting of the American Educational Research Association, New Orleans, LA.

Kleiman, G. (2000). Myths and realities about technology in K–12 schools. In T. Gordon (Ed.), *The digital classroom* (pp. 154–160). Cambridge, MA: Harvard Education Press.

Pearson, G., & Young, A. T. (2002). *Why all Americans need to know more about technology.* Washington, DC: National Academy Press.

Thurlow, J. P. (1999, April). *Teachers as technologists: Professional development for technology integration.* Paper presented at the annual meeting of the International Reading Association, San Diego, CA.

World Summit on the Information Society. (2005). *The digital divide at a glance.* Retrieved April 05, 2009, from http://www.itu.int/wsis/tunis/newsroom/stats

Zucker, A. (2008). *Transforming schools with technology: How smart use of digital tools helps achieve six key educational goals.* Cambridge, MA: Harvard Education Press.

| Needs Assessment
These are based on your current computer needs/abilities. | How many computers in my classroom do I have? _____ _____ _____ How many computers are in the lab? _____ _____ Do these computers allow me to utilize all of my computer skills? _____ _____ How many technology specialists are there in my school? _____ _____ Which software programs do I have access to? _____ _____ What are the computer skills of my students? _____ _____ | What technology skills do I currently have? _____ _____ _____ _____ What computer skills do I currently have _____ _____ What Web 2.0 skills do I currently have? _____ _____ What multimedia skills do I currently have? _____ _____ Which software programs do I currently know how to use? _____ _____ How can I use my skills to integrate technology into the curriculum? _____ _____ | Prioritize your needs 1. _____ 2. _____ 3. _____ 4. _____ 5. _____ |

Personal Technology Improvement Plan

Short-term goals *These are goals that can be achieved within a few months.*	Acquiring hardware/software goals • _____ • _____ • _____ • _____ • _____	Acquiring computer skills goals • _____ • _____ • _____ • _____ • _____	Prioritize your short-term goals 1. _____ 2. _____ 3. _____ 4. _____ 5. _____
Long-term goals *These are goals that take a year or more to achieve*	Acquiring hardware/software goals • _____ • _____ • _____ • _____ • _____	Acquiring computer skills goals • _____ • _____ • _____ • _____ • _____	Prioritize your long-term goals 1. _____ 2. _____ 3. _____ 4. _____ 5. _____
Resources *Identify sources of funding to acquire specific technologies and locations/details of professional development opportunities*	Sources of grant funding • _____ • _____ • _____ • _____ • _____	Location/details of professional development opportunities • _____ • _____ • _____ • _____ • _____	Prioritize acquisition of resources 1. _____ 2. _____ 3. _____ 4. _____ 5. _____
Implementation *Create a timeline of the steps required to achieve your goals.*	Implementation of short-term goals Month 1: Month 2: Month 3: Month 4: Month 5:	Implementation of long-term goals Year 1: Year 2: Year 3: Year 4: Year 5:	
Evaluation	Reflect on how successful you were in completing and implementing your short-term goals	Reflect on how successful you were in completing and implementing your long-term goals	Reflect on what skills/resources you need to take in order to successfully implement

Note. Adapted from Besnoy (2007).

About the Editors

Kevin D. Besnoy is assistant professor of education at Northern Kentucky University. He was a classroom teacher in Alabama, Maryland, and Mississippi before receiving his Ph.D. in gifted education from The University of Southern Mississippi. He has published in journals such as *Gifted Child Today, Roeper Review, and RE:View.* In addition, he has coauthored textbook chapters and has conducted research studies on how to integrate instructional technology into the classroom. His interest in instructional technology comes from having grown up around computers and his practical experiences with implementing them in the elementary, middle school, high school, and college classrooms.

Lane W. Clarke is assistant professor of education at Northern Kentucky University. She was a classroom teacher in New York, South Carolina, and Ohio before receiving her Ed.D. in literacy from the University of Cincinnati. Since then she has been a researcher and scholar on many issues surrounding literacy. She has been published in journals such as *Journal of Literacy Research, Language Arts, The Reading Teacher,* and *Journal of Adolescent and Adult Literacy.* She also has a coauthored book on struggling readers that will be published by Teachers College Press in Fall 2009. Her interest in technology has come from a grant and a pilot study that she is conducting with colleague Dr. Kevin D. Besnoy about enhancing reading comprehension for middle school students using Palm Pilots.

About the Authors

Todd Campbell is assistant professor of science education in the School of Teacher Education and Leadership at Utah State University. His research is focused on factors supportive of current reform efforts in science education and includes research ranging from investigations of teacher questioning strategies in science classrooms, recently published in the *International Journal of Science Education*, to technologies aligned with this reform. He is a former high school and middle school science teacher.

Grace Enriquez is assistant professor of language and literacy at Lesley University. Previously, Grace was a middle school language arts teacher and a literacy staff developer. A recipient of the American Association of University Women American Fellowship, her research interests involve the intersection of literacy and identity, critical literacy, literacy and technology, and children's and young adult literature. Her work has been published in *Reading Research Quarterly*, *Language Arts*, *Journal of Children's Literature*, and *The ALAN Review*. She has also coauthored a forthcoming book with Stephanie Jones and Lane Clarke on turning around reading instruction for teachers and students in grades 2–6.

Tirupalavanam G. Ganesh, a native of India, now a resident of Phoenix, AZ, works at Arizona State University. His current research aims at developing engagement models for creating learning experiences that are meaningful to youth and studying what works and why. His research interests include K–12 engineering education, use of visual data in research, and science, technology, engineering, and mathematics (STEM) education in the elementary and middle grades. He is the principal investigator (2008–2010) of Learning Through Engineering Design and Practice, a National Science Foundation project aimed at creating and testing informal learning curricula with underserved middle school youth while studying the impact of such long-term engagement for impact on student attitudes and interest in STEM subjects and careers. He teaches research methods at the Mary Lou Fulton College of Education. He has lived in Arizona since 1991 and enjoys the natural habitats of the southwestern United States.

Hui-Yin Hsu is assistant professor in the School of Education at New York Institute of Technology, where she coordinates the College Reading Placement Program. She received her Ph.D. from the University of Pittsburgh. Her professional interests have been in the areas of reading and diversity and global literacy, as well as new literacies of ICT. Her research has been published in national and international journals, including *Computer Assisted Language Learning*, *Multicultural Education & Technology Journal*, *TechTrend*, and *Journal of Online Interactive Learning*. Her Web site address is http://iris.nyit.edu/~hhsu02.

Christopher T. Inman is a doctoral student and graduate teaching assistant at The University of Alabama. His research interests include emerging technologies, distance education, and integrating technology into social science education.

Jesse Lubinsky is the technology coordinator and Chief Information Officer for the Irvington Union-Free School District in Irvington, NY. He previously served as a middle and high school teacher specializing in mathematics, computer science, and technology. He received a master's degree in educational administration from the College of St. Rose in 2008. Prior to entering the field of education, he worked in private industry as a technology consultant for Fortune 500 companies. He also has served on technology grant committees for the National Science Foundation. His interests are educational technology, computer science education, technology leadership, and helping teachers to bridge the disconnect between curriculum and technology. He is a Google Certified Teacher and is active in a variety of educational organizations at the state and national level. He currently resides in Westchester County, NY, with his wife and daughter.

Stephanie Anne Schmier is a doctoral candidate at Teachers College, Columbia University in the Department of Curriculum and Teaching and a National Academy of Education Adolescent Literacy Predoctoral fellow. Her research explores how youth take up new digital technologies, the ways in which adolescents' digital literacy practices travel across in- and out-of-school spaces, and the meanings that they make of these practices across multiple contexts in their lives. Stephanie has published in the journals *Language Arts* and *E-Learning*. She holds a bachelor's degree in psychology from UCLA and a master's degree in educational psychology from California State University, Northridge. Prior to her doctoral work, Stephanie was a classroom teacher and technology coordinator, as well as a literacy advisor in Los Angeles and New York City schools.

John Thieken worked for a short period of time as an engineer on completion of a bachelor's degree in mechanical engineering. Following his engineering career, he joined the U.S. military, were he served in Washington, DC. He later earned a master's degree in secondary education. He is going into his sixth year of teaching mathematics at Pinnacle High School in Arizona. He also is pursuing a Ph.D. in mathematics education at Arizona State University where he works on a National Science Foundation funded project titled Learning Through Engineering Design and Practice. His contribution to this project is in bringing engineering concepts to the K–12 arena by assisting with the design and development of project curricula. Upon completion of his Ph.D. program he intends to pursue an academic career in higher education.

Shiang-Kwei Wang is an associate professor in the Master of Science in Instructional Technology Program at the New York Institute of Technology. She received her Ph.D. from the University of Georgia. Her professional interests are in the areas of technology integration in K–12 learning settings, the impact of ICTs on learning attitude and performance and the design and development of interactive tools. Her articles have been published in *Educational Technology Research & Development*, *Journal of Online Interactive Learning*, and *TechTrend*. Her Web site address is http://iris.nyit.edu/~skwang.

Elizabeth K. Wilson is a professor in the Department of Curriculum and Instruction at The University of Alabama. Wilson, a former secondary social studies teacher, collaborates with classroom teachers to promote social studies education in her community. Her research interests in social studies education include teachers' beliefs and practices as well as technology. She has published articles in numerous journals. Wilson can be contacted at ewilson@bama.ua.edu.

Vivian H. Wright is associate professor of instructional technology at The University of Alabama. In addition to teaching in the graduate program, Wright works with teacher educators on innovative ways to infuse technology in the curriculum to enhance teaching and learning and has helped initiate and develop projects such as Master Technology Teacher and Technology on Wheels. Her research interests include K–12 technology integration and emerging technologies. She can be contacted at vwright@bamaed.ua.edu.